The Two Worlds of Jill

Patricia Aks

SCHOLASTIC BOOK SERVICES

New York Toronto London Auckland Sydney Tokyo

For Kathy and Michael

Cover Photo by Owen Brown

ISBN 0-590-31801-2

12 11 10 9 8 7 6 5 4 3 2 1   6   1 2 3 4 5 6/8

Printed in the U. S. A.   06

The Two Worlds of Jill

A Wishing Star Book

Chapter One

I keep telling myself I can handle it, but sometimes I wonder. I don't really know what it's like yet, and I don't know anyone else in my situation.

You see, my parents, after eighteen years of marriage — which seemed more like the Hundred Years War — and one child (that's me), finally split. I have to admit everyone's better off, including me. The only thing that scared me during the divorce proceedings was that I would be "awarded" to one parent, or worse, that I'd be forced to choose which parent I wanted to live with. I honestly do love them both, and the very idea of choosing sent me into a tailspin. Thank goodness it never came to that.

What happened was they *both* won me, and now I split my time between them — one month with my father, and one month with my mother. It makes a lot of sense because they're still my parents and the one thing I know they totally agree on is that they love me. But "joint custody," which is what this thing is legally called, has some unique problems. Some I knew I'd have to face, but a zillion others I never even thought of. Today was the first test, because it was my first day at my new school.

When I arrived there were these two efficient-looking girls, probably seniors, sitting at a desk in the hall, handing everyone a schedule and telling them where their homeroom was located. I was directed to a room on the second floor where all the kids seemed to be yelling at each other, telling about their summers. For a few minutes I felt a real pang for my old school in Westport, Connecticut, where I'd gone all my life. I was beginning to feel really sorry for myself when this girl came up to me.

"Hi, I'm Maggie Lawton," she said amiably. "Welcome." She had the exact opposite coloring of me — long blond hair parted in the middle, and warm brown eyes. (I have straight black hair and blue eyes.)

"Hi," I said. "My name is Jill Belmont. I guess I'm the only new person here."

"You won't feel new for long. This is a really friendly class."

"Who's our homeroom teacher?"

"That's Winslow," she whispered, tilting her head toward a roly-poly woman who wore horn-rimmed glasses over black-button eyes. She was shuffling papers around on her desk at the front of the room. "She's a character. I had her for Introduction to Science two years ago, and now we'll have her for biology. I can't imagine what she'll be like as a homeroom teacher."

"I think we're about to find out," I observed as I saw Winslow peer over her glasses and then pound her desk with her fist.

"Enough mingling," she announced in a brisk voice. "It's my turn to speak." She sounded stern, but her eyes were sparkling, and soon I discovered she had a sense of humor.

The first thing she did was pick up a piece of chalk and say, "You're much too old for what I'm about to do."

Then she turned to the blackboard and printed her name in block letters: WINSLOW. "That's so you won't have any excuse for misspelling." Then she added: MRS. "That's so you don't mix me up with Mr. Winslow — no relation — who teaches fourth grade. If you do wind up in a class where the subject is long division, and the teacher needs a shave, you'll know you've got the wrong Winslow."

Everybody broke up.

She gave us the usual pep talk, saying she was happy to see some faces she knew, and a couple that she didn't. "There are two new members of the class, I see," she said. "Jill Belmont and Carl Newman. Please stand up so we know which one is which."

We both stood up and there was a chorus of "Hi's." I was relieved that I wasn't the only one they were staring at. I glanced at Carl, who had the looks of a California surfer, and I wasn't surprised when Mrs. Winslow asked him where he was from and he said, "Sausalito, just north of San Francisco."

She asked me if I had always lived in New York, and I said my family had just moved into the city from Westport. I sat down quickly, glad that there weren't any more personal questions.

Winslow went on to explain that we would be studying biology with her, and that she was deadly serious when she said she wanted us to learn about the birds and the bees. "I don't appreciate anyone who goofs off on work, but even if you get F's, I won't hold it against you as a homeroom teacher. In that sense I'm two people."

Her saying she was two people gave me a funny feeling, because somewhere I thought that was what I might become. Then I remembered my father telling me how "well-integrated" I was, and my mother saying my sense of humor would see me through anything. Well, I thought to myself, it is the first day of school, and I am sort of nervous, and I shouldn't be so sensitive to my "situation."

"Pay attention, now," Winslow said, pulling me out of my private thoughts. She wrote the title of a book on the blackboard. "Buy this," she commanded, "and have the first three chapters read by Wednesday."

Everyone started scribbling down the assignment. "Now you can go back to mingling until the bell rings." She went back to shuffling papers on her desk as though we had all disappeared.

"Character, right?" Maggie asked me in a low voice.

"And how!" I said. "Thanks for warning me."

Just then the bell rang.

"What's next on your schedule?" Maggie said.

"Gym."

"Me, too. Let's get going."

As I followed Maggie out of the classroom, I thought that things were really going well so far. But I wasn't at all prepared for what would happen in gym. It would be my first zinger!

Chapter Two

"Take seats, girls, take seats," shouted a little gray-haired woman who was wearing a gray suit and Hush Puppies. She looked more like somebody's grandmother than a phys. ed. teacher. The only giveaway was a lanyard around her neck, but when I looked closely I could see that her eyeglass case was attached to it.

"I'm Mrs. Gabriel," she announced, "in case there are some of you who don't know me."

She started right in, explaining that there would only be girls in the class. There was an audible groan, but she ignored it and went right on talking. She told us what gear we should bring to keep in our locker — shorts, T-shirts, and sneakers.

"Also," she added, "you must wear a bra for sports — otherwise it's 'lag now, sag later.'"

This time there was a collective giggle, but that didn't stop her for a second. She continued telling us what the program would be — team sports for each semester, tennis outdoors in the spring and fall, gymnastics and swimming throughout the year.

The more I listened to Mrs. Gabriel, the more surprised I was that she would be in charge of athletics. Maggie, who must have known what I was thinking, whispered, "Don't worry. She's only in charge of scheduling. Mr. Jenkins is our regular coach. Wait'll you see him."

"Whew!" I said. "You must be a mind reader. I was worried for a minute." But that was a minor worry compared to what happened next.

Mrs. Gabriel droned on. "I'm going to pass out some blank cards. Please fill them out legibly with your name, address, and telephone number; who to notify in case of emergency; and your doctor's number."

Now what do I do? I thought to myself. I could write, "It depends." But I was sure Mrs. Gabriel wouldn't appreciate that, so I decided to play it straight, exactly like it was. I wrote: September, November, January, March, May, July; my address is: 120 Spring Street. October, December, February, April, June, August; my address is 30 East 81st.

My doctor was in Westport, so I decided to leave that blank. I was writing so long that Maggie looked at me in amazement.

"All she wants is your address, not your life history."

"It's complicated."

"How complicated can it be?" she asked, genuinely confused.

"I'll explain later," I said.

"Okay. Maybe we can walk home together after school. I live on Seventy-second Street. Where do you live anyway?"

"This is September. I live in Soho."

"Soho! How terrific! But that means we can't walk home together. How do you get there?"

"By subway. But October, December, February, April, and June, we can."

"Can what?"

"Can walk home together. In October I'll be living on Eighty-first Street."

"You mean you're moving."

"I am, but my parents aren't."

"Huh?"

"It's complicated."

"You already said that." I could tell Maggie was getting a little annoyed.

"Look," I said, "I know I sound crazy, but I'll explain everything as soon as this is over."

"Okay," Maggie said, softening. "I didn't mean to pry."

Before we could continue, there was a burst of applause. I looked up and saw a youngish-looking man, built like a quarterback, running toward Mrs. Gabriel. He smiled broadly when he reached her, and raised his hands for silence. "First I want to thank Mrs. Gabriel for attending to all the business details of the phys. ed. department. Without her, the whole athletic program would fall apart."

For the first time Mrs. Gabriel cracked a smile. Then she started to walk away. She stopped abruptly in her tracks, turned around, and said, "Leave your address cards in my office and look for your locker number, which will be posted on my bulletin board. Let's hope we don't have to use the emergency numbers. Good luck!" She marched off.

"Let's hear it for Mrs. Gabriel," the coach shouted, and started applauding, and the rest of us joined in.

"I gather that's Mr. Jenkins," I said to Maggie.

"You guessed it," she said just as he began talking.

"I'm Mr. Jenkins, in case some of you don't already know me."

There was another round of applause, and he seemed to bask in the reaction of the girls, waiting until it died down so he could continue. "I know I don't have to sell you on phys. ed. It's everybody's favorite class, next to lunch. There's one philosophy that guides us in all our sports — 'It's not how you play the game, it's who wins!'"

We all roared and then when we were relatively silent he said, "Only kidding. You know, I believe the most important thing is how hard you try, really caring. If you're lackadaisical about winning, you're just as much a bad sport as if you cheated in order to win. You really have to *care*, for yourself as well as for your teammates."

He went on, telling us that volleyball would be our first team sport, and everyone would play even though there were twenty in the class and there are only supposed to be nine on a side. There would be tryouts for the tennis team, and finally, he said, "Since I'm known as a man of action and few words, you can have free time till the bell rings. Don't forget Mrs. Gabriel's instructions, and I'll see you tomorrow."

Maggie and I were still on the bleachers when a skinny girl with auburn hair and freckles came charging over to where we were seated.

"Hiya, Maggie. Hope we can be tennis partners this year," she said, totally ignoring me.

"Hi, Sue," Maggie greeted her.

"The school has rented indoor courts so the team can play all winter."

"That's good," Maggie said.

"That means we'll get a lot more practice."

She still didn't look at me, and Maggie finally turned to me and said, "This is Sue Robbins."

She looked at Sue and said, "Say hello to Jill Belmont. This is her first day."

"I know. I'm in your homeroom class. Remember?"

"Hi," I said, wondering why she seemed angry.

"Hi," she replied without looking at me, and walked away.

"What's wrong?" I asked.

Maggie shrugged her shoulders and said, "She's like that. It's nothing personal."

Then as we started to get up, two other girls approached us.

"Hi, Jill, I'm Sandy List," the first one said.

She was small, had dark curly hair and a turned-up nose. "Hope you like it here. I started two years ago, and I still remember my first day. It doesn't take long getting used to, you'll be happy to know."

"So far it's been fine," I said.

"I've been here *forever*," the other girl drawled. "I'll *never* get used to it."

We all chuckled and then Maggie introduced us. "This is Serena Peters." She was tall and willowy and had green catlike eyes.

"Hi, Serena."

"Hello, Jill. What school did you come from?"

"The public school in Westport."

"Was it anything like this?"

"It was a lot like this. My father says this is the closest to Westport High — the main difference being this one costs money."

"My father talks about that, too," Sandy said. "But I keep telling him I only have high school, four years of college, and three years of law school. Then I'll support him in his old age."

"I told my parents I'm willing to drop out right now," Serena offered.

"Don't believe her," Maggie said to me. "She gets all A's without even trying."

"Can't help it," Serena agreed nonchalantly. She looked at her schedule and said, "I have math next, with Kasey. Anyone else going there now?"

"I have study hall next," I told them.

"Me, too," Maggie said. "We must be programmed together."

"And I have French," Sandy grumbled. "My

worst subject, but my mother insists that I take it. It's a sign of an educated person, she says. Yech!"

"I see you're getting along with her as well as ever," Serena observed.

Sandy nodded her head resignedly.

"Let's all sit together at lunch," Maggie suggested.

"Good idea," Sandy said. "You available, Serena?"

"I guess so. Although I was seriously thinking of checking out the new boy. Wouldn't want him to feel left out, after coming all the way from California."

"We'll see you at lunch," Maggie said, laughing.

The bell rang, and we all headed for the door.

Chapter Three

When Maggie and I arrived at study hall, a boy wearing horn-rimmed glasses was poring over *War and Peace* at a desk at the front of the room. He didn't bother to look up when we entered. As the room filled up with about twenty kids shouting at each other, he put his book down, pushed back his chair, and said in a surprisingly soft voice that got everyone's attention: "This is study hall. But since it's also the first day of school, and you obviously have nothing to study, you may do anything else for the next forty minutes — providing it's legal and not too loud. In other words, keep the decibel count down so we don't disturb the other classes. After today, of course, the 'silence is golden' rule is put into effect. I'm going to be the monitor here for the whole semester, and my advice is: if you don't want to use this place to do your homework, then write letters, try meditating, or go to sleep. Just don't make noise. My name is David Rowley, in case you have any problems."

He went back to reading his book, and Maggie and I sat down in the last row. There was a general buzz of conversation which gave us some privacy.

"I honestly didn't mean to pry," Maggie began. "But I'm curious about you living in Soho now, and living uptown in October, and your parents aren't moving."

"I don't blame you for being curious. The thing is, my parents are divorced. My mother lives in Soho and my father lives on the Upper East Side."

There was a pause, and then Maggie said slowly, "I get it. You mean you live one month with your mother and one month with your father."

"Exactly."

Maggie didn't say anything for a minute and I wondered if I had shocked her. I was relieved when she finally said, "That's a terrific arrangement. It's a lot better than cutting off one parent."

"I think so. At least it's terrific so far. This is the first month and I don't know yet what it'll be like to leap back and forth."

"It might be a lot of fun. At least you'll never be in one place long enough to get bored."

"That's true," I said, grateful for her support.

"Have you told anyone else?"

"It hasn't come up yet. The administration knows, of course, but none of the kids do."

"I won't say anything if you don't want me to."

"Eventually everyone will know, and in a way I'll be glad when they do. It's not a secret or anything."

"It makes you kind of interesting."

"I know. I just don't like feeling different."

"An adolescent hang-up," Maggie said, laughing. "My mother is getting a master's degree in psychology and she has a name for everything."

"That's convenient."

"Not always. But I'm learning to handle it."

"That's what I keep telling myself about life — I'm learning to handle it."

"This is getting heavy," Maggie said. "We haven't got that much time left, so maybe we should mix a little. C'mon, I'll introduce you to some people. Alex and Jimmy are the two best-looking jocks in the class, and they've been eyeing you ever since we sat down. It doesn't look like they have the sense to introduce themselves, so we might as well make the first move. Okay?"

"Okay," I agreed.

"Alex, the smaller one, is on the varsity swimming team. He's very funny, but he's not known for his tact."

"I can handle him," I said, and we both laughed as we went over to where they were now leaning against the wall.

The rest of "study hall" we spent gabbing

with them and when it was time for lunch, Alex and Jimmy insisted on joining us. Everyone was so friendly that my "new girl" feeling quickly faded.

After helping ourselves cafeteria-style, we sat at a table with Sandy and Serena. Alex began quizzing me about what school I'd gone to and where did I live. When he found out I lived in Soho, he said, "How inconvenient. Do you commute by helicopter, or do you plan to move?"

I gulped because I didn't want to make a public announcement, and so I mumbled something about living on Eighty-first Street next month.

"That's sensible," Alex commented.

"But the month after, I'll be back in Soho."

He looked at me for a minute as though I had flipped out, but before he could say anything, I quickly told him my parents were divorced and I was going to live one month with each throughout the year.

Alex's jaw dropped, and when he recovered *he* made a public announcement. "Hey, Jill here leads a double life — one month with mom and one with dad."

"Sounds like a good idea to me," Maggie said, coming to my rescue.

"Dreamy, I would say," Serena chimed in.

"Where do you like living the best?" Alex asked.

"I don't know yet. It's just started."

"You're what's known as a 'joint kid' I guess." Alex wouldn't let up.

"C'mon Alex," Jimmy admonished him. Jimmy was built like an athlete, but he had the sensitivity of a poet. He turned to me and said, "You have to forgive my friend here. We learned this morning that we'll be studying the Spanish Inquisition, and he's practicing being an inquisitor."

"I won't be a very good subject because I don't know the answers myself yet. My 'double life,' as Alex calls it, has just begun."

"I wish you luck," Jimmy said sincerely. He had the deepest brown eyes and I had trouble turning away from them.

"Thanks," I managed to say, hoping that would end the discussion.

I was glad when Sandy changed the subject and asked me if I was going to try out for the tennis team.

"I plan to. That's my favorite sport."

"Sandy is *numero uno* on the girls' team," Alex said. "And Jimmy is captain of the boys'. You're in very good company."

"I'm impressed."

"Maybe we can all play doubles at Randall's Island one day," Jimmy suggested.

"I'd love that," I said.

"I thought you didn't like mixed doubles," Alex said as he turned to Jimmy and gave him a raised-eyebrow look.

"I happen to have an open mind, and I'm very adjustable," Jimmy said, smiling.

Alex shook his head. "I can't believe it, I can't believe it," he mumbled.

"What's next on anyone's schedule?" Jimmy asked quickly, obviously unwilling to pursue the subject.

Everyone started babbling about where their next class was, and who they had for what, and before I knew it, the bell rang and it was time to go. As I headed for the door Maggie caught up with me and put her hand lightly on my arm. "I think you've made a conquest," she whispered. "Everyone's been after Jimmy, but he's never shown an interest in anyone. This is a first for him."

"You mean it?"

"I mean it. But beware of Sue Robbins. She's had her eye on him ever since fifth grade, but he's never even looked at her."

"Thanks for warning me," I said. "I'll play it cool."

"That's the only way."

As I climbed the stairs to my next class, I thought that I'd only been in school a few hours, and already I had new friends and a possible romantic intrigue. It was all very exciting, but I was glad when my first day was over and I could be "alone" on the subway. Besides everything else, I had to get used to living with just my mother in a loft in Soho.

Chapter Four

When I got home from school my mother, wearing blue jeans and an old shirt, her wavy, dark hair tied back with a scarf, was in the middle of the floor surrounded by cartons. She was carefully unwrapping a collection of paper-weights, which she says is her passion in life. I think she must have at least fifty of them in all different shapes, sizes, and materials.

"Hi, sweetie. How'd it go?" she asked as soon as I'd let myself into our loft.

"Surprisingly good." I climbed over some cartons and bent down to give her a peck on the cheek. "One girl, Maggie, especially made me feel right at home."

"I'm so glad," she said enthusiastically. "Give me a hand, will you? I've been trying desperately to plow through these cartons, but it looks like a losing battle."

I helped her up and she threw her arms around me as though I'd just returned from some remote part of the world. "Was the subway ride okay?" She looked genuinely concerned.

"No problem. It's not the rush hour then, and it gives me a chance to think."

"Great," she said. "I know this is going to work out. If you love this place even half as much as I do, I know you'll be happy here."

"I'm gonna try," I said, and I meant it. I knew living here meant a lot to Ronnie — my mother's real name is Veronica, but all her friends call her Ronnie and that includes me. Being an artist, she often talks about the right environment and even though she had a studio in our house in Westport, it was never right for her.

"How about some cappuccino with whipped cream? I think we both deserve a treat."

"I'd love it," I said.

"I'll go fix it and you go look in your room. Then tell me what you think."

"O-oh," I sighed, smiling. "You've done something creative."

"Go see," she said as she ducked into the kitchen.

My "environment" is small and the previous tenant had built a loft bed which I inherited. Underneath the bed is a built-in desk. It's all very compact, and tiny, compared to the rest of the loft.

Actually, the loft is huge and one reason Ronnie rented it was because it has a northern

light and she can work at one end of it. It's
decorated in what can only be described as
"eclectic" — a little bit of everything including
a Tudor chest and bean bag chairs. Depending
on your view, it's either comfortable or cluttered.
Fortunately, it's big enough to absorb all of
Ronnie's impulse buys.

The walls are covered with her paintings,
which tend to be large abstracts in wild colors.
There wasn't enough space in Westport to hang
more than one in a room, but now that problem
is solved. My room is too small for her paintings, and I was looking forward to browsing
around Soho on Saturday to pick something
out.

Ronnie's surprises are sometimes a little hard
to take, so I was prepared for the worst as I
stumbled over cartons into my room. It was
late afternoon so there wasn't much light coming into my window, but it didn't matter. The
"surprise" was a day-glo psychedelic poster
hung on the wall opposite my loft bed. It
seemed to shoot off red and orange sparks. It
flashed through my head that maybe I could
get a shade for it to keep the light out. Then
I noticed there was an Indian-print spread on
my bed in subdued colors, and that really did
appeal to me.

After I recovered from the shock of the
poster, I went into the kitchen where Ronnie
was whipping cream.

"How do you like it?" she asked.

"Great," I said, even though that was only
half true.

22

"I couldn't resist that poster, even though it's a little loud."

I knew she loved it and I didn't want to appear ungrateful so I joked, "It's so loud that I may need earplugs to get to sleep."

"You do like it, sweetie?" she asked as she poured the coffee.

"Sure," I said agreeably. "And I love the spread."

"Let's have this in the dining room," Ronnie said, and carried the cups out of the kitchen and placed them on a round, heavy oak table, one of the few pieces of furniture she wanted from our house in Westport.

"Dining room?" I queried.

"Wherever this table is located is the dining room," she explained, putting down the cups.

I looked at her quizzically, and she went on, "Wherever we decide to put the bean bag chairs will be the den. And the desk and book shelves will designate the study. We don't have enough furniture yet for a living room."

"I get it," I laughed. "Since it's one humongous area, we won't know where we are except by the furniture."

"You got it!" she said appreciatively. Then she took off her scarf and shook her long hair loose. For the millionth time I was struck with how youthful and good-looking Ronnie is. She actually looks like she could be my older friend rather than my mother. And she treats me that way, too. It's flattering to be treated as an equal, especially when we're alone, but I was to find out that "playing adult" with Ronnie's friends wouldn't always be the greatest. But on a one-to-one basis, like now, it was fine.

I told her about all my classes, and having lunch with the kids in the cafeteria, and about some of my teachers.

"Any cute guys?" One thing about my mother, she never messes around getting to the point.

"As a matter of fact, there were a couple. One is a new guy, who lived in California, and he looks like he travels only by surfboard. But I didn't get a chance to talk to him — yet. The other one is Jimmy, and Maggie tells me he's really hard to get."

"But he likes you," Ronnie surmised.

I shouldn't be startled anymore when my mother knows what happens even before I tell her.

"That's what Maggie says."

"He obviously has good taste, besides being cute," she said, grinning.

"What did you do all day?" I asked.

"When I couldn't stand these cartons another minute, I went out to get groceries, and bumped into Marsha Keene, who I hadn't seen since we took art history at college. She and her husband run a gallery, and she was so excited to learn I was moving in here."

"Maybe she'll give you a show." Ronnie had been in group shows in Westport, but I knew her heart was set on having her own show.

"That's exactly what I was thinking. Anyhow, I promised to invite her and her husband, George, over as soon as this place is settled."

24

"We better work on these boxes some more, otherwise we'll be playing leapfrog forever and never be able to have anyone over."

"You're right," Ronnie sighed. She picked up her scarf from the floor and tied back her hair. As she pushed back her chair, she said, "Marsha mentioned that they have a son, Jason, one year older than you. He's lived and gone to school in Soho most of his life. Marsha said he'd love to show you around."

"That's nice," I said indifferently as I started clearing away the dishes. And I didn't give it any more thought.

Chapter Five

I'd only been at my new school a couple of weeks, but it felt much longer. I seemed to fit right in. I've always frowned on cliques because they seem to be snobby, but I guess it's inevitable that you want to be with some people more than others, and unless you're running for president, you can't pretend to like everyone equally. I guess what I'm trying to do is justify why I hung out mostly with Maggie, Sandy, and Serena. And Maggie soon became my closest friend of all.

My favorite subject has always been sociology. It combines history, anthropology, and the study of human behavior. I lucked in with our teacher, Mrs. Carson, who is from Belize. She's very open and friendly and talks about herself. I soon learned that she was a widow with two children, and she came to this country three

years ago because she believed the opportunities for herself and her children were greater here than in Belize, even though she is black.

One of our first assignments was to write a personal history as though we were explaining to someone from the opposite end of the world what our lives were like. "Describe your school, your family, vacations, jobs — and anything else that influences you. Later we'll read about the lives of people your age in places as divergent as Alaska and China. The enormous differences will give you fresh insights, I hope, into why it is often difficult to find a common ground for understanding."

"Is it okay to discuss our sex lives?" Alex asked. Everyone laughed, including Mrs. Carson.

"Of course, Alex. That's also a part of life."

"But will the papers be confidential?"

"I promise you they will be. I'll tell you some of the conclusions that can be drawn, but no one will be embarrassed. You can write anything you want."

Actually, I was glad Alex had asked that question because now I knew I could write without inhibition. In fact, I couldn't wait to get started.

"The papers are due one week from today," Mrs. Carson went on. "After I've read them, I will schedule individual conferences. To me the best part of teaching is the students. I love the subject matter, but *you* are what makes my job interesting."

"Right on!" Alex piped up.

Mrs. Carson laughed along with the rest of

us. The remainder of the hour she talked about our reading assignment, which was on family life in various cultures.

As soon as I got home that afternoon I settled down to write about my life, pointing out how living in Westport was a different world from Manhattan, and that Soho was a separate world from the Upper East Side. I went on to describe what my parents did, how I spent my summers, the subjects I studied, and everything else that someone at the opposite end of the world might like to know. I called my paper "Different Worlds," and it went on for five pages.

When it came time for my conference, Mrs. Carson told me it was one of the most interesting papers she'd read.

"I never knew anyone in a joint custody situation, but I can certainly see the advantages. And you seem to be dealing with it very well," she said.

"So far it's been easy. I like Soho a lot, and my mother is so much fun. Next month I move uptown to live with my father. That'll be very different."

"I know it will take some doing, but I'm sure you can make it work."

"I hope so."

"Your paper was so well written and thoughtful that I would love to share it with the class. But that might make you uncomfortable. Actually, we will be discussing marriage and divorce in different cultures, and at that time we'll talk about custody arrangements in a general way."

"By then everyone will know about my living in two places and it'll be a lot easier to talk about. In fact, it's getting easier already. I mean, when everyone takes it for granted, it will no longer seem weird."

"I think you'll do just fine, and please let me know how things are going. If you need any moral support, I'm here to help you."

"That's good to know," I said, and I meant it. Mrs. Carson was so easy to talk to I knew I could turn to her if I had a problem.

Then she asked me if I was going to sign up for any extracurricular activities. I told her I was trying out for the tennis team and that I was considering joining the photography club.

"I wish you would," Mrs. Carson said enthusiastically. "I happen to be in charge of that club, and we have room for one more person."

"That does it! I'd really like to join."

"Wonderful! The next meeting is Thursday after school, room 308. That's right next to the darkroom."

"I'll be there."

That afternoon as I rode the subway downtown, I thought about all the things that had happened to me since I'd moved to New York — I honestly liked my new school; I already had made some good friends; Mrs. Carson was definitely going to be my favorite teacher; and as always, I got along great with my mother.

I'm really lucky, I thought, and things are going better than I expected.

Chapter Six

When I got home, my mother was unloading the last of the cartons that contained books. "Hi, sweetie," she said, "you're just in time. We have about fifteen minutes till countdown."

"What do you mean?" I asked.

"Dump your things in your room and help me with these." She was holding a book in each hand, and kissed me on the cheek.

"Who's coming?"

"Marsha and her son. They'll be our first official guests and they're coming for tea. Do you think the place is presentable?"

"I think it looks terrific. I can't believe you've gotten rid of all those moving boxes finally."

"Marsha called this morning and when we decided to get together I worked like a Trojan to get things finished."

"I better make my bed. I didn't have time this morning."

"I already made it for you. Hope you don't mind."

"Course not." As I walked into my "environment" I wondered why everyone, including Ronnie and myself, were always concerned about making an impression. I put my book bag under my desk and hung my jacket in the closet. Then I ran a comb through my hair, put on some lip gloss, and made a last-minute inspection of my appearance in the full-length mirror, which is on my door, and went into the "den."

Ronnie was standing on a stepladder, reaching to the top shelves. "Hand me the rest of the books, and then we're finished. I can't believe it!"

When the last carton was unloaded, Ronnie got down from the stepladder and folded it, while I took the empty carton into the incinerator room. When I returned, Ronnie had put the ladder in the broom closet and was twirling around the center of the loft. "Perfection!" she shouted.

Her enthusiasm was contagious. "Super!" I agreed.

"Now let's hope Marsha likes my paintings."

"She will if she has good judgment!"

"I can always count on you, Jill," Ronnie said lovingly.

"I just hope her son isn't a nerd."

"Don't worry. If you don't like him, you never have to see him again."

"That's true."

Just then the buzzer sounded and Ronnie said, "I'll get it. Will you put on the teakettle?"

"Sure," I replied, and headed for the kitchen.

While I was putting in the water, I heard Marsha exclaiming, "Oh, Ronnie, I can't believe we're neighbors. This is so wonderful."

"Come in, come in," Ronnie said.

"This is Jason," Marsha said.

"Hello, Jason. Your mother didn't have to introduce us. I could tell in a minute you belong to Marsha. You two look exactly alike."

"Practically clones. Fortunately my mother is very good-looking."

They all laughed. *Fresh kid*, I thought to myself, and got some mugs off the shelf.

"Hey, Jill, we have guests," Ronnie called.

"I'm coming," I said, walking out of the kitchen.

Ronnie was hanging their jackets on a coatrack that looked like antler horns attached to a broomstick. It was one of her impulse buys that happened to be practical because we don't have a hall closet.

"This is Jill." My mother turned to introduce us.

I could hear Jason whistle under his breath, and then mumble, "To think I didn't even want to come here!"

"Speak up," Marsha said to him.

"Hiya, Jill." Jason extended his hand.

"Hi, Jason." I shook his hand a few seconds longer than necessary because I couldn't stop looking at him. He had the most penetrating brown eyes I'd ever seen. He also had a great smile that seemed to have a melting effect on me. *No nerd he*, I thought to myself.

"And this is my old friend Marsha," Ronnie announced.

"Hello," I said, managing to take my eyes off Jason.

"Let's sit down," Ronnie suggested, and led the way.

"You've done fantastic things here," Marsha commented. "I always remembered you as being one of the most talented art students and was sure I'd be reading about you in some of the art journals. What happened?"

Marsha had the same Mediterranean good looks as Jason and was obviously just as outspoken.

"What happened was I got married, settled down in suburbia, and didn't spend as much time as I should have painting."

"I love your work," Marsha enthused as she gazed at a huge canvas that covered a white wall. "You must have others."

"I do, I do. Let's have some tea and then I'll show them to you. They're in my studio, which is behind that screen." She pointed to the far end of the loft.

"I can't wait to see them," Marsha said impatiently.

"Why don't I fix the tea and you can show your paintings," I suggested.

"Good thinking, Jill," Ronnie said.

"And I'll help in the kitchen," Jason volunteered as he got up to follow me.

I led the way into the kitchen and promptly turned off the boiling water.

"It's one of the few times my mother's been right," Jason muttered, standing very close to me.

"What do you mean?" I asked as I put some tea bags into a china teapot.

"I mean she had to talk me into coming here. She said your mother is an old friend, and that she had a daughter — that's you — and that you'd just moved to Soho and I should be a welcoming committee."

"And you didn't want to come, right?"

Jason nodded his head.

"Can't say that I blame you."

"But look what I would have missed."

"Me, too," I said, looking into his eyes and reaching for the teakettle at the same time. I missed the handle completely.

"Ouch!" I screeched, and jerked my hand away.

"Let me take over," Jason said authoritatively. "I'm very big in the tea department. But first, let me see the damage."

He gently took my hand and examined it. There was a tiny red mark, and he lifted my hand to his face and brushed his lips over it. "Better than butter," he boasted.

"I'll get some cookies out. That can't get me into trouble," I said, pulling my hand away and trying to cover my embarrassment. I put everything on a tray and Jason carried it to the round table that designated the dining room.

We sat down and I asked, "How do you like it?"

"Straight," he answered.

"Help yourself to cookies," I said, and poured the tea.

There was what seemed a long silence and I noticed Jason staring at me. I looked at him expectantly and when he still didn't say anything, I said, "What's wrong?"

"You're amazing-looking."

"I am? No one's ever said that before."

"I'm known for my originality."

"And your modesty, I'm sure."

Then we both laughed, and Jason asked, "Where do you go to school?"

I told him the name of my school and he groaned. "Oh, no. Why do you have to go *uptown* to a private school, when you could be going to Stuyvesant, which is public and *downtown*?"

"It's a compromise."

"Between what and what?"

"Well, it's a lot like the school I went to in Westport, even though it is private."

"But couldn't you find a downtown expensive school?"

I found myself on the defensive. "I'll be uptown next month."

"You just moved, Jill. What's the matter with you?"

"It's the arrangement." He looked bewildered and I thought, *Here it goes again.* I was right in the middle of explaining when Ronnie and Marsha pulled up chairs to join us. Ronnie was all smiles, so I knew Marsha had liked her paintings.

"It's all set then," Marsha was saying. "If you can have two other canvasses ready by Christmas time, I can promise you a one-woman show."

"That's terrific," I said. "Let's drink to that." I held up my cup.

"And let's drink to uptown versus downtown," Jason chimed in.

Marsha and Ronnie simultaneously looked at each other, raised their eyebrows, and shrugged their shoulders. Then they went right on talking about the art show Ronnie would have. I wanted to participate in the discussion, but was too busy thinking about what Jason had said — "uptown versus downtown." I don't know why that remark bothered me so much, or why, in fact, *he* bothered me so much. The only thing I knew for sure was that I'd have to see him again. When it came time for them to leave, Jason said to me in an offhand manner, "My mother says one of my welcoming functions is to show you Soho. How about going out Saturday?"

"You don't have to continue welcoming me," I said haughtily.

"Only kidding," he said gently. "I'd love to show you Soho." Then he beamed those eyes on me and I could feel myself weakening. "Is it a deal?"

"Deal," I gasped, unable to say anything else.

"Is nine o'clock in the morning too early? That's when a well-organized tour begins."

"Nine's fine," I said, knowing I would have agreed to anything.

As soon as they left, and we heard the elevator door close, Ronnie exclaimed, "Isn't Marsha great? And she really liked my work. I'm so excited."

"That's super," I told her.

"What d'ja think of Jason?" Ronnie asked.

"Interesting," I said noncommittally.

"Handsome, I'd say," my mother said, munching on a cookie. She glanced at me knowingly, but didn't pursue the subject. She knows when I clam up that it means I don't want any questions.

"I've got to get to work right away, in order to finish two canvasses by December. No time for gabbing."

"I'll clean up," I offered.

"Thanks, Jill. I don't know what I'll do without you next month." Ronnie suddenly seemed very sad.

"There's always the month after," I said, trying to sound cheerful.

"You're right! That's the only way to look at it."

When she headed for her "studio" I sank down in a chair, thinking I'd have one more cup of tea. *Uptown versus downtown,* he'd said, *one of my welcoming functions, look what I would have missed, I'd love to show you Soho, you're amazing-looking, better than butter.*

No one had ever affected me so strongly and so quickly. It was very unsettling. And those fabulous eyes! I couldn't wait till Saturday.

Chapter Seven

The last Saturday in September turned out to be a perfect Indian summer day. I waited downstairs in front of my building because Ronnie was still sleeping and I didn't want to disturb her. Actually, I hadn't spoken to Jason all week and I was a little anxious that he might have forgotten about me. But promptly at nine he appeared.

"You're a woman of your word, and prompt besides," he greeted me. His tousled black hair was still wet from the shower he'd obviously taken, and it fell over his forehead. *He is handsome*, I thought.

"And you're a man of your word." I thought I'd better use my voice because looking at him had a tendency to make me freeze.

"Do you know anything about Soho?" he asked. We started strolling.

"Practically nothing."

"You've had a very sheltered life, I guess."

"Do you know anything about Westport?" I countered. He did have a way of putting me down.

"What's to know?" he asked, but didn't wait for an answer. He went right on talking. "The first thing you should know about Soho is it's about twenty-six blocks and is a historic landmark. That means that these cast-iron buildings must be preserved. A lot of them were used originally for manufacturing, but now they've been converted into lofts and studios, and mostly people in the arts — painters, dancers, actors, and musicians live here. They're the most interesting people anyway. That's why Soho's so great. Too bad you have to live uptown at all."

"Hey, wait a minute. Uptown has some interesting people, too." I was thinking about my father.

"Like who?"

"Like my father. He's a lawyer and even though he's not artistic, he's still interesting."

Jason ignored that and went right on rattling about the charms of living downtown. He pointed out the most famous restaurants as we walked along West Broadway and up some of the side streets. There seemed to be a zillion of them.

"There's something for everyone here," he said. "Chinese, French, Japanese, cafés, cabarets, pubs. Much more interesting than the Upper East Side."

I didn't say anything. In the first place, I didn't know that much about the Upper East Side yet, and in the second place, I didn't want to spend the day arguing.

"Now I'm going to show you the best food store in the world. Actually, it's a food emporium."

"I'm willing to try anything."

Jason put his hand on my arm and pulled me into a brightly lit store, filled with some of the most exotic-looking foods I'd ever seen.

"Wow!" I shouted, genuinely impressed.

"You can have anything here — from quail eggs to butterfly wings. What would you like?"

"I'll settle for a pastry," I said, looking at a delectable selection and pointing to a raspberry tart.

"Make it two," Jason told the amazingly slender woman behind the counter.

I reached in my pocket for some money, but Jason grabbed my arm and said, "This is on me."

"That's silly," I protested.

"I'm the tour director. You do what I say."

"If you insist."

We stopped at a café, ordered coffee, and ate our tarts while Jason mapped out the rest of the walking tour, which included galleries, boutiques, and museums.

He did seem to know Soho like the palm of his hand, and we weaved in and out of places for a couple more hours. By mid-afternoon I was beginning to fade. Jason noticed and suggested I go to his place and play some records.

"My folks are away for the day, and we won't have to worry about making too much noise. Every time I play the stereo, they're convinced I'm hard of hearing. I keep denying it, but George — he's my father — says if I keep it up, I'll go deaf, to say nothing of what it will do to his and Marsha's ears."

I couldn't help laughing, and Jason asked me what was so funny. "That's exactly the kind of thing my father warns me about. I think their generation must have been born with very sensitive ears."

"Just one of the many gaps. Anyhow, here's our chance to blast some music. I've got some new records I'd like you to hear."

"I don't think so," I said hesitantly.

He didn't seem to hear me. "Let's get going," he said. "It's getting chilly and you look like you could stand some of my hot cocoa. Another specialty of this tour."

"But your parents aren't home."

"So what?"

"So I don't think I want to go to your place without anyone there."

"Are you kidding?"

"No, I honestly don't want to."

"How old are you, Jill?" He sounded annoyed.

"You know I'm fifteen."

"You sound about ten. With some ten-year-old's hang-ups."

"They're not hang-ups. It's just not what I want to do."

"Maybe I'm just too old for you, or too sophisticated. I'll be seventeen next month, and you are the youngest girl I've ever even looked at. I guess I should have known better."

"I can go home by myself," I said stonily, although my feelings were really hurt.

"I'll walk you to your building. After all, that's part of my assignment."

"Don't do me any favors."

"I'm not. But I wouldn't want you to get lost."

I knew he was being facetious because we were only about two blocks from where I lived. I started walking briskly, but he kept up with me. When we got to my building, I turned to Jason and said, "I had a great time — till now. And thanks for everything."

"I had a great time till now, too," he said. His voice mellowed. "I know you're moving this week and won't be back for a month. Maybe by then you'll grow up. If that happens, call me." Then, before I knew what was happening, he put his hands on my shoulders, pulled me toward him, and kissed me right on the mouth.

I was so surprised that when he let me go I couldn't say anything. He looked at me very hard and neither of us said a word. Then he turned away abruptly and said, "See ya, kid."

I don't know how long I stood there, but I suddenly noticed it was getting dark, and I went inside and waited for the elevator. When I got into the loft, my mother was busy painting.

"How'd it go, Jill?" she asked.

"Interesting," I answered as I kissed her on

the cheek. Then I walked into my room. My mother knows that "interesting" is my code word for not wanting to talk.

I sat down at my desk, knowing I had to master my Spanish verbs for a test we were having Monday, but all I could think of was Jason. I really liked him, I thought, but I wasn't sure how much. Had I blown the whole thing? Was I acting like a ten-year-old? He had me completely confused, and to add to my problems, I had only two more days of the month left in Soho. On Tuesday I planned to take a suitcase of clothes uptown, and move into my father's apartment for *his* month.

Chapter Eight

I arrived at my father's apartment after school on Tuesday as planned, and a big, friendly-looking woman let me in. "You must be Jilly," she said with a thick Viennese accent. "I'm Marie, who comes every afternoon to clean and cook."

"Hello, Marie," I said as she took my suitcase and ushered me into the living room.

I'd never been to the apartment before, but it looked familiar because it was furnished with all the early-American antique furniture that we had in Westport. The apartment even had a fireplace, and the chintz-covered chairs and sofa were grouped around it just as they had been in our house.

"Come, I'll show you your room," Marie said, "and help you unpack."

I followed her as she went on babbling about

what a lovely room my father had had decorated for me, and how pleased he was with the results. I let out a sigh when I saw what had been done, and I hoped Marie didn't notice. Actually, the room was very pretty — all pink and white and matching curtains and bedspread, with Grandma Moses-type paintings on the walls. But as they say in the decorating magazines, it wasn't *me*. I mean it would have been great for a little kid about seven years old, but it was too frilly and unsophisticated. It flashed through my head what Jason would have said, but fortunately he'd never see it.

Marie had opened my suitcase and was starting to take out my clothes. "I'll do that," I told her, hoping I didn't sound rude. "Otherwise I won't know where anything is."

"Such a smart girl!"

I had to smile because Marie treated me as if I were seven years old, too.

"When does my father get home?"

"Always at six. And always he has dinner at six-thirty."

"Before I unpack, I'd like to see the rest of the apartment."

"Sure, sure." Marie seemed so happy that she could do something for me. "Come, I'll show you."

First I followed her into the kitchen, which was small but compact, and something delicious was cooking. "That smells wonderful," I said.

Marie was all smiles. "A roast stew. One of my specialties, because you're here."

"Oh, thank you."

"Such a sweet girl," Marie remarked, and I realized I could do no wrong in her eyes.

Then she led me into my father's room, which was fixed up like a study. The walls were lined with books and it had a black leather chair and hassock for reading, and a daybed. It was almost a duplicate of our den in Westport, but this doubled as a bedroom. It made me feel nostalgic and right at home, all at the same time. I had so many different feelings, I wondered if I'd ever be able to sort them out.

"Nice, no?" Marie asked.

"Yes, very," I said.

"Now I go into the kitchen. If you need me for anything, just call."

"Thank you, Marie. I will."

I went back to my room and started hanging my clothes on the pink velvet hangers, and putting things in the chest of drawers that had been lined with pink and white paper. Everything was so perfect and tidy, it almost made me uncomfortable. Ronnie was so laid back about housekeeping, and having meals on time. I knew my father wasn't nearly so relaxed and I'd have to adjust.

Now I could see that my parents' different attitudes toward life were probably one of the reasons they couldn't get along, no matter how hard they tried. They just couldn't change their personalities or the way they'd been brought up. Actually, I could see advantages to both lifestyles. Ronnie was more easygoing, but I knew that my father had provided me with a structure that made me know I could always depend on him.

When I finished putting my things away, I settled down to do my homework. I had an algebra assignment. Algebra is my least favorite subject, but to my amazement I could do the problems without too much difficulty this time. I thought to myself that maybe I was inspired by my highly organized room. Before I knew it, it was six o'clock and I heard my father's key in the door.

I ran out to greet him. He had his briefcase in one hand, and a bunch of flowers in the other, but he still managed to squeeze me in a hug. I was so happy to see him that I let out an unexpected squeal of delight.

He was smiling, and asking a million questions, and saying he hoped I liked my room. Marie stood there, clapping her hands and saying, "Oh, it's so wonderful, so wonderful." You would have thought that we'd been separated for more like thirty months rather than thirty days.

"These are for you, dear," my father said. "Now you've got to find something to put them in."

I took the bunch of flowers and carefully removed the wrapping.

"They're beautiful," I said, sniffing the miniature red roses.

"I really missed you," he remarked.

"Me, too, Daddy."

"I find a vase," Marie said, taking the flowers from me, and she disappeared into the kitchen.

"I hope you had a good time in Soho, but not so much that you didn't want to come uptown," my father said seriously as he hung his coat in the hall closet.

"Soho was great, but I was still looking forward to being with you this month," I told him honestly.

"Good girl. I know things will work out. I'm going to wash up. Then I'll fix a drink. Do you want a Coke or something?"

"I'll have a Coke. Why don't I fix your drink?"

"You know how?"

"Of course, if it's not too fancy."

"Can you make a martini on the rocks?"

"Coming right up," I said.

"Very good." He sounded quite amazed as he walked into his room.

As I went over to the bar, which was built into the bookcase, I couldn't help chuckling because anytime I did anything the least bit grown up, my father seemed astounded.

When my father came back into the living room, I had just finished pouring in the vermouth, and then went to the fridge to get a bottle of Coke.

"Perfect proportions," he said, sipping the martini as I brought my Coke into the living room and sat opposite him.

"Maybe I should be a chemist," I suggested.

"You seem to have the magic touch." My

father was peering at me over the rim of his glass and frowned.

"What's wrong?" I asked.

"We're not having a picnic, you know."

"Oh, this," I said, holding out the bottle. "You mean I should use a glass."

"That's what we do in civilized society," he said, half-kidding.

I certainly wouldn't tell him, but for the past month I'd been drinking Cokes out of bottles. Ronnie wouldn't even think about that being bad manners. In fact, she'd be glad because it would mean one less glass to wash. But I helped myself to a glass at the bar, and my father asked me questions about school.

Marie came in to tell us dinner was ready, and I continued telling my father about all my courses, and how much I liked sociology, in between exclaiming to Marie how delicious everything was, and she muttering under her breath, "What a perfect little girl," which made both me and my father have trouble not laughing.

We were on dessert, a delectable homemade chocolate roll, when my father said, "I wanted to show you the city Saturday, but I'm working on a case, and I've got to have my brief ready by Monday. There's no way I can get out of it."

"That's okay. The kids at school want me to do something with them, since this is the first time I'll be uptown on the weekend."

"That's good. But you can have dinner with me. I'm playing squash at five-thirty and you can meet me at the club. There's a new Italian restaurant I want to try. Marie is off weekends, so it's a good time to go out."

"Sounds wonderful. Unless you want me to make my special lasagne."

"You cook?" he asked in amazement.

"I've just learned how to make a few dishes, since I've been living in Soho."

"We'll save that for another time. For your first weekend here, I think we should go out."

After dinner, my father said he had to work on his case and went into his room. I offered to help Marie with the dishes, but she would only let me clear the table and insisted on doing everything else herself.

I wandered into my room and idly flipped on the television. One of my favorite programs had just begun, but I couldn't concentrate. I was too busy thinking about my family and my new life. The change from Soho to uptown was dramatic, but luckily I seemed to be adjusting.

Chapter Nine

Saturday morning I woke up about nine-thirty, and still half asleep, stumbled into the kitchen. There was a note from my father Scotch-taped to the fridge:

> Jill dear,
>   Have gone to the office to do some research and will be there all day in case you need me. Am leaving your allowance on the hall table plus a ten-dollar bonus. Buy something special today for yourself! Meet me at six at the club.
>
> Love,
> Daddy

I poured some cornflakes and milk into a bowl, and sat on the kitchen stool, slowly eating and grateful to be alone. I really do like people, but when a zillion things are happening I sometimes just like to sit and think.

I had just finished my cereal when the phone rang. It was Maggie, firming up our plans. We were to meet Sandy and Serena in the junior department of Bloomingdale's at eleven o'clock. They would take me on a tour of the store, we'd have lunch at a café that specializes in omelets, investigate the record store on Lexington Avenue, and do anything else that I wanted.

"Terrific," I exclaimed when Maggie finished describing our plan of action. Then I told her about the bonus my father had given me and that I had to spend it that very day on myself.

"That shouldn't be too difficult," Magie said. "Sandy and Serena are great at figuring out how to spend money."

Then I heard some noises in the background, and Maggie was saying, "Be quiet."

I said, "What?" because I thought she was talking to me.

She explained that she was talking to her kid brother, who was being a pest, as usual, but that it was her turn to walk the dog and she had to hang up. "I'll see you later. Remember, second floor, junior department."

"Later," I said, and hung up.

I cleaned up the kitchen, made my bed, and got dressed in my jeans and my favorite red knobby sweater. I was in a really good mood, delighted at the prospect of having some extra money to spend, but also amazed. My father is usually very strict about not letting me spend more than my allowance. He thinks it's important to learn how to budget, and plan ahead for gifts and extras.

I still had time to walk the twenty-odd blocks to Bloomingdale's. It was a perfect fall day, and even though I missed being in Westport, where I'd probably be playing tennis outdoors now, I thought about it less and less. There was something exciting about just walking in the city.

When I took the escalator to the second floor, Maggie was waiting for me. A few minutes later Sandy and Serena arrived, and we greeted each other like long-lost friends. No one would have believed we'd seen each other the day before.

"What'll we do first?" Sandy asked.

"I have to buy a present for my mother. It's her birthday next week," Serena told me.

"Have you decided what to buy?" Maggie asked.

"She loves blouses, so I'll go pick one out and meet you wherever you want."

"I want to see the model rooms. Jill, that's something you'll love," Sandy said.

"I'll meet you on the fifth floor then," Serena announced, and went off.

The model rooms were unusual, each one representing a motif from a different country. The Indian decor was the most exotic, with dramatic cloths billowing from the ceiling. The futurama room was all silver and chrome and you'd have to be a space cadet to feel comfortable just standing in it. My favorite room was contemporary Danish, furnished with beautiful teakwood tables and chairs, and a desk that had such perfectly clean lines it would inspire anyone who used it. It occurred to me that if my parents ever let me choose what I wanted, instead of what they liked, it would be this.

Serena met us, carrying a shopping bag, and said, "Mission accomplished." She took a fast look at the rooms while Sandy told me that she wanted to be a decorator and what she would do different in her own home. Her mother kept everything magazine-perfect, which drove Sandy crazy because she was afraid to sit down half the time for fear she might mess something up.

Then we investigated other parts of the store, until Maggie said we should get to the omelet place soon or we'd never get in. We trudged over to a small restaurant on a side street that was already filling up. When we had given our order I told everyone about the bonus I had to spend, and Sandy explained, "If it were me, I'd buy a plant for my room. My mother hates plants because they need care and I think if a leaf fell off she'd throw the whole thing out."

"I'd buy records," Maggie said. "I can never have enough, and Linda Ronstadt has a new album out."

"I don't think my father would appreciate that," I commented. "He only likes classical music."

"What about your mother?" Sandy asked.

"She'd go for it. But I'd have to wait till next month."

"If I had to spend money, I'd get earrings," Serena said. "I think I have a pair to fit every mood and every occasion. Like right now I'm wearing my Saturday-with-the-girls pair." She held back her long hair so we could see her small gold loops.

"That's not a bad idea," Maggie remarked. "I love earrings, too, and they come in all prices."

"But I don't wear earrings," I said.

"You don't wear earrings?" Sandy shouted in such a loud voice that the people at the next table stared at us. Sandy covered her mouth to hide her embarrassment while we all giggled.

"They're not even pierced," I went on.

"You're kidding," Serena drawled. "I've had pierced ears since I was twelve."

"You always were a leader," Maggie said good-naturedly.

"But there's no question, Jill. That's what you should do," Sandy went on.

"That's right," Maggie agreed. "That's the perfect way to spend your bonus. And there's a jeweler just down the street where you can have it done."

"Does it hurt?" I asked, getting really interested.

"Not at all. It just feels funny for a minute," Sandy said.

"First you pick out the earrings," Maggie explained. "They have to have gold posts so you don't get an infection."

"And leave them in for a month. After that, you can wear anything you want in your ears."

"Including these," Serena said, dipping into her shopping bag and coming up with a small package. "After I bought the blouse, I couldn't resist going by the earring counter. I guess I'm addicted." She unwrapped the package and held up some feather earrings that I could never imagine wearing.

"You could get away with those," Maggie observed, "but I wouldn't have the nerve."

"You get used to it," Serena said.

"You'll first get tiny gold ones, Jill," Sandy explained. "They'll seem tame after these birds Serena will have dangling."

"You talked me into it," I said, "but I am a little nervous."

"Don't be," Maggie instructed. "We'll hold your hand."

"It's not like having a baby," Serena said so seriously that we had to laugh.

"I'll be brave," I promised.

After we left the restaurant I followed the girls down the street to a small jewelry store where a sign in the window read, *Ears pierced free with one purchase of 14-karat gold earrings.*

Inside the store, a man with twinkly blue eyes, wearing a gray smock, which made him look half-artist and half-doctor, greeted us. "Who's the victim?" he asked.

"Me," I croaked.

"Nothing to worry about," he assured me. "I've already punched six pairs of ears this morning and haven't lost a customer yet."

The girls laughed, but I could only manage to smile weakly.

"First, pick out a pair of these," the jeweler

said, and opened a velvet case which had dozens of small gold earrings. I picked out a pair of gold studs.

"Perfect for a beginner," Serena commented.

Then the artist-doctor pointed to a high stool at the far end of the store and I sat down.

"My name is MacIntyre, but my friends call me Mac," the jeweler said as he dabbed something that was probably antiseptic on my earlobes. He kept up a running commentary while he prepared to "operate." Then he picked up what looked like a paper punch, I closed my eyes, and the whole thing was over in minutes.

Maggie and Sandy were watching from a distance and both applauded. I got up from my chair, held back my hair, and glanced in the mirror. "You've done it!" Maggie exclaimed.

"Welcome to the club," Sandy added.

We walked to the front of the store where Serena was leaning over the glass case that exhibited jewelry. She glanced at me long enough to say, "Congratulations." Then she turned back to the case, and said, "I have to have these." She pointed to a pair of silver loops.

"I thought you had this size," Sandy remarked.

"Not in silver. But I guess I've had my quota for today. Maybe I'll come back next week, if I pick up any money baby-sitting."

"We always have a supply of these and new ones coming in," Mac told her.

"I'm glad to hear that," Serena said. Then she spotted another pair that struck her fancy.

They were jade dangles. "O-oh," she sighed, "there's another pair that I can't live without."

"We better leave before Serena loses control," Sandy advised.

"You're absolutely right," Serena agreed. "I don't know what I'd do without such good friends."

I couldn't tell if she was being sarcastic or not, but I thought I was lucky to have good friends so soon.

I paid Mac my "bonus" and had to add some from my allowance. It's worth it, I thought. It's time I started looking more sophisticated.

Our next stop was the record store on Lexington, where we lingered over the new listings, and finally Maggie bought a new country-western album.

It was almost five o'clock and I had to get uptown to change my clothes. My father would never approve of me going out to dinner in jeans. I explained all this and said good-bye to the girls. "Thanks for showing me around today. I really like it uptown."

"This is only the beginning," Sandy said.

Then I started home, thinking what a great time I'd had. Not wanting to spoil everything by being late for my father, who hates to be kept waiting, I walked faster, but I still could take in the cityscape. It was that time of day when the buildings were clearly silhouetted against the sky which had a soft pink glow. I thought of what Mrs. Carson had said at our last photography club meeting. She had advised us to have a camera ready to take pictures at all times. "You never know when something unexpected will happen, something you didn't anticipate that you'd like to 'freeze' on film."

I thought how right she was, that I would have loved to have a permanent reminder of this extraordinary skyline. Then Mrs. Carson had added in an offhand manner that in life you never know when something unexpected will happen, for which you'll be totally unprepared.

Chapter Ten

When I got home I changed into my red plaid skirt, white blouse, and black velvet jacket. I hadn't worn clothes like these for a whole month and it occurred to me that I had two "different" everything, including two separate wardrobes. If I'd gotten dressed to go out to dinner with Ronnie, I'd be wearing my best faded jeans.

I took the bus down to the forties, where my father's club is located. I was actually fifteen minutes early, and sat down in the lobby to wait. I was only there for about five minutes when a very preppy-looking guy sat down opposite me. He looked like he'd been born in a button-down shirt, striped tie, and dark blue blazer. His straight blond hair was short and perfectly combed. His classic features and robin's-egg blue eyes made him look like he'd walked out of an ad. I would have expected him to be very snobby, but he started talking to me right away.

"Hi," he said. "I'm waiting for my father. How about you?"

"Me, too."

"You're waiting for my father?" he asked grinning. *At least he has a sense of humor,* I thought.

"No, *my* father. He's playing squash."

"Mine, too. I'm going out to dinner with him because my mother is visiting my grandparents in Florida."

"I'm going out to dinner with my father, too."

"Now don't tell me your mother's in Florida. At this rate, we might turn out to be brother and sister."

We both laughed out loud at that, and I couldn't help noticing that he had a toothpaste smile that definitely belonged in a TV commercial.

"My mother's not in Florida," I said.

"You make her sound mysterious," he remarked in such a way that I felt I had to explain further.

"My mother lives in Soho."

"Don't you live there, too?"

"Half the time."

"Huh?"

"My parents are divorced."

His jaw dropped visibly. Finally he recovered enough to say, "You live half the time with one, and half with the other."

"That's right. I move every month."

"And this is your father's month."

"You got it," I said.

"That's really too bad."

"No, it isn't," I said defensively.

"I don't approve of divorce." Now he was beginning to sound as arrogant as he looked.

"The divorce wasn't up to me." I was annoyed with his attitude.

"Do you actually enjoy living in Soho? That's the place for Bohemians."

"That's crazy. My mother lives there and she happens to be an artist. That doesn't make her Bohemian!" I was really getting mad, and he noticed.

"I'm sorry," he apologized, looking so crest-fallen that I believed him. "I don't really know anyone who lives there, and I shouldn't make snap judgments."

"You've led a very sheltered life," I said, borrowing a line from Jason.

"You're probably right." He seemed so contrite that instead of being angry anymore, I was almost beginning to feel sorry for him. "I didn't mean to get so personal and I don't even know your name." He moved over to where I was sitting and extended his hand.

"My name is Jill Belmont," I said, and shook his hand.

"Hi, Jill. I'm Paul Bennett. Forgive my bad manners. I know I shouldn't have said all those things. It just surprised me."

"That's okay," I said, thinking it's hard to stay mad when someone admits he's wrong.

Then we told each other where we went to school, and Paul seemed pleased that mine was on the Upper East Side. He went to an all boys' school that still required ties and jackets. When I expressed surprise he accused me of having as many preconceived ideas as he did. I admitted he'd scored on that one.

We were so involved that neither of us noticed our fathers approaching until they were only a few feet away. Mr. Bennett, who was a larger and craggier edition of Paul, cleared his throat and said, "Hello, son. I'm glad you two have met because we're all having dinner together. Paul, this is Mr. Belmont."

"Hello, sir." Paul stood up and shook hands with my father.

"Hi, Daddy," I said, standing up also. My father gave me a kiss on the cheek and introduced me to Mr. Bennett.

"Mr. Bennett and I were playing squash together and when we discovered we were both meeting our offspring, we decided we should join forces."

"Good idea," Paul agreed.

"I knew you'd think so," his father said. "Paul's afraid that if I get him alone, I'll start questioning him about his summer plans."

"Dad, it's only October. You don't expect me to look now for something next summer."

"It's never too early to look ahead. If you want a job as a counselor, you better know it soon. Camps start hiring almost as soon as the camp season's over."

"Yes, Dad," Paul said resignedly, and I could see immediately that it wasn't *his* fault if he was so stuffy.

My father suggested that we eat in the taproom, and Mr. Bennett agreed, saying, "Best roast beef in town."

Dinner went okay and I could see that our fathers had a lot in common. They'd been classmates at college, and belonged to the same eating club.

As we were leaving the taproom, Paul pulled me aside and said he hoped he could see me again. "There's a dance at my school two weeks from tonight. Could you come?"

"I'd love to," I replied, "but I'll have to check it out with my father." The minute I said that I was embarrassed. I mean I'd never have asked my mother's permission to go to a dance. I'd just tell her and she'd tell me to have a good time. "My father likes to know my plans," I added quickly.

Paul seemed to understand perfectly, and said he'd call me during the week to make sure it was okay.

We dropped Paul and his father on Sixty-third Street, and I was thinking what a nice time I'd had when my father suddenly blew up.

"Jill," he exploded, "I thought I could trust you."

"What do you mean?" I asked, trying to think what I'd done.

"Do I have to monitor every penny you spend?"

64

"I don't know what you're talking about." I
was totally bewildered.

"These!" he shouted, pointing at my ears. "I
didn't give you extra money for that."

"They're just tiny little studs."

"In the first place, I don't like earrings on
young girls, and second, I never thought you
would have them pierced without my permission.
You're certainly too young for that!"

"I'm not too young," I protested. "Almost
every girl in my class has pierced ears. The
friends I met today couldn't believe I'd waited
this long."

"Next thing, you'll be getting a ring for your
nose, just because your friends do."

"That's not true!" I felt awful, because I'd
tried so hard to please my father — making my
bed before I left, cleaning up the kitchen, wearing the right clothes for meeting him for dinner,
making sure I was on time. But somehow I
never thought that he might not approve of how
I'd spent my bonus. I never thought he'd be so
angry.

It went through my head that my mother
would have approved, but I knew it wouldn't
be fair for me to use that as an argument. In
order to keep peace, I mumbled something about
being sorry, and by the time my father had paid
the taxi and we got upstairs, he seemed to have
calmed down. Dad loses his temper fast, but
fortunately gets over it quickly. I've learned
the best way to handle him is just get off the
subject.

"Paul has asked me to go to his school dance two weeks from tonight. Is that okay?" I was fully aware of playing the "good little girl" role.

"Paul's a very nice young man. I'm sure you'll enjoy going with him."

"I had a really nice time tonight, Daddy. Thanks a lot."

"I enjoyed it, too, dear," he said. And then he added, in case he thought I'd forgotten, "Just don't let me catch you wearing anything bigger than those pinheads in your ears."

"Don't worry!" I said, relieved that the crisis was over.

That night, as I tried to get to sleep, I reviewed everything that had happened. If I was totally honest, I knew I wasn't sorry I'd had my ears pierced, no matter how mad it made my father. The other thing I knew was I was looking forward to seeing Paul again. Maybe he was a little stuffy, and almost too polite, but it would be a nice change from know-it-all Jason!

Chapter Eleven

The next morning my father apologized again for having to work all day, and told me that he'd treat me and a friend to a movie. I was about to accept his offer, when Maggie telephoned and asked me to come over for brunch. "Brunch is my father's specialty," she explained. "He makes French toast, bacon, sausages, and fresh-ground coffee. Also, it's the one time he insists that my mother stay out of the kitchen."

"Hang on. I'll ask my father if it's okay."

"Who's Maggie?" my father inquired when I told him she had invited me over.

"A friend from school." I covered the receiver with my hand so that she couldn't hear me. "She's the one who's been so helpful to me from my first day."

"I guess it's okay. Just make sure you're home by six."

"It's okay," I told Maggie, feeling dumb because I had to ask my father's permission for everything.

"Good. Be here by noon. You'll get the full treatment from my brother, Billy, who's eleven years old and an expert in being a pain. His specialty is my friends."

"Can't wait," I said. "It'll be better than going to the movies."

"Who said anything about movies?" Maggie asked.

"I'll explain later."

Maggie lived in a big co-op apartment located just a few blocks from where we lived. She actually had the door open to her apartment when I got off the elevator so I'd know which direction to go, and she immediately dragged me into the kitchen where her father was bustling around.

Mr. Lawton had reddish hair, looked like a younger version of Danny Kaye, and was very good-natured. He was complaining that someone had hidden his favorite spatula, and that he couldn't cook without the proper equipment, and therefore it wouldn't be his fault if the French toast tasted like lead instead of ambrosia. When he paused for breath, Maggie introduced me, and Mr. Lawton, who was in the process of breaking eggs, waggled his little finger at me and said, "You must be a special friend of Maggie's. Only her favorite people are privileged to partake of my Sunday brunches."

"I'm honored," I said.

"Now, out of the kitchen. I need all my powers of concentration to make this concoction come out right."

Maggie and I scurried out of the kitchen and plopped down on the couch in the living room.

"Where's your mother?" I asked.

"She doesn't make her appearance on Sunday until my father calls her into the dining room."

"You mean she plays queen for a day?"

"Actually, it's more like empress."

"And where's your brother?"

"Right here!" a voice piped up from behind the couch.

Maggie and I both jumped. "I wish you wouldn't do that," Maggie snapped.

"But your friend wanted to meet me. Right, friend?" He smiled, and looked exactly like a cute chipmunk. He was hard to resist.

"Hello, Billy. I'm Jill."

"Pleased to meetcha," he said, and stuck out his hand for me to shake.

"I've heard about you," I said.

"If it's from Maggie, it must be all bad."

"Not *all*," I told him, smiling.

"What'd she tell ya?"

"Look, Billy," Maggie groaned before I got a chance to answer, "why don't you get lost?"

"You mean disappear?"

"If you're good we'll take you and Gladstone to the park later."

"And if I'm not good . . . ?"

Maggie ignored him and turned to me. "It's

not easy to have a private conversation in this house, unless I hide in the closet."

"And then, who knows, I might be listening from a shelf."

"You're funny," I remarked.

"You're cute," Billy said.

I couldn't help laughing, but Maggie was frowning. "Come on, Jill," she sighed wearily. "I'll show you my room. That is my turf, and nobody, including Ermantrude, our cat, or Gladstone, our poodle, is allowed in without my permission."

"What she's really saying, Jill, is that she wants to keep me out. I can take a hint."

"Remember," Maggie said, standing up, "good now, zoo later."

We were heading for Maggie's room when Mr. Lawton, wearing a frilly apron, popped out of the kitchen. "Five minutes till countdown," he announced. "Prepare the troops."

"I'll get mother," Billy volunteered, and scooted past us.

"And we'll wash our hands," Maggie said.

I followed her into her bedroom and gasped when I looked around. It was exactly the kind of room I would have liked. It had a studio bed covered in a navy blue and white print, white shutters on the window, and a solid navy blue easy chair. The desk and bureau were Danish modern. The rug on the floor was deep red.

"This is perfect!" I exclaimed.

"What is?" Maggie asked innocently.

"This room. It's exactly what I would like to have."

"Oh," she said, "I guess I'm used to it."

I thought then that if I didn't like Maggie so much I might be jealous. Everything seemed so easy and normal for her. I even envied her having a kid brother who, though he was a pest, I knew she liked. And she took it all for granted.

I was thinking these things when her father shouted, "Come on, troops, before it gets cold."

We hurriedly washed our hands and went into the dining room. Maggie introduced me to her mother, who was already seated at one end of the table. Not only did she act like an empress, she looked like one, too. She had a cameo complexion, and dark gray eyes, and it was hard to imagine her *not* being waited on. She was wearing a long, green velour hostess gown, a single strand of pearls, and she looked like she should be at a state dinner. Her streaked blond hair was held back with combs.

"How do you do, Jill?" she said when Maggie introduced us. "How do you like living in New York?"

She seemed genuinely interested, and I told her how much I was enjoying the city.

Then Mr. Lawton, who had dished out the French toast and sausages, said, "Isn't anyone going to comment on this glorious repast?"

"It's spectacular, Allan. You've outdone yourself."

"Super," I chimed in.

"Better than ever," Maggie added.

"Yummy," said Billy.

"That's more like it," Mr. Lawton said. "Now you may continue your conversation and I'll fix another batch."

There was a lot more kidding around with Mr. Lawton, and Billy trying to impress me, and Mrs. Lawton trying to make me feel at home. *What a neat family*, I kept thinking.

Chapter Twelve

After we'd finished clearing off the table and loading the dishwasher, Maggie and I escaped to her room. I couldn't wait to tell her about being invited to the dance at Paul's school.

"Far out," she said. "You've only been here a few weeks, and already you've got an interesting love life."

"Not exactly," I said. I had told Maggie about Jason, and how he'd made me feel like I belonged in kindergarten. "I might not ever see Jason again, and I hardly know Paul."

"You will, though. At the rate you're going, you'll have more guys than Serena."

"I'm not looking for quantity. I'd settle for just one good one, like Seth."

Seth was Maggie's O.A.O. (one and only) and they went out together whenever possible. Seth was a junior and went to our school on a scholarship, so a lot of his free time he spent working in the supermarket. Maggie's problem was that her mother didn't think Maggie should see Seth exclusively.

"Tell me about Paul," Maggie said, throwing her long legs over the arm of the easy chair.

I was about to describe him when there was a knock at the door, and before we could ask who was there, Billy burst into the room.

"Zoo time?" he asked, trying to look innocent.

"Later," Maggie growled. "If you leave us alone for another thirty minutes, I promise we'll take you. Deal?"

"Deal," Billy agreed, and backed out of the room.

"Whew," Maggie breathed. "Now you can see what it's like having a kid brother. Pain, heh?"

"Actually, I think your family is great."

"You do? Well, they are, sort of."

"What do you mean, sort of?"

"I know you won't believe this, but sometimes I envy you."

"Me?" I was honestly shocked.

"It's hard to explain. Because even though I love my parents and everything — I'd even miss not having that bratty brother — I think it might be terrific to have a place to go to live when things get hairy around here."

"I suppose there are advantages," I said thoughtfully. "Although at the moment I can't seem to think of any. Compared to me, your life is so *normal*."

"Who cares about normal. Look at my problem, for example. I really only like Seth, but my mother gets annoyed when I don't do what she calls 'circulate.' But I also know that my mother doesn't like Seth because he isn't from the right social class. His father is a carpenter and didn't even go to college."

"How does your father feel?" I asked.

"That's the whole point. My father doesn't care about things like that. He knows Seth is a talented musician, in addition to being very smart, and he respects him for working and being on a scholarship. My mother doesn't think that's nearly as important as having a father who's gone to an Ivy League school."

"So you think if you could live with your father, you wouldn't get bad vibes about Seth from your mother, at least for the month you were living with him."

"That's right." Maggie was silent for a moment and looked very thoughtful. Then she said, "But that wouldn't be ideal either, because, although you'd never guess it, my father's a workaholic and he thinks I don't study enough. He says since I have the brains there's no reason I shouldn't have an A average."

"Does your mother care about that?"

"Not at all. She's mainly concerned that I should have fun. If I had your arrangement, I'd get away from my father's pressure to get all A's — at least for a month — but I'd feel a lot more relaxed about seeing Seth. The next month I might worry about not 'circulating,' but at least I wouldn't have to study so much."

"You make it sound so simple."

"I know it's not, and besides it's never going to happen. I mean I'm not going to suggest to my parents that they get divorced just so I can divide my time between them."

That made us both laugh, and then Maggie said, "My father says they've been married sixteen years and they're still going crazy together."

Before we could continue, there was a pounding on the door and then Billy appeared with the dog on his leash.

"Time's up!" Billy announced. "Me and Gladstone are ready."

"Okay. We'll be right with you," Maggie said.

As we got up to go I said in a low voice, "I still think you're lucky."

"I know I am," Maggie whispered back, "but then so are you."

That gave me a lot to think about. As we walked to Central Park, Billy was ahead of us trying to teach Gladstone to heel, and I tried to sort out my thoughts. Just a few hours ago I'd actually felt jealous of Maggie and her perfect life. Now I knew it wasn't so perfect. *Whose is?* I wondered.

"What are you thinking?" Maggie asked, after a long silence.

"Nothing," I answered.

"Oh, come on. Tell me."

"You first," I said.

"I was thinking that nobody's got it made."

76

"You must have read my mind," I said, "because that's exactly what I was thinking."

"Maybe that's why we're good friends."

"Probably. We're certainly on the same wavelength."

"Hey, before this gets too philosophical, we better pay some attention to Billy. He's a mile away now."

"No problem," I said. "I think he's adorable."

"You do? Well, I guess we can't agree on everything."

"You know you don't mean that."

Maggie grinned sheepishly. "Maybe you can read my mind, too."

"Let's get going. He's almost out of sight."

We both started running and for the moment, at least, I stopped thinking about myself.

Chapter Thirteen

The next couple of weeks my father and I settled into an easy routine, with Marie treating me like a princess and my father treating me like a little kid. One night he invited a lawyer from his office and his wife, the Danburgs, over to dinner. My father insisted that I change from jeans into a skirt before they arrived, and as usual, I didn't give him an argument.

Thinking about it later, I didn't see why it mattered what I wore because after I was introduced to the Danburgs, they practically ignored me. Mr. Danburg was a small, trim man with iron-gray hair, who never stopped talking. My father had told me before he arrived that he was one of the foremost tax lawyers in the country. His wife was even shorter than he, mousy-looking, and seemed in awe of him. She hardly said a word the whole evening.

When I first met them, Mr. Danburg asked me the usual dumb questions about how old I was and where I went to school. During dinner, my father and Mr. Danburg became involved in discussing a fine point of tax law. I'm always impressed with my father's knowledge and his ability to express himself.

As soon as dinner was over, I excused myself, saying I had to do my homework, which was true. I had a paper due for my soc. class the following week, and I hadn't decided what I would write. Mrs. Carson had told us to pick out an ordinary incident in our daily lives and develop on it in such a way that it could be representative of our society. I had the perfect subject now — "Male Chauvinism." I had just witnessed it firsthand, and could prove how it was practiced in my house. Poor Mrs. Danburg, I mused, she's never allowed to speak. But then, I thought, maybe it's her fault just as much as her husband's. Why doesn't she assert herself? As I started writing, it all spilled out easily, but when I was finished I changed the title to "Woman's Role in Male Chauvinism."

I hadn't had what could be called an "enjoyable evening" with the Danburgs, but it certainly proved to be valuable. Mrs. Carson gave me an A on the paper and even read it before the class. It stimulated a lot of discussion, most of the boys saying it's the woman's fault that she takes a backseat, and the girls arguing that society forces her to take such a role.

When the bell rang, Mrs. Carson asked me to stop by her desk on my way out. After the class had gone, I went over to her and she said that I should submit the paper to the school newspaper, with the idea of getting it published on the *Opinions* page. *Opinions* consists of articles written by the students who are not on the paper, and gets more mail than any other section.

"I couldn't do that," I said.

"Why on earth not?" asked Mrs. Carson.

"My father would see it then."

"What's wrong with that? It's an excellent paper and I would think you'd be proud to show it to him."

"Well," I hedged, "I don't think he'd like me using his dinner guests as a subject for publication."

"You don't actually use their names. You refer to them as 'one couple.' And besides, you have many other examples."

"I don't know," I said. "I don't want to risk him getting angry."

"Well, it's your decision, Jill. I think you've done a fine paper and I hope one day you'll change your mind about letting your father see it. I think he'd love it if you would."

"You do? You don't think he'd get mad?"

"Perhaps you misjudge him. Maybe, in fact, you're taking the role of the woman you describe, who is victimized because she won't assert herself."

"You mean I should let him know what I feel?"

"Exactly. You have definite ideas. Why not share them with him?"

"I'm not sure I'm ready."

"You will be, Jill. I have confidence in you."

"I appreciate that."

"Now you better hurry or you'll be late for your next class."

"Thanks for everything," I said, picking up my canvas bag, and then rushing out of the room.

I didn't think about my conversation with Mrs. Carson at the time, because I knew that no way would I share that paper with my father.

Chapter Fourteen

The last Saturday of October was symbolic of my "uptown" month. During the day, I hacked around the city with Serena, Maggie, and Sandy. We ate hot dogs at Züm Züm, treated ourselves to ice cream sodas at Rumplemayer's, and saw *Treasure of Sierra Madre* at the Museum of Modern Art.

I had to be home at six to have dinner with my father. He knew I was going to the dance with Paul and arranged for Marie to make a stew that we could heat up for supper. He told me he planned to play bridge with friends after I left.

Paul had arranged with me early that morning to pick me up at ten minutes to eight. At seven forty-nine the bell rang and I ran to open the door. Paul was wearing a tweed jacket, shirt and tie, and chinos. His idea of "informal"! He looked scrubbed and I wondered if he *ever* had a rumpled look or needed a haircut. Fortunately I had changed from my jeans and T-shirt to a Swiss blouse and red dirndle skirt. I didn't want to look "Bohemian," even though Paul had told me it was a disco dance.

"You look great," Paul said to me as I let him into the apartment. I couldn't help wondering if he was just saying that to be polite or if he really meant it.

Then my father came out of his room and shook hands with him.

"Good evening, sir," Paul said.

"How are you, Paul? Jill told me you were picking her up at ten to eight, and I'm happy to see you're a man of your word."

I had a feeling my father was leading up to something, and I was right. The next thing he said was, "You know, Jill has to be home by midnight, or she turns into a pumpkin."

I was embarrassed that my father had said that because everyone I knew had a much later curfew than that on Saturday night, but Paul didn't blink an eye.

"Don't worry, sir. I'll make sure she's home by then."

"That's fine. Now, you two have a good time and I'll see you later. If I don't leave soon, I'll be late for my engagement."

We said good-bye and as soon as the door closed behind us I turned to Paul and said apologetically, "My father is very old-fashioned. He has these standards about being prompt and getting home on time."

"He's absolutely right," Paul said without hesitation. "I can't stand waiting for people, so why should I make people wait for me."

"You're right about that," I agreed.

"And what's wrong with telling your father you'll be home at a certain time? That way he won't worry."

"Possibly," I said noncommittally, but deep down I thought he sounded more like a school principal than a guy I was going out with.

Then he changed the subject completely. We were alone in the elevator and he looked me over carefully. "I like your red combs. They match your skirt perfectly," he observed.

"Thank you," I said, amazed that he noticed that I was wearing combs to hold my hair back — which I don't usually do — and especially that they matched my skirt. I hadn't even planned it that way.

"Do you know anyone who'll be at the dance?" he asked as we headed toward his school, which was just a few blocks away.

"Only my friend Serena." I told him that she was one of my friends who had shown me around the Upper East Side, and that next month I was going to show them around Soho.

"I hope you'll show me Soho next month, too. I think it's time I got educated."

"Of course I will," I said, pleased that I could act as a guide for this born-and-bred New Yorker.

"And I'd like to meet your mother."

"Sure," I said, again not knowing if he was being polite or just plain curious.

When we got to his school, we went directly to the gym where the band was blasting away. The gym was dimly lit by flashing lights, and the floor was packed with couples.

A few guys yelled "Hi" to Paul when we came in, and he tried to introduce me, but it was too noisy for me to catch their names, and impossible to hold a normal conversation. Then the music got softer for a minute and the emcee announced over the mike that the band would play the Hustle.

"Let's go," Paul shouted, pulling me onto the floor. "That's my favorite."

O-oh, I thought. I'd never done the Hustle, but I thought maybe I could fake it. I obviously wasn't too successful because Paul, who seemed like an expert, shouted in my ear, "Look at my feet, and see if you can pick up the basic step."

I tried to follow him, but was relieved when the band finished that number and went into music that didn't require a set pattern.

"This is more like it," I said loudly as I tried to do my own thing.

"Hey, don't forget you've got a partner," Paul shouted back.

I couldn't help smiling at the thought that if it were up to him we'd probably be doing the foxtrot or the waltz.

During the break we pushed our way over to the food and drink bar. There was a huge spread of potato and corn chips, Ritz crackers with assorted dips, store-bought cookies and brownies, and a variety of soft drinks.

"Yech," Paul commented as he looked over the possibilities.

I helped myself to a handful of corn chips and a Coke. "What's wrong?" I asked.

"Pure, unadulterated junk food."

"I suppose you'd prefer celery and lettuce," I remarked.

"You guessed it. And that teeth-rotting stuff you're drinking! How can you?" He was smiling, but I thought he was half-serious.

"I suppose you'd prefer carrot juice."

"My favorite!" he said, picking up a bottle of plain soda and reading the ingredients. "At least this won't destroy me."

"You're serious about junk food, aren't you?"

"Deadly. But not just for health reasons."

"Why else?"

"I happen to be a *bon vivant*."

"A what?"

"It's French. It's someone who likes the good life. Good food, good wine, that type of thing."

He did sound a little obnoxious and I tried to get even by saying, "But junk food — *es muy divertido*."

"What's that?"

"It's Spanish. It means it's a lot of fun."

"*Basta!*" Paul said, upmanshipping me.

"What's that?"

"Italian for 'enough.'"

"You win," I admitted. "I don't know Italian."

"C'mon," he said grinning, and grabbed my hand. "The band is about to begin, so let's find an empty spot on the floor before the great gray mass takes over."

As we walked to the center of the floor, we bumped into Serena. She introduced me to Stephen Green, a classmate of Paul's, who was dressed exactly like him. He was tall, skinny, and had straight black hair. He couldn't seem to take his eyes off Serena for a minute, even when he was talking to us. We all greeted each other with as much enthusiasm as though we had accidentally met in the middle of the Sahara desert. Then the music began and it was impossible to talk in a normal voice. "We'll look for you at the next break," Paul yelled, pointing toward a far corner of the gym.

"We'll never find them," I said as I watched them fade into the crowd.

"Don't be too sure. I think I could spot those earrings Serena is wearing anywhere."

"Those feather earrings? I think they look great on her."

"Dégeulasse!" he said.

I knew that was another French word, but I wasn't going to give him the satisfaction of asking him to translate. Besides, I knew from his frown that it meant something derogatory.

Actually, we did manage to find them at the next break, and I could see that Stephen and Paul had a lot in common. At one point, Stephen told Paul he hoped his family was planning to go to Davos over Christmas vacation, like last year. Paul said his father had made reservations, but he was involved in some real estate negotiation. "If the deal isn't finished by December first, my father is cancelling."

"Quel dommage!" Stephen sighed.

I looked at Serena and we both shrugged our shoulders. I wondered if they thought that sprinkling their conversation with French phrases made them think they were sophisticated.

The music started again and the conversation was cut short. Paul and I finally managed to get it together on the dance floor and I completely lost track of time. But at quarter of twelve, right in the middle of a dance, Paul stopped cold, tapped his watch, and shouted, "Time's up!"

I had forgotten about my curfew, and was both disappointed and grateful that Paul remembered. Sometimes, he reminded me of an Eagle Scout and I wondered if he ever broke a rule.

On the way home Paul told me what a great time he'd had.

"I had a great time, too," I said.

"Will you promise to show me Soho?"

"I promise."

When we got to my floor, Paul walked me to my door and looked at his watch. "Two minutes to go," he observed.

"You are a man of your word," I said, and we both smiled.

I was sure that he'd try to kiss me, and I would have let him. But to my surprise — and disappointment — he just grasped my hand and shook it firmly.

"Thanks for a wonderful time," I said.

"I'll call you," Paul promised, slowly releasing my hand and backing away.

I opened the door to our apartment quietly, not wanting to disturb my father, but he immediately called to me from his bedroom. "How was the evening, Jill?" he asked.

"Great," I answered, warding off any further questions.

"You can tell me about it in the morning. I'm half asleep now. Good night, dear."

"Good night, Daddy," I said, happy to be alone with my thoughts.

As I got ready for bed, I wondered about Paul. My intuition told me he liked me, but he seemed almost too good to be true. *Well, I've got to give him a chance*, I thought, and what better place to see what he's really like than in Soho. I couldn't really picture him there, but he would certainly add a new dimension to my "downtown" life.

Chapter Fifteen

It was the first of November and I was ready to leave the apartment. My knapsack was on my back, a suitcase in one hand, and my book-bag in the other.

"Be sure to call me, Jill," my father said as I stood at the door.

"Of course I will," I assured him.

"Can you manage all this?" he asked worriedly.

"No problem," I said.

Then he opened the door for me, waited with me for the elevator, and gave me a bear hug just before it arrived. "It was wonderful having you here, and I'm looking forward to next time," he said.

The elevator door opened and it was already filled with several people. "Thanks for everything, Daddy," I whispered, and crowded into the elevator.

I had actually left for school a little early because I was hoping that I wouldn't get a lot of questions about why I was carrying a suit-case. It's like having a leg in a cast and every-body asks what happened. When you're carry-ing a suitcase, they want to know where you're going. Of course, my close friends knew I was moving downtown, but naturally most kids, even if they knew the situation, wouldn't remember that this was the first of the month and that's why I looked like I was going on a trip.

I hoped to get to my homeroom where I could dump my suitcase in the closet without being stopped. But just as I was about to walk into the main entrance, Alex and Jimmy ran into me.

"Where you going?" Alex asked. "This is the beginning of the week, not the end. It's custom-ary to travel on weekends."

"I'm just moving some things," I told him, not in the mood for being teased. No matter how on top of the situation I was, I still was sensitive about having two separate homes.

"Moving things?" He looked thoughtful for a minute. Then he slapped his hand on his head, and said, "Oh, I forgot. You lead a double life, and this is switch-time."

There wasn't much I could say to that, but Jimmy, who seemed to sense that Alex was making me uncomfortable, said, "Hey, Jill, let me help you with that." He took my suitcase with one hand and held the door open for me with the other.

"Thank you," I said, smiling at him. It flashed through my mind that I hadn't seen much of Jimmy since that first day. I remembered his offhand remark about playing tennis, but he'd never followed up on it. Maybe he was just a slow starter like Maggie had warned me, or maybe he didn't like girls yet. Serena, who was an expert on the subject of men, told me there were guys like that, but that when they fell they really fell hard.

"I'll lug this upstairs for you if you want."

"Please do. I want to leave it in my homeroom closet till after school."

"Gotcha," he said, and led the way.

"The bell hasn't even rung. I'm not going in yet," Alex yelled behind us.

"Later," Jim called back.

My homeroom was empty and I thought that this was the first time we'd been alone. Maybe he would show a little more than polite interest, I hoped. Instead, all he did was shove the suitcase in the closet and announce that he had to rush to the lab to check on the guinea pigs.

"The what?" I asked.

"We're conducting an experiment to determine the effect of vitamins on guinea pigs, and it's my turn to check them out."

"How do you do that?"

"We check their weight and the condition of their fur and things like that. We're supposed to make tests at the same time every day."

"Sounds like fun," I said, a little sarcastically.

Jimmy glanced at the clock on the wall at the front of the room. "I've really got to run."

"Don't forget to take their pulse," I joked as I sat down in one of the classroom chairs.

"See ya 'round," Jimmy said, hurrying out the door.

As I watched him disappear, I thought this was the first time I'd ever played second fiddle to a pig! But whatever my feelings were about Jimmy, I had to put them on the back burner for the time being. There wasn't time for me to sort them out now. I had an algebra test coming up that morning, and every spare minute I looked over the practice problems that Mr. Thorp had told us to study.

Mr. Thorp has white hair and wears steel-rimmed glasses, and has worn the same light gray suit every single day. He always has chalk marks on the back of his jacket from rubbing against the blackboard. He blends so perfectly with the room that I'm always surprised when I see him in the halls or the lunchroom. He reminds me then of a plant that's been uprooted.

As I've mentioned before, math is my least favorite subject, but Mr. Thorp is in love with it and his enthusiasm is contagious. He talks about the "romantic elegance" of solving problems. I personally don't see anything romantic or elegant about formulas, but Mr. Thorp is so unhappy if we don't do well, that I try extra hard.

When I thought about Mr. Thorp, I wondered if he ever had problems about his parents or his love life. I'm sure if he did, he'd just have dug into a math book and forgotten about anything personal.

Ronnie had told me that she gets so involved when she's painting that the whole world could cave in and she wouldn't notice. And my father can go for hours, even forgetting to eat, if he's involved in a legal case.

I wished I could get into something. Maybe that would make me stop thinking about my personal problems. It seemed as soon as I started getting comfortable in one situation, I was thrust into another. Things were going so smoothly with my father, and now I had to leave. I was actually beginning to enjoy the schedule and being pampered by Marie. And now all that would change.

Sure I was happy at the prospect of living with my mother, but it meant shifting gears. Maybe I wasn't as adjustable as I thought. Is it possible, I wondered, to have "culture shock" within one city?

Chapter Sixteen

When I arrived at the loft after school I let myself in with my key, thinking I'd surprise Ronnie. She didn't know exactly when I'd arrive and I figured she'd be working alone, which is usually how she spends her days. She likes to take advantage of the light, and even though she loves people she saves her socializing for the evening.

Therefore I was surprised when I heard voices, and as soon as I opened the door I saw at least six women sitting around. They were all wearing pants or jeans and half of them were stretched out on the floor. I suddenly felt overdressed because I happened to have on a full wool skirt, which was easier to wear than to pack.

I stood at the door a few seconds before anyone noticed me. Then someone saw me standing there and said "hello." Six pairs of eyes were on me, and Ronnie leapt up from the floor and let out a whoop. "Jill, darling, you're home!" She threw her arms around me and kissed me on both cheeks. I felt a little self-conscious because everyone was watching.

I dropped my suitcase and bookbag and hugged her back. "Hi, Ronnie," I said. "It's great to see you."

"Jill, I'll help you put your things in your room," she offered, picking up my suitcase. "Then you must meet everyone."

"I thought you'd be alone working," I said in a whisper as I followed her. My "environment" seemed very small and alien after my spacious room in my father's apartment.

"Ordinarily I would be," Ronnie explained. "But I'm part of this consciousness-raising group and we meet one afternoon a week. I had it here this week because I knew you'd be coming home and I didn't want you walking into an empty place. I was sure you wouldn't mind."

"That's okay," I said. I knew she meant well, but personally I would have preferred being alone for a few hours than having to mix with my mother's friends.

"Why don't you leave everything for now, and you can unpack later. I think you better get out of that skirt. The one thing we don't have enough of are chairs."

"Okay," I said. "I'll be right out after I change."

"I can't wait to hear everything about your stay with Tim, but we'll get to that later. Just tell me if it's working okay."

I knew that the "it" she was referring to was the joint custody arrangement, and I didn't want to suggest that it was anything but perfect. "It's fine," I assured her.

"I'm so glad," she said. "And I'm so glad you're here, Jill. I've looked forward to it all month. Also, you're just in time to give us a fresh point of view."

"What is it you're talking about?"

"We're discussing how women must take risks and do their own thing, even if it threatens their relationship with men."

"I'm not exactly an expert on the subject," I remarked.

"Well, maybe you'll think of something," she said, and left the room.

I closed the door behind her and started to change my clothes. I thought of myself as a squeezie doll that I'd had in first grade. It could be shaped in a million different ways — short and fat, long and thin, or even made to have a head bigger than its body. *That's me,* I thought, pulling off my sweater and putting on an old T-shirt, *doing what everyone expects me to do.*

When I came out of my room, Ronnie introduced me to everyone by their first names and they immediately treated me like an adult. It made me feel strange — half flattered and half uncomfortable. Greta, one of the women who had short, curly gray hair and friendly green eyes, and was leaning against the couch, patted the floor beside her and said, "Pull up a piece of rug."

"Thanks," I said, and slid down beside her.

Then a woman named Betsy, who had long, wavy blond hair, and wore lots of makeup, and looked like an aging teenager, offered me a cigarette.

"I don't smoke," I told her.

"You're lucky," Betsy said. "I didn't either until a year ago when Jerry went out for a carton of milk and never came back."

"You mean he left you?" I said, trying to act cool.

"You guessed it. We'd been married for three years, but things started going bad after the first six months."

"That's awful," I muttered, embarrassed that a contemporary of my mother's would be telling me such personal things.

"That's not the worst," she continued. "When he left, I didn't know it for sure, but I found out about a week later that I was already two months pregnant."

"Wow," I said, losing whatever cool I was pretending to have. "What d'ja do?"

"A month later, I had a miscarriage. To this day, I don't know if I'm happy or sad about that. Sometimes I'm sorry, sometimes I'm not."

She looked forlorn and I couldn't think of anything profound to say, so I made some dumb remark about "everything happens for the best."

"I suppose," she said, and lapsed into silence.

Then a woman named Maureen, who looked like a fashion model and wore high heels with jeans that she seemed sewn into, spoke up. "You don't know when you're well off, Betsy. I've got two kids under five, a husband who's never home when he says he will be, and nothing to do all day but take care of the house. Sometimes I'm tempted myself to go out for a carton of milk — permanently."

Everyone laughed, but there was a note of desperation in her voice and it triggered off a lot of comments from the group. I just sat there like a lump and listened, hoping no one would notice me. Then Greta suddenly seemed aware of my presence. She turned to me and said, "How would you have felt if your mother or father had skipped out one day without even saying good-bye."

"Awful," I answered.

"That's what I think," Greta agreed, and to my relief everyone continued talking, so interested in expressing their own point of view that they didn't ask me to elaborate on mine.

Finally the group broke up, promising to meet next week at Betsy's house. I was relieved to be alone with Ronnie. It took me a while to recover from hearing the confidences of these women, but my mother didn't seem to notice. As I helped her empty ashtrays and plump up pillows, she went babbling on about how much she missed me, how much work she'd done for her art show that was coming up, how the consciousness-raising group proved to her that the options open to women today complicate their lives, but that she would never have it any other way. Then she stopped what she was doing and said, "Let's sit down a minute. I'm always exhausted after these meetings, and besides, I want to hear about you."

She flopped down on the couch and I sat cross-legged opposite her on a huge floor pillow. Then she asked me about living on the Upper East Side and how school was going.

I told her everything I thought she'd like to hear, including going to the disco dance with Paul who'd never even been to Soho and thought it might be inhabited by aborigines.

Ronnie cracked up when I said that and then suggested that I should invite some kids over just to prove that I didn't live in an uninhabitable jungle.

"As a matter of fact," I said, "I thought I might invite them over this Saturday."

"Wonderful," Ronnie enthused. "We'll get some pizza and I'll make my special vegetable salad."

"That'll be great," I said, pulling my hair back.

"What a minute," Ronnie gasped. "Isn't there something you haven't told me?" She was staring so hard at my ears that I couldn't pretend that I didn't know what she was talking about.

"Oh, these," I said casually, pulling at my ear.

"You got them pierced," Ronnie exclaimed. "That's terrific. Now I'll always know what to buy you. A girl can't have too many sets of earrings."

I had to smile when she said that, partly because she was pleased that I'd had my ears pierced, but mostly because her reaction was so completely different from my father's.

I couldn't seem to stop grinning, and finally Ronnie said, "What's so funny?"

"Nothing," I answered. "I'm just glad that you're happy that I had it done."

"And your father wasn't," she said knowingly. As always, Ronnie could read my mind.

I didn't say anything, because I didn't want to make waves.

"Never mind," she said. "It's much ado about nothing."

"Hey, what's for dinner?" I asked, wanting to get off the subject.

"Well, I thought I might whip up a couple of frozen delights for us, but since it's your first day home, I think we should splurge. Why don't we go to Sloppy Joe's for some chili?"

"Love it," I said. "I haven't had it all month."

"I'm sure of that," Ronnie said, smiling.

Then I chuckled, finally feeling relaxed and getting used to being *here* with my mother, rather than *there* with my father. No matter how discombobulated I might get, I knew I enjoyed living with both of them.

Chapter Seventeen

I tried not to think about Jason now that I was back in Soho, but I wasn't too successful. Everything reminded me of him. And then, when we were having our pecan pie, Ronnie dropped the fact that she'd visited Marsha's gallery the previous week and had seen him.

"He asked how you were and said you should call him when you get here."

"He did?" I couldn't hide my excitement. Then the way we had parted came back to me and I must have frowned because Ronnie asked me what was wrong.

"Nothing, really. It's just that *he* should call me."

"That's silly, sweetie. Today it doesn't matter what gender calls first."

"In this case it matters, and it has nothing to do with gender," I growled.

"Whatever you say," Ronnie said, and shrugged her shoulders.

"Anyhow, this Saturday I'm going to give my Introduction to Soho course."

"Who're you having?"

"I think I'll ask Serena to bring Stephen, who's a friend of Paul's, and then Paul won't be the only guy. And of course I'll invite Maggie and Sandy. Maggie won't bring anyone because Seth works every Saturday, and Sandy says she's between men."

"Sounds like just the right number."

"I'll call as soon as we get back home."

"What's the big hurry?"

"I want to make definite plans." Then I thought hard for a minute and confided, "I want to make sure they like it here."

"I know they will," Ronnie said reassuringly. "If anyone is ever bored in Soho, it's their own fault."

"You're probably right, but this Saturday, I feel responsible."

"It's lucky you have some of your father's genes," Ronnie said. "In fact, you're a good influence on me."

"I am?" I was a little embarrassed. Sometimes I thought that Ronnie wanted me to be older than I was, just the way I thought my father wanted me to be younger, but there wasn't much I could do about that.

When we got back to the loft, we mapped out a plan. Naturally, I had to include a number of places Jason had taken me, but he'd never have the satisfaction of knowing. I thought we should go sightseeing in the morning and come back to the loft for lunch.

"I don't know what we should do in the afternoon. Another three hours of walking is too much," I groaned, remembering how exhausted I'd been.

"I've got it!" Ronnie exclaimed. "You may be tired of walking, but you won't be too tired to roller-skate."

"Roller-skate?"

"There's a new rink that's supposed to be sensational. Maureen told me about it. She says when she wants a break from her domestic routine she hires a baby-sitter and takes off for the rink."

"That's a super idea," I said. "The only problem is nobody has skates."

"Don't worry about that. You can rent them at the rink, and I'll treat."

"You will? That's great. I just hope I remember how its done. I haven't been skating since I was about ten years old and all I can remember about that was losing my key."

"No problem about that now. Everything's attached."

"I know that," I said. "And I can't wait to try it. I'm going to invite everyone for Saturday right now."

I went into the kitchen and made all the phone calls. I managed to reach everyone and they all agreed it was a terrific idea.

That night, as I tried to fall asleep, my head was spinning with all that had happened. It took a while for me to get used to my loft bed; I still

104

felt peculiar about being included in Ronnie's consciousness-raising group; I was worried about readjusting my inner time clock so that I would get up a half hour earlier in order to take the subway. But I did enjoy being with Ronnie, and now I couldn't wait for Saturday. It was like having an unexpected party.

Chapter Eighteen

On Saturday I couldn't sleep late because I wanted to straighten things before the gang arrived. Ronnie knew exactly how I felt and helped. When everything was reasonably neat — no matter how hard we tried there were always magazines and art journals strewn around — Ronnie asked, "What should I wear?"

I was about to answer when I realized she was kidding me. The last thing Ronnie cares about is what she wears.

"Wear your best jeans," I advised, chuckling.

"For the occasion, I think I'll wear the ones without the holes."

"That's very good," I said. "I wouldn't want to shock Paul. I have a feeling he's never seen his mother in anything but a dress with a Peter Pan collar."

"He can't help that," Ronnie pointed out, and I realized that my mother wasn't even a snob about snobs.

"I'll make some coffee," I said. "They're not supposed to be here until ten, but for Saturday that's the crack of dawn."

"Go ahead. And when they get here, heat up some of those natural bran muffins I have in the freezer. We want the troops to be fortified before they venture forth."

"Good idea," I said, and went into the kitchen to get things ready.

Promptly at ten o'clock the bell rang and my friends piled into the loft. I introduced them to Ronnie, who greeted them so warmly that they seemed to feel right at home. Then there was a lot of ohhing and ahhing about the loft, and although I had pretended to myself that it didn't matter what they thought I was really pleased that my friends were so enthusiastic, including Paul.

"Can we see your room?" Maggie asked.

"Sure," I said, "but it'll have to be single file. It's not what you would call roomy."

I led the way and everyone crowded into my environment.

"Where is it?" Paul asked facetiously.

I didn't bother to answer, but was happy when Maggie said, "I think it's terrific. Not one bit of wasted space."

"What's it like sleeping on top of a ladder?" Paul asked.

I supposed he was being funny, but I didn't want to give him the satisfaction of thinking I cared what he thought — which I did. But before I had a chance to give him a snappy answer, Ronnie shouted, "Who's for coffee?"

We trooped out of the room and gathered around the round oak table, where Ronnie poured coffee into mugs. Then she passed the muffins around.

"These look delicious, Mrs. Belmont," Paul said as he helped himself to one.

"Speciality of the house," my mother said. "But please, Paul, call me Ronnie."

"You mean it?" Paul gulped.

"Well, not if it means you're going to choke to death."

That made everyone loosen up, but I could see Paul was embarrassed. Just a minute ago I'd been annoyed with Paul because he'd made some snobby remark, and now I was feeling protective. "We better get started soon," I warned, wanting to save him. "We can't hang around here too long or we'll be off schedule. Bolt down your coffee and let's go!"

As soon as we got downstairs, Sandy said, "You are so lucky."

"Why?" I asked.

"You've got so much freedom."

"Yes," Stephen added. "Your mother really treats us like her equal. My sister, who's two years younger, had the biggest fight with my mother last time she was home from boarding school because she thinks she's too old to curtsey."

"Perhaps she's in training for visiting the Queen," Serena suggested.

"I hate to tell you," Paul said, "but that's exactly the way my parents feel. They think curtseying is a sign of respect."

"Oh, no," I groaned. "Even my father wouldn't insist on that."

"See how well off you are," Maggie muttered, so that only I could hear. She never failed to remind me that everyone had problems.

"And your mother's the greatest. If I ever called my mother by her first name, I think she'd disown me!" Sandy said.

"I'm so used to it, I don't think about it anymore." Then I said, "Listen, you guys didn't come here to study family behavior. Let's go see some galleries before it rains." It was a mild day for November, but the skies were overcast.

"Lead on," Paul said, taking my arm through his.

"Follow me," I ordered, and headed for West Broadway, where the action is.

I led them into different galleries that specialize in various kinds of art — pop art, Hispanic, Indian, as well as a photography exhibit. We had trouble getting Sandy to leave a place called Let There Be Neon.

"I can't believe it," she said. "You can actually turn a line drawing into neon. How is it done?"

"Let me explain," Stephen said. "In neon art, neon or argon gas is in a vacuum through which an electrical charge passes."

"But what makes it light up?" Sandy wanted to know.

"Illumination is caused by the electrical charge passing through inert gas."

"I'm impressed," Serena said.

Stephen looked so pleased with her reaction that I thought he might faint. It was probably the first time she had ever given him any encouragement.

"Where else can neon be used?" Sandy asked.

Stephen pulled himself together, and without taking his eyes off Serena answered, "Practically anywhere — furniture, clocks, sculpture. It lasts about thirty years and uses very little electricity."

"It's fantastic," Sandy said. "I could look at it forever."

"You can come back another day," I promised. "Now we've got to go on. There are two more places we have to see, and then we have to have lunch in order to be in time for the afternoon skating session."

Our next stop was something called the Bar Room. It was a series of brass bars spread out on the floor of an otherwise empty room.

"Is this supposed to be art?" Paul asked.

"I guess you'd call it experimental. I like it," Maggie told him.

"Doesn't exactly turn me on," Paul said. "In fact, none of this abstract art does much for me. I like to be able to recognize what I'm looking at."

"I thought you wanted to be educated," I said, half-kidding. "That means you have to have an open mind."

"I can't get excited over a bunch of blobs."

I was tempted to say that I'd avoid showing him my mother's work, because she specialized in blobs, but I didn't want to embarrass him. I thought to myself that Paul really was square and probably would never be able to overcome his prejudices.

The last place we visited was the New York Earth Room. It was actually an empty room with an earthen floor and bare, stonelike walls. A hush fell over us as we entered and, although there was nothing specific to look at, it was surprisingly peaceful.

On the way back to the loft, Maggie said, "That was an amazing experience. It makes me want to be a set designer more than ever. I mean, you can see how the atmosphere of a place can set a mood."

"I never thought of it that way," I said, "but I see what you mean."

"If you lived in the Earth Room, you'd have to use your imagination for everything," Serena pointed out.

"Personally, I'd be happy anywhere if there was a TV. Just so long as I could see the Knicks," Paul said.

"Oh," I groaned, "you're hopeless."

"Not hopeless, just honest."

"You are that," I agreed, and suddenly it occurred to me that I was the one who was being intolerant.

"Can you imagine the Earth Room decorated with neon furniture?" Sandy asked with a straight face.

"And a few brass bars on the floor," Maggie added.

"It wouldn't be dramatic enough for me," Serena said.

Then we all laughed, realizing the absurdity of the conversation, and I thought to myself that even though we had different reactions, the expedition so far had been very successful.

Chapter Nineteen

Ronnie had everything ready for lunch when we arrived. The table was set, the pizza was being kept hot in the oven, an enormous salad was prepared, and a huge pitcher of chilled apple juice was on the table. As soon as we sat down to lunch, Ronnie wanted to know everything we'd done. We told her all the places we'd been, and she admitted we'd covered some galleries that she didn't even know existed.

"I've got to see the Earth Room after what you've told me," she said enthusiastically. "And the neon art. Sounds fascinating."

"It is," Sandy said. "I wish my mother would see it."

"Why wouldn't she?" Ronnie asked.

"Because she's not interested in going below Forty-second Street if she can help it — and she wouldn't like it anyway."

"You have to have an open mind," Paul said, and winked at me.

At least he can laugh at himself, I thought, and smiled at him. Ronnie had said to me a million times that if you have a sense of humor about yourself you can survive.

After we finished eating, we all pitched in and did the dishes. As Serena was sponging off the table, she said, "Ronnie, I hope you'll come with us."

"I'd love to," Ronnie said, drying the wooden salad bowl, "but I have to do some work today. I have an opening next month and I'm finishing up a canvas."

"Can we see what you're doing?" Sandy said.

"I never thought you'd ask," Ronnie said, smiling. "My studio is behind that screen." She started walking toward the far end of the loft and we trailed behind her.

Here goes, I thought, *I'll see how polite Paul can really be.*

A huge canvas of white, red, and black abstract shapes was leaning against the wall and Ronnie pulled it out so that everyone could see it. It seemed like forever before anyone spoke. Then Sandy broke the silence and said, "That's dramatic. I'd give anything to own something like that."

Then everyone else made appropriate comments and wanted to know how long it took her to do a painting, and had she changed her style over the years, and who was her favorite artist.

I noticed that Paul was the only one who hung back and said nothing.

"Well, what do you think?" I asked him in a low voice while everyone else was babbling.

"Never seen anything like it," Paul answered, his eyes twinkling.

"You're very diplomatic," I told him, and couldn't help admiring the fact that he knew his own mind.

Then Ronnie said, "I love having you here, but I don't want you to be late. You're welcome back anytime."

As we got ready to leave, and a couple of girls disappeared into the bathroom, Ronnie pulled me aside and slipped me some money. "These are for renting the skates," she said, "and have a great time."

"Thanks a million," I said, and gave her a peck on the cheek.

Finally we were shoving out the door, which Ronnie held open for us as we waited for the elevator, and everyone seemed to be shouting, "Thank you, Ronnie," at the same time, except for Paul who said, "It was lovely, Mrs. Belmont."

"Ronnie," Stephen corrected him under his breath.

"You can't undo sixteen years of conditioning in one day," Paul said, and I noticed that not even Stephen had an answer for that. And I thought at least he's consistent, and not trying to please everybody. I wished I could be more like that.

We took a bus uptown and walked West on Eighteenth Street toward the rink. On the way I discovered that not one of us had been roller skating for years. "Don't worry," Stephen reassured us, "it's like swimming. Once you learn, you never forget."

When we got to the rink, it was like entering another world. It had the same atmosphere as a disco — crazy lights that flickered and loud music that generated excitement. After we paid the admission, we handed in our shoes in exchange for the skates, rented two lockers into which we dumped our belongings, sat down on the benches, and laced up our skate shoes. I stood up tentatively, waiting for the others.

Paul seemed very confident as he pulled himself up. "Lean on me," he directed, as he held out his hand to Sandy and Maggie, who seemed glued to their seats.

"I'll bring up the rear," Stephen said, linking his arm with Serena's and extending his hand to me.

"You mean we'll bring you up," I said, laughing.

Amid groans and yelps and giggles, we managed to reach the rail of the rink. Everyone else looked like an expert, whipping around at a great pace. Some of the skaters were going backwards, and a few in the center, which was roped off, actually performed acrobatic stunts.

"Who wants to join me?" Paul asked, glancing at all of us, but his eyes finally resting on me.

"I think I'll just look for a minute," I told him.

"Me, too," the rest of the girls chimed in.

"It's you and me, Stephen," Paul said, and started off with Stephen stumbling behind.

It wasn't long before Paul was far ahead of Stephen and looked like he'd been skating all his life.

"He's terrific," Maggie said to me as we watched him picking up speed.

"I guess he's a natural. I know he's quarter-back on his school football team, but I didn't know he'd be good at all sports."

"That's usually the way," Sandy said. "Probably schussed down an entire mountain the first time he went skiing."

"But look at Stephen. He's not what I'd call coordinated," Serena groaned. We watched Stephen inching his way around the rink and couldn't help giggling.

"We shouldn't be making fun of him," Maggie said between giggles, "seeing that's the way I'll be."

"You're absolutely right," I agreed.

"Besides," Serena added, "he'll have some brilliant explanation. He may not be athletic, but he sure is smart."

"Between the two of them we have the perfect man," Sandy said.

Just then Paul glided into the rail where we were standing. "Can't stay planted here all day," he said. "I'll take you around and promise you won't fall. Who's game?"

"Me," Sandy said, grabbing Paul's arm and letting him guide her onto the rink.

"I'll give each of my harem a turn," he announced, laughing, as he and Sandy rolled off.

"It's ridiculous to wait. I'm going to try by myself," I said, screwing up my courage.

"We can always hang on to the rail," Maggie commented.

"Let's go," Serena added, and clutching the rail we managed to get ourselves onto the rink.

I stayed close to the rail and slowly circled the rink. By the time I was on my second round, I actually edged away from the rail and was feeling more secure. I was so intent on watching my feet that I didn't bother to notice what was going on with my friends.

Then, because the rink was so crowded I hardly noticed that someone was shadowing me. I figured some other slow skater was using me to run interference. That's why I was totally surprised when a familiar male voice said, "Don't look down, Jill. You'll never learn."

I glanced behind me and almost toppled over from the shock. "Jason!" I screamed. "What are you doing here?"

With that, I stumbled, but Jason quickly grabbed me around the waist with one hand and held my hand with the other, so that I regained my balance.

"Whew," I breathed. "That was a close one. Thanks for saving me."

"Always glad to help a damsel in distress," he said, still holding his arm around my waist.

"Do you mind if we stop a minute?" I pleaded. "I'd like to catch my breath."

"Okay," he said agreeably, and I let him guide me off the rink and toward some benches off to the side where I collapsed.

He sat down beside me and looked me over with those piercing eyes. Then he flashed that headlight smile. I felt weaker than ever, and I knew it wasn't from having almost taken a spill.

"This is the last place I thought I'd find you. What are you doing here anyway?" he asked.

"I'm with some friends," I explained.

"Some of your Upper East Side buddies?"

"You guessed it," I said, trying to ignore his sarcasm.

"Were you going to call me?" he asked. "I told your mother to tell you to."

"I know," I said, avoiding answering the question.

"Well, I'm glad I bumped into you," he admitted. "The problem is, I'm with a friend and she'll think I got lost if I don't go look for her."

"Oh," I said, idiotically, feeling a pang of jealousy. "I'm with someone, too."

"You already told me that," he remarked, making me feel more foolish than ever.

"We better split then," I suggested, trying to show my indifference.

"Let's take one more spin together. After all, if you're thrown off a horse, you're supposed to get right back on."

"You're right," I said, not wanting to be left alone on the bench.

I held tightly onto his arm as we made our way to the rink.

"Be loose," he ordered, "look straight ahead and don't crouch. You don't want to look like Groucho Marx."

That made me laugh, and by following his instructions I really did manage to start rolling. We circled the rink three times and then the music stopped.

"Clear the rink," a voice shouted over the loudspeaker. "Only boys for now."

"Why are they doing that?" I asked Jason. "I was just getting warmed up."

"Because it's getting too crowded and if everyone's on the skating area at the same time there's bound to be a collision."

He took my hand and escorted me off the rink. The first person I saw was Paul, who was leaning against the rail.

"There you are," he said in a disapproving tone. "I've been looking for you."

"Oh," I said, trying not to sound as flustered as I felt. "This is Jason, who lives in Soho. His mother's a friend of Ronnie's."

I turned to Jason and said, "This is Paul. Paul's father and my father knew each other in college and they play squash together." The minute I said that I felt stupider than ever. I mean, why did I have to explain everything in such detail. It sounded as though I was apologizing to Jason for knowing Paul and to Paul for knowing Jason.

While I was fretting about my idiocy, Paul and Jason were exchanging "hi's" and then the announcer repeated, "Gentlemen only for this round."

"See what you women libbers have accomplished," Jason quipped. "I remember the days when it was 'Ladies first.'"

"Go skate," I said, chuckling.

He rolled backwards onto the rink and gave me a small wave. I waved back and turned to Paul. "You better go," I suggested, "or you'll miss your turn."

"I guess you can take care of yourself," Paul said, sounding a little miffed, and started off.

I watched him increase his speed along with the music, and wondered where Maggie, Sandy, and Serena were, when they suddenly surrounded me, each one offering me a candy bar. It looked as though they had raided the candy machine.

"We decided to take a break and buy some refreshments, but you were so involved talking to some strange guy that we didn't want to interrupt," Sandy explained as we edged our way to the benches and sat down.

"That was thoughtful," I said, mysteriously.

"Well, who is he?" Serena asked.

"That's Jason — my Soho friend," I said.

"Thought so," Maggie said, remembering what I'd told her about him.

"He's really cute," Sandy observed, offering me some gumdrops.

"If you like the type," I said, popping some candy into my mouth.

"You prefer the preppy type?" Serena asked. I knew she was referring to Paul.

"Don't know what type I prefer," I answered honestly.

"Well, you don't have to decide yet," Maggie said.

"Fortunately," I agreed, and thought to myself that I couldn't seem to make my mind up about anything lately.

We watched the skaters spinning around and I couldn't help comparing Jason and Paul. Jason's dark wavy hair brushed the collar of his pale blue cotton shirt that he wore open. I couldn't decide if he unbuttoned it that way to show off his chest or to display a gold chain that had an enamel medallion attached to it. He seemed sewed into his faded jeans, and moved around the rink with the ease of a cat.

Paul, on the other hand, was wearing his chinos and a navy cotton turtleneck. A lock of his otherwise perfectly groomed hair fell over his forehead — the only indication that he was expending any effort. His prowess on skates was remarkable and I couldn't help admiring him.

Paul, preppy, polite, and a little uptight, versus Jason, a freewheeling spirit, and not just a little bit rude. I liked them both for some things and didn't like them for others. They probably felt the same way about me. I already knew, for sure, that Paul didn't approve of me skating off with Jason.

All these thoughts were whirling through my head as fast as the skaters. Then the music slowly faded and a voice sounded over the loudspeaker, "Clear the floor. Next will be couples. Choose your partners."

The four of us — Sandy, Maggie, Serena, and me — were still seated on the benches when the boys rolled off the rink.

"Over here, over here," Sandy yelled, waving frantically at Paul, who came toward us and immediately sat down beside her. I happened to be sitting in the middle, so I didn't think he was purposely ignoring me.

Stephen, who was one of the last ones off, looked all around and finally spotted Serena, who had stood up and waved. He managed to reach us just before the music started up again.

"I think I'll sit this one out," Stephen announced. "Rest the old calf muscles."

"Good thinking," Serena said. I could tell she wasn't that keen on skating.

I noticed then that Paul was guiding Sandy toward the rink, without even a glance at me. Was he trying to make me jealous? Maybe. But I didn't care. Or did I? Anyway, Stephen was now sitting with us and I didn't feel like a complete wallflower.

Then I noticed one couple whipping around, and I literally caught my breath. It was Jason and his "friend." If I ever thought before that I wasn't his type, this clinched it! She, whatever her name was, was poured into a lipstick red leotard that showed off her perfectly proportioned figure and long legs. Her long dark hair swished behind her, and her dark eyes glistened in her olive-colored skin as she sped around. She didn't wear much makeup except for a slash of red across her lips, which matched her leotard. I had to admit she was smashing.

Besides that, she and Jason moved together as though they'd been training all their lives for the Olympics. It was impossible not to notice them, and I couldn't help hearing some guy who was behind me say to the girl he was sitting with, "Take a look at the girl in red. Maybe if you wore something like that it would improve your skating."

"If I looked like that in a leotard, I wouldn't have to improve my skating," the girl said, laughing.

I personally didn't think the situation was so funny. There was Jason and his partner, their arms wrapped around each other's waists, knocking everyone out with their good looks and their grace. I looked at Paul, who was holding Sandy's hand, and the two of them were laughing. And then there was me, warming the bench.

Maggie must have sensed how I felt because she tried to get me involved in Stephen's conversation with Serena. He was saying something about how the music combined with the whirling motion of skating had a mesmerizing effect on the sensibilities.

"Do you agree?" Maggie asked me.

"Uh, yeah, very interesting," I said, not for a minute understanding what he was talking about.

No matter how hard I tried, I couldn't take my eyes off the rink. It seemed like a year before the "couples" were asked to "Make way for the ladies."

"C'mon," Maggie said, standing up, "it's our turn."

Serena stood up, too, saying, "I have to try out Stephen's 'mesmerizing sensibilities' theory. Besides, we didn't come here just to sit. Come on, Jill."

"Nothing ventured, nothing gained," I said, trying to sound a lot more lighthearted than I felt.

As I approached the rink, Jason and his partner came toward me. "Hey, Jill," he called, "I'd like you to meet Gloria. Gloria, this is Jill. I told you about her."

That's interesting, I thought, *he's told her about me, but he's never told me about her.*

"Hi, Jill. I've heard a lot about you," Gloria said. Was she making sure that I didn't miss the fact that they'd talked about me?

"Hello," I said, trying to look pleasant.

"How do you like living here?" Gloria asked.

"Good," I answered, hoping I didn't sound stupid.

"We don't want to hold you up," Gloria said, looking at the skaters. "I've had it for today."

"It's so crowded," Jason explained, "that Gloria and I are going to split."

"We're going to leave soon, too," I said, and immediately thought whatever I said to Jason today seemed to come out wrong.

"Remember, Jill, keep your head up." Then he and Gloria made a perfect turn in place and headed for the checkroom, while I bumbled my way to the rink.

I tried to concentrate on my skating, and soon felt confident enough to try going backwards. When Maggie, Serena, and Sandy passed by, they each commented on how good I was. For a while I even managed to stop thinking about Jason and Gloria.

When the music stopped and I rolled off, Paul said to me, "You're doing very well."

"Thanks," I replied, not sure whether he was just being his polite self. I was sure he'd seen Jason and Gloria leave, so he could no longer feel threatened.

Maggie came up to us and said, "Would you believe it's five-thirty already? It's my uncle's birthday and we're all going to his house for dinner. I promised I'd be home by six-thirty at the latest. I hate to break this up."

"Don't worry," Paul said, "I have to leave, too. Let's mobilize the forces."

When we were all finally assembled, we turned in our skates for our shoes, and gathered our belongings from the lockers. I walked everyone to the subway stop, where they would catch the train for the Upper East Side. They all thanked me profusely for a wonderful day, and we said good-bye.

I walked alone to my bus stop, thinking it had been quite a day, but I couldn't help feeling let down now that it was over. Somehow, I felt disoriented — as though I didn't know where I belonged. Part of me wished I was going uptown, too, but another part of me was relieved that I could go home to Soho.

When the bus came after a few minutes, it was almost empty. I took a seat in the middle, next to a window, and watched the skies darken. It started to drizzle, and I thought the atmosphere was reflecting my mood. Or was it the other way around?

Why do I have so many questions, I wondered as the bus made its way toward Soho. *Why am I trying to please everyone? When will I ever really be me?*

Chapter Twenty

I didn't hear from Jason for almost ten days
— not that I really expected to — but I couldn't
stop thinking about him. Then one day, as soon
as I got home from school, he called to ask me
to come to a mime show that was in the Village.
I couldn't help thinking that Gloria had come
down with pneumonia or something at the last
minute and that was why he was stuck with a
ticket.

"I'll collect you at seven-thirty," he said.

"No, you won't," I told him.

"Why not?" he asked. "You're not standing on
ceremony, I hope, just because I'm asking at the
last minute."

"I've got homework to do — at least two
hours' worth."

"C'mon Jill," he pleaded. "Be a sport and let
your homework ride for once. You can always

do homework, but the mime show will only be here two more nights."

"I have to finish a Spanish report that's due tomorrow."

"If you stopped arguing with me now, you could hang up and finish it before seven-thirty."

"I also have a zillion problems in algebra, and three chapters to outline in history."

"I think you should change schools," he said, and I could just see him grinning.

"You would say that," I groaned, "when what I really need is sympathy."

"If you ever get your priorities straightened out, call me. My philosophy is 'fun now, work later.'"

"I'm sorry, Jason. I've just got too much to do."

"I heard you," he answered. "Sometimes, Jill, I think you're too good to be true."

"I'm glad you called," I said, feeling my heart sink.

"It only cost a dime," he replied, and I knew he was no longer grinning.

There was a long pause, and I didn't know what to say, but I didn't want to hang up either.

"Well, you better not waste any more time," he said, and I could hear the irritation in his voice.

"Good-bye," I said slowly, "and thanks a lot for asking me."

"Don't mention it," he said, and hung up.

I held on to the receiver as though it were a lifeline. *I really blew that one*, I thought. *Prob-*

ably I should have gone. It wouldn't have killed me to be late with an assignment for once.

"Rats!" I roared aloud, and slammed down the receiver just as Ronnie was coming into the kitchen.

"What's wrong, sweetie?" she asked, opening the fridge door, but not looking too concerned about me.

"Jason asked me to go to the mime show in the Village tonight and I told him I couldn't," I told her.

"You should have gone," Ronnie said casually, getting some lettuce out of the vegetable bin.

"How could I?" I asked angrily. "I've got tons of homework."

She pulled out a few tomatoes and without looking at me said, "You could have stayed up late finishing your assignments, or gotten up early. I hear the mime show is great and I wanted to go myself."

"Thanks a lot," I said, and slammed out of the kitchen.

"Hey, hang on," Ronnie called after me. "It's not that serious."

"It is to me," I muttered, and disappeared into my room.

I realized I was being childish, which was exactly the image I was trying to shed as far as Jason was concerned. Well, maybe he was right. Maybe I was too young and inexperienced for him.

On the other hand, my father would have

approved of my decision. He believed in the "work now, play later" theory. If I'd been living uptown now, he wouldn't have allowed me to go and that would have upset me, too.

I went into the bathroom and splashed some cold water on my face so that I would calm down. Then I wandered back into the kitchen, where Ronnie was intent on tossing the salad.

"Hey, I didn't mean to get mad at you," I apologized. "It's not your fault that I didn't go out with Jason tonight. I'm just mad at myself for not thinking fast enough."

"Don't worry," Ronnie said. "Next time you'll be ready for him."

"I'll probably never see him again," I said, sulking.

"Yes, you will," Ronnie said. "Marsha's invited us over for Thanksgiving."

"She has?" My spirits lifted considerably. "Why didn't Jason mention it?"

"Probably he doesn't know it yet. She just invited me today and maybe didn't get a chance to tell him. He does go to school, you know."

"Doesn't act like it," I said. We both realized how silly that sounded and laughed out loud.

Ronnie always has a way of getting me out of a bad mood, and now I was ready to get off the subject of Jason.

"What's Daddy doing Thanksgiving?" I asked. I knew that my alternate months didn't necessarily include vacations and holidays, which had to be decided separately. It said in their divorce agreement that vacations and holidays would be decided "in the best interests of the child."

"Since it's only one Thursday, I thought you would rather stay here, but —"

"I would," I said, interrupting her. "It seems dumb to leave for one day."

Ronnie was busy scraping carrots over the sink and didn't look up when she said, "But I spoke to Tim today and he said Aunt Deborah and Uncle Scott were driving up especially from Boston to spend Thanksgiving with him — and hopefully you, too."

"What d'ja tell him? I don't see how I can do both."

"As a matter of fact you can." Ronnie was glancing sideways at me to see my reaction. "You see, Marsha wants us before one o'clock, and Tim doesn't want to have dinner till six. He said something about Marie not wanting to get there early, and Deborah and Scott won't arrive till mid-afternoon. You can get there by six and plan to spend the night."

"It's okay," I said, knowing Ronnie wanted to keep peace between me and Daddy. Besides, I didn't want to hurt anyone's feelings.

But as I set the table for dinner, I thought, *What does it mean, in the best interests of the child?* When it comes right down to it, they decide what's best for them, and maybe it suits me. Somehow, I didn't believe that that was what the court had in mind at all.

Chapter Twenty-one

Nothing brought home my schizzy existence as much as Thanksgiving Day. It was a study in extremes, and although it didn't seem so funny at the time when I met Maggie at the Mall in Central Park the next day and told her about it, she cracked up.

Marsha is a vegetarian, so that meant instead of turkey we had a veggie casserole as a main dish. Just so we'd know it was Thanksgiving, she served cranberry sauce and stuffing as well. Under the circumstances, it didn't make too much sense.

As soon as we arrived Jason asked me if I'd finished my homework, and before I could come up with a snappy answer, added, "You really missed a good one." I knew he was referring to the mime show.

"I needed that," I said, trying to keep it light.

"Never mind, you'll learn," he said, helping me off with my jacket.

"Jason, you could introduce us," a man wearing jeans and a work shirt, and growing a beard interrupted.

"Oh, sorry. This is George, who under that disguise is my father."

"How do you do?" I tried not to show how surprised I was that Jason treated him with so little respect. But it didn't seem to bother George at all.

"Hi, Jill," he said, "I'm so glad you and Ronnie could come over."

"Make yourself at home," Marsha shouted from the kitchen. "I'll be right with you."

George helped Ronnie pull her poncho over her head, and then planted a kiss on her cheek. "How's my favorite artist?" he asked.

"Terrific," Ronnie answered.

Marsha, her long black hair tied in a single braid down her back, burst out of the kitchen holding a tray, and yelled, "Sit down, sit down."

We followed her into the center of the loft and she put the tray down on a huge, round black table. I was about to sink into a black Naugahyde chair, but she threw her arms around me and said, "Welcome, welcome." Then she released me and did the same thing to Ronnie. It was hard not to feel comfortable here, and I was beginning to understand why Jason could be so loose.

I sat down and looked around, and thought I'd never seen such a spectacular room. All the furniture was black, the floors were black slate, and the walls were painted white. The only color came from the paintings which covered the walls.

"This room is fantastic," I said.

"You've obviously inherited your mother's good taste," Marsha said. She passed me the tray of hors d'oeuvres, which consisted of peanut butter on Ritz crackers, and chunks of cheddar cheese with toothpicks stuck in them.

"Would you like to see the gallery?" Jason asked. "It's one flight down."

"Sure," I said.

"Now or later?" Jason asked.

"Better go now," I replied. "I have to leave on the early side."

"Don't tell me," Jason groaned, slapping his palm against his forehead and looking pained. "You've got homework."

"That's something my son has never heard of," George said.

"Come on," Jason urged, pulling me out of my chair, "let's go downstairs before we get into an academic discussion."

"Academic?" Marsha laughed. "I thought that was a dirty word around here."

"So why do I get practically all A's?" Jason answered with a smirk.

"Good genes, I guess," George said.

"Or else he's got the teachers buffaloed," Marsha suggested.

"Probably a combination," Jason said, and hurried toward the door, laughing.

"Don't forget the keys," Marsha shouted to us as we were halfway out. "They're on the hook over the sink."

"Thanks for reminding me, Marsh," Jason said, and went back for the keys while I held the door.

We walked down a flight of stairs and Jason opened the door to the gallery. He flipped on the light and I could see it was the exact layout of the loft upstairs.

"This is a group show of still lifes," Jason explained. "Runs the gamut from representational to abstract. Which do you like?"

I looked around at the paintings and was immediately drawn to a misty watercolor of vaguely defined flowers. "I guess I'm somewhere in the middle," I answered.

"Figures," Jason said.

"What's wrong with that?" I asked defensively.

"Nothing. You really are too sensitive, Jill. It's fine to be in the middle, providing you mean it and you're not hedging."

"I mean it and I'm not hedging," I said definitively. *Certainly not about art*, I thought to myself.

"Okay, okay," Jason said. "Now let me show you the back room, which is actually the office."

I trailed after him into a small room off the main gallery. The light reflected from the outer room so that I could see a desk and a couple of chairs. I wondered why he didn't put the light on, but I should have known.

He stopped abruptly, turned around, and put his arms gently on my shoulders.

"Do you care if I kiss you?" he asked.

"No," I said quickly. "I mean yes."

"You mean no, you don't care, or yes, you do?"

"I don't know what I mean," I replied idiotically.

"I'll solve the problem," he said, and pressed his lips against mine.

I didn't exactly push him away, but I didn't think I encouraged him either. Then he pulled back and smiled at me in the shadowy light.

"That's better," he said.

"Better than what?" I asked.

"Just better," he said, ending the conversation.

"I thought you were going to show me this room." I tried to sound nonchalant about what just happened.

"Oh, yeah. I almost forgot." He reached for the light switch next to the door.

"Very nice," I said, looking around at the wide, formica-topped desk and the chrome and leather pull-up chairs.

"You're very nice, too," Jason said. "And I like your eyeshadow."

"You're very observant." This was one of the few times I'd worn anything more than lip gloss, but I guess I wanted to look more sophisticated knowing I would see Jason, so I'd borrowed Ronnie's eyeshadow. The problem was, I'd have to remember to wash it off before I went uptown.

"You should always wear it," he remarked.

"Guess so," I said, noncommittally. The last thing I wanted to do was explain why I couldn't wear it all the time.

"Well, the gallery tour is over. If we don't go back upstairs soon, they'll think we've been kidnapped." Jason flipped off the light switch.

"Lead on," I said as he took my hand.

Trudging up the stairs, I kept wondering what Jason thought of me. Did he consider me just a silly kid, who didn't know her own mind? Or was he really interested in me? What about Gloria, the red flash who probably never concerned herself about whether some guy liked her or not. Was he crazy about her, and did I really care?

Jason was right about one thing, I had to stop hedging!

Chapter Twenty-two

We settled down at the table as soon as we got upstairs, and the next few hours raced by as I sampled Marsha's haphazard meal. I didn't want to make it obvious that I was saving room for the uptown feast.

There was a lot of bantering back and forth between Jason and his parents. The fact that they treated him like an adult didn't faze him at all. They didn't even object when he poured himself a third glass of wine.

We talked about Ronnie's opening, which was scheduled for two days before Christmas.

"Better give me the list of people you want to invite," Marsha said. "I like to send out the invitations at least three weeks ahead."

"How many can I have?" Ronnie asked.

"The gallery holds over a hundred," George

said, "and if we want more, we have them in shifts. That means half the invites say three to six, and the other half six to nine."

"I'll show you the invitations," Marsha offered, pushing back her chair. "Come with me."

Ronnie went with her, and George started clearing the table, saying, "I'm going to put away the leftovers. You guys can help later with the dishes."

We were the only ones left at the table. "Inviting people in shifts is very clever," I remarked to Jason.

"It's called staggering," Jason explained.

"Sort of what I'm doing today," I murmured. I'd been trying to let him know why I had to leave, but was unable to come right out and say it. He had no idea I would be spending the night uptown because I didn't have an overnight bag. I kept two of everything essential in both places.

"What do you mean?" Jason asked.

"I mean," I said, looking at my watch, "I'll have to be uptown by six o'clock. It's known as a split holiday."

I thought he might say something sympathetic, like maybe it was too bad I had to leave early. Instead, he just shook his head and said, "Why do you let it happen?"

"Do I have a choice?" I said.

Before he could answer, Marsha and Ronnie had returned to the table. Ronnie shoved an invitation under my nose and said, "What do you think?"

The invitation had one of her black and white abstracts on the cover, and inside, in distinguished type, details of the showing.

"It's beautiful," I said. "Can I send some to my friends?"

"Of course, sweetie. As many as you want," Ronnie said. Then she and Marsha went into the kitchen to help George.

"You mean we're going to be blessed with the prom and preppy set," Jason whispered to me.

"Just because they live above Fourteenth Street, doesn't mean they're not normal," I rasped.

Before we could get into a real argument, George appeared with a tray and started to load it with dishes. "Many hands make light work," he commented. "Hint, hint."

"I think he's trying to tell us something, Jill. Like maybe we should help the old folks." He turned on that electric smile and I couldn't stay mad at him for long.

I got up to help clear as Marsha came out of the kitchen. She announced that she would provide some entertainment to make our burden lighter, and proceeded to get out her guitar. Then she accompanied herself on some country-western songs.

"You're really good," I complimented her after she finished one song.

"To tell the truth, Jill, I was always torn between whether I should pursue a career in music or in art. I love both."

"Then she met me, an art freak, and the decision was made for her," George said.

"Don't believe him, Jill. The decision was *weighted* when I met him, but it wasn't made for me."

"Okay, Marsha, we know you're liberated," Jason observed.

"Be quiet," Marsha said, smiling at him. "I don't need to hear it from you."

"Why not do another number?" Ronnie suggested.

"That's the best idea yet," Marsha said, and started strumming away while we finished cleaning up.

I could have stayed there all day, but it was almost five o'clock and I knew I had to get ready to leave. Ronnie sensed my reluctance, and said, "I'll blow you to a taxi. I don't like the idea of you waiting around on a deserted subway platform today." I told her I accepted and then I went into the bathroom to comb my hair and grab some tissues that I would use in the taxi to remove my eye shadow.

When I came out I thanked everyone for a wonderful time and after Jason helped me with my jacket, Marsha, George, and Ronnie kissed me good-bye. Jason volunteered to wait with me for a taxi and the two of us left.

It was dark and chilly and the streets were deserted. I was really glad that Jason was with me.

"Well, Jill," he said, as we strolled toward the corner, "I was glad you could come today — even though you have to leave now."

"Me, too."

"Your downtown month is almost over. But I'll see you the day of Ronnie's opening."

"That's not for more than three weeks," I said. It just slipped out and I immediately regretted saying it.

"You mean you can't wait," he teased me.

"Course I can," I said, trying to recover my indifferent pose.

"Maybe I'll give you a break, and venture forth into your neck of the woods."

"I'll protect you if you do," I offered. "And then you can meet my father."

"Hey, you make it sound serious."

"No," I protested, "it's just being civilized."

"You mean you have to have your father check me out before you can go out with me?"

"Don't be silly," I lied, but thought that was exactly what I had to do.

"Here comes a cab now," Jason said, waving it down.

The cab drew up to the curb and Jason opened the door. Then he pressed my arm and kissed me on the cheek.

"Thanks for waiting with me," I said as I climbed in.

"Always the gentleman." He blew me a kiss as the taxi took off, and I gave the cabbie my uptown address.

It was hard to figure Jason out, I thought, as I looked in my hand mirror and rubbed my eyelids with a tissue. The eye shadow came off easily, and I wished it was just as simple to change my psyche. Sure, I was looking forward to seeing my aunt and uncle, who didn't have children of their own, but they couldn't be more different from Marsha and George and Ronnie. After spending the afternoon with them it wouldn't be so easy to assume my "good little girl" role again. But, of course, I was going to try.

Chapter Twenty-three

Marie answered the door and threw up her hands in excitement, shouting, "It's Jilly. It's Jilly. Your father was just beginning to worry. Come, come, your aunt and uncle are already here."

Then my father came to the door and gave me a hug. "Good girl," he murmured. "You're on time. You know how Aunt Deborah is about being punctual."

Runs in the family, I was tempted to say, but knew my father wouldn't appreciate any fresh remarks.

Marie took my jacket and hung it in the front closet and I went into the living room. Aunt Deborah was sitting on the sofa, holding a long-stemmed glass of wine in one hand and a caviar hors d'oeuvre in the other. "Jill, darling," she said in her lockjaw voice, "you're here. It's wonderful to see you. Give me a kiss, will you? I can't possibly extricate myself from this sofa."

"Hi, Aunt Deborah," I greeted her and bent down to kiss her cheek.

Aunt Deborah always looked so perfect. She was wearing a tissue-thin beige wool dress and a single strand of pearls. She had the same chiseled features as my father and blond hair that she wore severely pulled back in a bun. She was so uptight that she made my father look like a swinger.

Uncle Scott was at the bar, pouring himself a drink. He was a stockbroker and the only thing he seemed comfortable talking about was the economy. His black hair was flecked with grey, and he had a perpetual sunburn — a barbershop tan, Ronnie once explained to me.

"Hello, Jill," he said, coming toward me, still holding the scotch bottle and his glass. He leaned over them to kiss my forehead.

"Hi, Uncle Scott. It's been a long time," I told him.

"Certainly has," he answered. The problem with me and Uncle Scott was I didn't know enough about stocks and bonds to ask the right questions and he didn't know what to say to anyone under thirty.

He went back to the bar and said, "What'll it be?"

"Cranberry juice," my father answered for me. "There's some right there."

"In a long-stemmed glass, please," I added, thinking at least I'd graduated from having a

Shirley Temple. I wondered what my father would think if he'd seen how Jason behaved.

I helped myself to the canapes that were on the coffee table. There were shrimp and lobster chunks and fresh caviar on toasted bread triangles.

"Sit down, Jill dear," Aunt Deborah said, "and tell me how you like living in New York."

"It's great," I answered, which was what I always told her about everything.

"I know it's wonderful up here, but what about downtown? I must confess, I never get down there."

"It's super," I replied, not wanting to get into a "My Two Worlds" discussion. Sometimes, I thought, Aunt Deborah's not too tactful. I mean, I had enough trouble keeping together my own United Nations.

Before she could ask any other probing questions, Marie, holding a huge turkey on a silver platter, announced that dinner was served. Everyone commented on how gorgeous the bird looked and Uncle Scott, who's a camera freak, yelled, "Hold it," took his instamatic out of his pocket and rapidly snapped a few pictures. Then we sat down at the table and my father proceeded to carve while Marie passed around the rest of the dishes, which were traditional down to the last homemade cranberry mold.

My father and Uncle Scott got into a discussion of how to curb double-digit inflation, and Aunt Deborah asked me what the girls were wearing in my class. When I told her jeans were practically the uniform for boys and girls in my school, she just shook her head in dismay.

We were on the mince pie when my father said, "Well, Jill, we have a surprise for you. Aunt Deborah and Uncle Scott and I plan to go to Aspen over Christmas, and we know you'll want to come. How's that sound?"

"Great," I said, without even thinking.

"We'll be leaving as soon as your vacation begins, which is the twentieth of December."

"O-oh," I muttered. "Can't go then."

"Why not?" Aunt Deborah asked. "I can't believe anything would stand in the way of your spending ten days in Aspen."

"My mother's art-show opening is on the twenty-third," I said.

"You can miss that," Uncle Scott snapped. "The show will be there a while, I'm sure."

"Well, I don't know," I said. "I think she'll be very disappointed."

"Not if you explain, dear," Aunt Deborah insisted. "She wouldn't want you to give up a ski trip."

"I don't know," I said, hesitantly. "Maybe she would."

"You've got to be kidding," Uncle Scott said.

"We'll talk about it later," my father intervened, sensing that I was getting very uncomfortable. "Now, who's for a little cognac?"

"Can't hurt," Aunt Deborah said, and pushed back her chair.

Before he poured the cognac, my father put on a record that my aunt and uncle had given him. It was the Boston Symphony Orchestra playing Ravel, and it fitted my bittersweet mood perfectly. Here I was being offered a trip to Aspen, which some kids would die for, and part of me didn't even want to go. I knew it wasn't a life-or-death decision — just another complication in my double life.

Chapter Twenty-four

The following day, Friday, there was no school, and Maggie called first thing in the morning and said I had to meet her in Central Park at the entrance on Seventy-second Street. Presumably we would have lunch together, but the minute we met we decided to go on a starvation diet and walk around instead. I started to tell her the details of my Thanksgiving, and she could only see the funny side until I came to the part about Christmas vacation.

"Wow," she exclaimed. "That's a tough one. But I think I may have a solution."

"Tell me," I demanded.

"On the other hand, my solution might complicate your life further."

"What are you talking about?" I asked impatiently.

"One of the reasons I was so anxious to see you today was to tell you about it."

"Hurry up," I urged.

"You won't believe this, but my folks said I could invite some kids up to our place in Vermont over Christmas. I wanted you to be the first one I asked."

"Oh, no," I whined. "I'd love that, but how can I?"

"Anything's possible," Maggie replied optimistically. "I hope Sandy and Serena can come, too."

"That sounds like so much fun," I said. "When are you going?"

"My father will drive the station wagon with my mother and all our junk, including my brother. I said I'd volunteer to go on the bus with my friends so they'd have plenty of room. Be more fun on the bus anyway, I figure."

"But when?" I asked.

"The twenty-first," she sighed. "That means you'll miss the opening."

"This is getting too much," I groaned. "At least if you were leaving after the twenty-third, I'd have a good excuse for not going to Aspen. Now everyone will be insulted."

"You are in a bind," Maggie agreed, "but we'll think of something. Who are you supposed to be with over the holidays?"

"Both," I said. "Depending on what's convenient."

"For you or for them?" Maggie asked.

"I sometimes wonder," I replied. "My first

split holiday was yesterday, and I could barely manage that for twenty-four hours. I don't know how it's going to work over a couple of weeks."

"I can see your problem," Maggie said sympathetically.

It was a crisp but sunny morning, and the park had attracted a lot of bicycle riders, runners, skateboard riders, and roller skaters. We were walking by a playground that was filled with toddlers being pushed on the swings and guided down the slides by their mothers and fathers and an occasional nanny. I couldn't help thinking how lucky these kids were to be so carefree and have all their decisions made for them.

I guess I must have looked forlorn because Maggie said, "You don't have to decide this minute. Why don't you let things ride for a few days and then everything might fall into place."

"You're right," I agreed, trying to smile. "There are just too many possibilities."

"It's called an embarrassment of riches," Maggie said, laughing.

"That's a good way of putting it. To tell you the truth, I was even looking forward to spending the holiday in New York."

"That can be fun, too. But for now, be a nonthinker. It's weeks off so let's not talk about it. I promise you everything will work out."

"You mean I'll wake up one day and it will be like ordering from a Chinese menu. I'll take two from column A and two from column B. . . ."

"That's exactly what I mean."

"You make it sound so simple."

"Not simple, but definite. You'll see."

"I hope you're right, Maggie," I said solemnly.

"Don't be so serious," Maggie pleaded. "In fact, let's stop talking about it."

"I am getting a bit self-centered," I admitted. "And you haven't told me yet about your Thanksgiving."

"It was half great," Maggie said. "We had my grandparents, my aunt and uncle, and three male cousins."

"Three male cousins," I repeated. "Sounds interesting."

"If you like them twelve and under," Maggie chortled. "Actually, they're a lot of fun. And the dinner was spectacular."

"So what was the other half?"

"The other half was that I was supposed to meet Seth at five and go to a movie. But nobody had left yet. I cornered my mother in the kitchen and told her I really had to leave."

"And she said 'no way.'"

"She was adamant. She said my relatives didn't come all the way from upstate New York to have me leave early. She said I should just call Seth and tell him I'd meet him later or not at all."

"What did you do?"

"I didn't have a choice. I called Seth and told him I'd meet him at six at the coffee shop on Eighty-sixth and Madison. That meant we'd be too late for the movie, but the important thing was we would be together."

"That's not so awful. And you're lucky, you didn't have to make a choice."

"That's one way of looking at it," said Maggie thoughtfully. "I guess everyone's problems seem a lot easier to the person who doesn't have them."

"That's for darn sure," I agreed. "But I thought we weren't going to talk about problems."

"We're not going to talk about *your* problems," Maggie explained. "That doesn't mean we can't talk about mine."

"Unfair, unfair," I yelled, and trotted off ahead of her.

"Hey, wait up," she called after me, and ran to catch up. I slowed down and we were running side by side. "Let's head for the polar bears," Maggie said, huffing. "They look like they have all the answers."

"You're on," I said, picking up speed.

We jogged in tandem toward the zoo and I kept thinking of *Aspen, Vermont, New York. What should I do? What should I do?* The first thing I knew was to ask Ronnie. She rarely waffled on anything, and maybe some of that decisiveness would rub off on me!

Chapter Twenty-five

When I arrived at the loft, Ronnie was sitting at the large oak table, a bunch of invitations spread out in front of her.

"Hi, sweetie," she said as I bent down to kiss her cheek. "You're just in time to help me address envelopes."

"For the opening?" I asked stupidly.

"Of course," she answered. "By the way, you can have as many invitations as you want to send to your friends. I don't even know a hundred people."

"Sure," I said, hanging up my jacket.

"You don't sound too thrilled," Ronnie commented. "What's the matter?" As usual I couldn't hide anything from Ronnie even if I wanted to.

"I've got a problem," I groaned, and slunk into a chair opposite her.

Ronnie froze, her pen in midair. "What's wrong, honey? Did something happen yesterday?"

"In a way," I mumbled.

"What is it?" she asked urgently.

"Daddy wants me to go to Aspen over Christmas with him and Aunt Deborah and Uncle Scott," I blurted out.

"What's so terrible about that?" Ronnie said relaxing, and went back to addressing an envelope.

"They're leaving on the twentieth," I muttered.

"You mean you'd miss the opening." Ronnie looked crestfallen.

"If I go," I said quickly.

"Do you want to go?" she asked evenly.

"I don't know," I said miserably. "And besides that, Maggie's invited me to Vermont with her family and some other kids."

"You certainly have a lot of invitations," Ronnie said in a monotone.

"But I want to go to the opening."

"Nobody's stopping you," Ronnie remarked, and concentrated very hard on her penmanship.

For the first time that I could remember I felt Ronnie was cool toward me. It seemed to last all weekend, although maybe I imagined it. Actually I didn't see much of Ronnie the next two days because she was busy finishing up a canvas, and I had to complete my photography club assignment of city scenes. Maggie's theory that things would fall into place didn't seem to be happening.

On Monday I had to move uptown. I packed some things and went into Ronnie's room to say good-bye. She was still half-asleep, and mumbled something about saving some invitations for my friends in case I changed my mind. Then she rolled over and went back to sleep.

I knew she'd been working very late and was probably exhausted and that was why she hadn't gotten up to have breakfast with me. At least that's what I kept telling myself. I mean, my mother couldn't stay mad at me forever if I happened to miss her opening. Or could she?

I was upset when I left the house, and it was one of those days when things were destined to get worse. Everything that could go wrong did, starting with the fact that I had to wait longer than usual for the subway. That meant I got to school just as the bell rang and everyone saw me lugging a suitcase. I hurried up the stairs to my homeroom and pretended I didn't hear when anyone asked me where I was going. I jammed the suitcase into our homeroom closet, but couldn't avoid Sue Robbins, who was sitting in the front row, watching me.

"What's the big hurry?" she asked me. "That was only the first bell."

"No hurry," I answered. "Just wanted to dump my suitcase."

"You act like it's stolen goods," she remarked.

"Nope," I said casually, and started to walk toward the back of the room where Sandy was sitting.

"Going someplace exotic?" Sue called after me.

"To the back of the room," I shot back and immediately regretted acting so snippy.

"Snob," Sue said under her breath, but loud enough for me to hear. I didn't really blame her. Even though Sue wasn't one of my favorite people, I thought I could at least be civil.

Sandy was all smiles as I approached. "Hey, Jill," she enthused, "isn't it great about going to Vermont over Christmas? Maggie called me last night."

"It's great," I said in a flat tone.

"You don't sound like you mean it," Sandy observed.

"I'm not sure I can go," I said, and sank into the chair next to her.

"Can't go," she gasped. "You wouldn't fink out on a trip like this. Maggie says there's a room downstairs that has bunk beds and sleeps eight — more if we bring sleeping bags."

"Terrific," I said dully.

"What's wrong with you, Jill? Even my folks, who are gung-ho on spending holidays together, say I should go. They know how much I love skiing and wouldn't want me to miss out."

"Lucky you. Your life is so simple. I suppose Serena's going, too."

"I don't know. I haven't spoken to her, but I can't imagine her not going. Who in their right mind would refuse such an opportunity?"

"Thanks a lot," I muttered.

"Sometimes I wonder about you," Sandy said despairingly.

"You just don't understand," I told her. "I'll explain later."

"Sure," Sandy said. She pulled her French grammar out of her book bag and buried her head in it, indicating the conversation was over.

The second bell sounded and Maggie and Serena, babbling away, came toward us.

"I just told Serena about Vermont," Maggie said.

"You're going, aren't you?" Sandy asked, stuffing her book back in her canvas bag.

"If it's humanly possible," Serena said. "Isn't everybody?"

"Maybe not everybody," I sighed, trying to ignore the lump in my throat.

"You can't go?" Serena sounded surprised.

"I want to, but I may not be able to," I murmured.

"There must be a way," Serena insisted.

"That's what I say," Sandy agreed.

Then the final bell rang and I felt spared, at least momentarily, from any further discussion about what seemed to be my increasingly fragmented life.

Chapter Twenty-six

During lunch period I avoided sitting down with my friends in the cafeteria. I grabbed a yogurt and explained to Maggie, who was standing in the food line next to me, that I was going to develop my film in the darkroom, so that it would be ready for me to make prints after school. Each member of the photography club was to have at least twenty prints ready for the next club meeting on whatever subject they'd chosen. The members would vote for the five best from each person's group, and those would be exhibited in the library.

"Don't worry about it," Maggie said. "I'll see you later."

I think she probably knew I could have used my study hall time to work in the darkroom, but I couldn't face any more questions about Christmas vacation, and going during lunch was a legitimate cop-out. I was grateful that she didn't let on and I could escape for a while.

I went up the stairs to the darkroom, which was on the third floor, and put the film in the developer and set the timer. While I waited for the chemicals to take effect, I bolted down my strawberry yogurt. When the timer went off, I removed the negatives and hung them on a line with what looked like miniature clothespins. I knew they would be thoroughly dry by the time I returned after my last class to make the prints.

I finished everything just before the bell rang, and I'd been so engrossed in what I was doing that my problems had temporarily submerged. Now they immediately surfaced and I wondered how I'd be able to concentrate on my next class, which was history. Our teacher, Mr. Berger, looks like Woody Allen and has a similar sense of humor, except when it comes to work. Then he's a perfectionist and he's convinced that the way to keep us on our toes is to give a lot of tests — every Monday and every Thursday. The Thursday ones go on our record and count toward our final grade; the Monday ones are for our own use and can't be held against us. That was especially fortunate because for the first time that Monday I couldn't concentrate. I'd get halfway through a question and my mind would start wandering. I was happy we were allowed to mark our own papers and that nobody could see mine. As soon as class was over, I scrunched up my test and tossed it in the trash basket.

My last class was English with Mrs. Clark, a dumpy little old-fashioned teacher with frazzled gray hair, who can be fascinating when she talks about literature. However, she insists that we learn perfect grammar, and devotes one day a week to the subject — always on Monday. I think maybe she likes it as little as we do and wants to get it over with.

One of her techniques is to read a sentence that has a mistake and ask us what it is. The class was almost over and I thought I had been spared her calling on me, but I was wrong again.

"Jill, what's wrong with the sentence I just read?" she asked.

I was really embarrassed because I hadn't been listening. I couldn't ask her to repeat it because she had warned us the first day of school that if she had to repeat things it would take her twice as long to teach us anything. Therefore I was forced to say, "I don't know."

"Tch, tch," she sighed, and wrote something in her attendance book — probably a goose egg, or n.g. for no good — beside my name.

I slumped down in my chair while she called on Sue Robbins who said brightly, "There's a dangling participle."

"Correct," Mrs. Clark said. Then the bell rang and she told us to have our reading assignment, *Catcher in the Rye*, completed by Friday.

I slunk past Mrs. Clark's desk and out of the room, thinking that the whole day had been a bummer. It had started with Ronnie not having breakfast with me; then the subway train being late; Sue asking pointed questions about my suitcase; Sandy suggesting I was a fink; flunking a practice test in history; and finally not paying attention in English so that I looked like a knucklehead.

As I trudged up the stairs to the darkroom I thought about all the stories I'd heard about kids who didn't do well in school because of problems at home. I never quite believed it because I thought everything could be kept separate. Now I realized that I'd been naive about that. A problem at home can absolutely destroy your ability to function at school — and what had happened to me today was a perfect example. If I continued like this I could guarantee getting all F's.

On my way to the darkroom I glanced in on my soc. classroom, which is located right next door. Mrs. Carson, who was working at her desk, caught my eye and smiled. "Hello, Jill. How are things going?" she asked.

"Fine," I lied. "I'm just about to make some prints. I'll have enough ready for the next meeting."

"Good," she said. "I'll be right here checking some papers if you need any help."

"Thanks," I said, "but I think I can manage."

Once in the darkroom I put the developing solution in the tray, removed the film from the "clothespins," put it in the enlarger, and was ready to print. The first print I made was of a group of buildings taken from the window of my father's apartment. I was disappointed to see that the images were very blurry, probably because I had moved the camera. I dumped the print in the stop-bath and then in the fixative, thinking that the way things were going that might be one of my best prints. Besides, I had to have at least twenty to choose from.

My next print was of a mounted policeman going through traffic on Fifth Avenue. This was a great improvement over the first print, as far as being clear, but the policeman's face was in a shadow from his cap. I decided to make the print again, this time "holding back" the dark area by using my hands as a mask between the enlarger light and the shadow.

When I finished developing it, there was a fuzzy outline of my hand around the policeman's head. Obviously I hadn't moved my hand enough, and the print looked worse than ever. I was so frustrated and angry that I threw the dripping print on the floor and watched as it slowly turned black.

The whole thing was too much for me and I started to cry. There were some paper towels on the sink. I grabbed a bunch and tried to muffle the sound, but even that didn't work, and soon I was sobbing out loud.

The next thing I knew, there was a knock on the door and it slowly opened. Mrs. Carson stood for a moment, looking totally bewildered, and then put her arms around me while I cried uncontrollably, my head buried in her shoulder. Finally I seemed to gain control and she led me toward her room while I hid my face in the fistful of paper towels that I was clutching.

When we got to her room she closed the door and I collapsed on a front-row seat.

"Jill," she said, half-smiling, "I know that

remembering all the steps in developing film can be difficult, but I've never seen such a violent reaction."

"It's not the film — it's everything," I grumbled.

"You mean life is getting you down." Mrs. Carson took a box of tissues from the bottom drawer of her desk and sat down beside me.

"It's already got me down," I told her, and grabbed some tissues and blew my nose. "I seem to be getting everybody mad at me. And all I'm trying to do is the right thing."

Then I told her about all the possibilities for Christmas vacation.

"What do you really want to do?" she asked me.

"I don't know. My mother will be hurt if I miss her show; my father will be insulted if I don't go to Aspen; my friends will think I'm a fink if I don't go to Vermont."

"Once you figure out what you want to have happen, the next step is to make it happen."

"I'm a wimp," I said miserably.

"That's the last thing you are, Jill. You've managed your new life very well up to now. There are bound to be obstacles along the way."

"I know that, and I always thought I could handle them. Now I'm not so sure. Even my school work is slipping."

"When did that start?" Mrs. Carson asked, looking concerned.

"Today," I answered.

Then she laughed and said, "I don't think

that's a pattern. Everyone has bad days. Some days I know I teach a lot better than others."

"Honestly?" I said.

"Honestly," she replied. "No one is perfect, and you shouldn't expect yourself to be."

"What should I do next?" It felt good, finally, to unburden myself to somebody I thought had all the answers.

Just as I was thinking that, Mrs. Carson said, "I don't have all the answers, but I think the important thing is to decide what *you* want."

"Even if it's a selfish decision?"

"The selfish decision may turn out to be the right decision. Taking a stand is sometimes painful, but in the long run it can be for the best."

"I'll try," I said thoughtfully. "At least I feel better now that I've talked to you. I even think I'm ready to face the darkroom again."

"That's good. And I'll be here at least another hour if you need any help."

"Thanks for everything," I said, getting up. "I think I'm beginning to see things a lot more clearly now."

Maybe that was a little bit of an exaggeration, I thought, as I headed for the darkroom. But at least Mrs. Carson seemed convinced that I wasn't a wimp; that I didn't have to be perfect; and that mainly it was for me to decide, however painful, what exactly I wanted.

Chapter Twenty-seven

That night at dinner my father asked point blank if I was going to Aspen with him. He said Uncle Scott had already made the reservation and if I wasn't going, he would tell him to cancel.

"I don't know," I said for the millionth time. "Maggie also invited me and some other kids to Vermont over Christmas vacation. They're leaving the twenty-first."

"And you'd rather do that?" His voice was steely.

"I don't know," I repeated.

"You better decide soon, Jill," he warned. "Otherwise the decision will be made for you. I think a week from today is a reasonable amount of time in which to make up your mind."

"Okay," I muttered, hoping that by some miracle I'd come up with an answer by then.

"Let's talk about something else now," my father said, his voice softening. "What happened in school today?"

"Not much," I hedged. "I developed some prints for the photography show. Some of them aren't too bad."

"When can I see them?"

"They're in school now, waiting to be chosen for the library exhibit, but I'll bring home some copies."

"I'd love to see them," he said. Then he proceeded to tell me how when he was a teenager he had a job one summer as an assistant cub reporter on a local newspaper in a small village outside Boston. One of his duties was to set up camera equipment for the reporter he was assisting.

"On a story covering a fire, I got so excited that I actually dropped some of the equipment. The man I was working for said I was responsible for him missing some great candid shots, and the next thing I knew I was fired. That turned me off from taking pictures for a long time. Since then I've never messed around much with photography, but maybe it's not too late for me to learn. Do you think you could give me a lesson one day in developing?"

"Sure," I said, "it's easy." Then I proceeded to tell him the various steps.

By the time dinner was over, I was feeling relaxed and happy to be with my father again, but it didn't solve anything. I even thought that if I could stay really mad at one of my parents, it would make my life easier.

The next few days were relatively peaceful. I managed to put the vacation question on the back burner and was almost ready to relinquish my part in making a decision. After all, my father said if I didn't come up with an answer by Monday, it would be out of my hands. That would be the easiest way out. Then whatever was decided, I could say it wasn't my fault because my father had insisted on doing whatever he wanted me to do. Deep down, I knew it was a cop-out, and even childish, but I was tempted to let it happen.

I'd practically come to a decision *not* to make a decision until Saturday, the night of the school play. Then there was a series of events that was to change everything.

Guys and Dolls was the musical comedy that had been in rehearsal ever since the semester began, and there was so much enthusiasm for it that seats had to be reserved in advance. Maggie and Seth were sitting together next to Serena, Sandy, and me. It must have been fate that Jimmy, Alex, and Carl were sitting directly behind us.

Alex, in his usual outspoken manner, said in a loud voice, "Aren't we lucky to be sitting behind the best-looking chicks in the class."

"Careful how you refer to us," Serena cautioned him, tilting her head in his direction.

"*Women* is the preferred handle," Carl remarked.

"That's better," Sandy agreed.

"Under the circumstances, I would say *dolls*

is the best description," Jimmy said, and we all laughed.

"That's perfect," I said admiringly, and pivoted around in my seat so I could see Jimmy. He had such sensitive good looks, and his eyes especially were so expressive. I personally thought he was the cutest guy in the class, and nice besides. Also, he was still available, although I knew plenty of girls would have liked to change that situation — including me.

I was thinking about this when the lights dimmed and the orchestra began playing the overture. Then the curtain rose and the show began.

The amusing story of a good-looking gambler falling in love with a beautiful Salvation Army worker was totally absorbing and the audience applauded enthusiastically after the first act. During the intermission we all went out to the lobby and somehow Jimmy had maneuvered me into a corner.

"A bunch of us are going to Out of Sight after the show. I hope you can come," he said.

"Is this an invitation?" I asked, surprised at my own coyness.

"You know it!" he said boldly.

"In that case, I'd love to," I answered, trying not to show how excited I was.

Out of Sight is the local hamburger joint that serves as a disco at night. It would be the first time I'd be there after sundown, and I couldn't wait.

When I got back to my seat, Serena whispered

to me that Carl had asked her, and Alex had asked Sandy to have a Coke later at Out of Sight.

"Maggie and Seth are going, too," she said, and looked at me expectantly.

"Jimmy asked me." I nodded my head, half-smiling and trying to be cool.

Serena didn't say anything, but she gave me a friendly wink.

The show was so good that in one way I was sorry when it was over. In another way, of course, I couldn't wait because this would be the first time I would actually be going out with Jimmy. There were a lot of curtain calls and a standing ovation for the cast, and finally the audience broke up and wandered out of the auditorium.

Alex, who had assumed the role of ringleader, urged us to hurry so we could all sit together at Out of Sight. He ran interference for us through the crowd and we were some of the first to arrive.

Out of Sight consists of two rooms. The first room is long and narrow and has a string of booths against one wall and a soda fountain opposite, behind which is the kitchen. An open archway leads to a large room where there are red and white plastic-covered tables surrounding a reasonably sized dance area. Music is taped in from strategically placed loudspeakers. Small vases of plastic flowers grace each table, and although the ambience could only be described as tacky in the harsh light of day, at night the dimly lit room actually looked romantic. Or maybe it was just reflecting my mood.

Alex and Carl pulled two tables together so that eight of us could sit together. The music was coming from all sides and somehow a Coke appeared in front of me along with an order of French fries. I didn't remember ordering anything, but I was so carried away with excitement, and so relieved from the tension of the past few days, that if a gorilla had served me I probably wouldn't have noticed. In fact, everyone seemed in a terrific mood and as the place filled up, the noise increased and the music was louder. I began to feel really heady. Everyone at our table danced with everyone else, but the best of all for me was dancing with Jimmy.

I knew he was shy with girls, but the atmosphere seemed to loosen him up. He even went so far as to say, "You're a terrific dancer. Think of all the time we've wasted not going out."

"Whose fault is that?" I asked, remembering that he'd never followed up on his offer to play tennis.

"I'm guilty," he admitted, "but all that's going to change. Will you help me mend my ways?"

"I can try," I answered. He slowly squeezed my hand, gazed deeply into my eyes, and for a minute I felt he was casting a spell over me.

Then he broke the silence with what might as well have been a bomb. "What are you doing over Christmas vacation?" he asked.

"Oh, no, not you, too," I groaned.

I must have looked stricken because he said, "What's the matter? You look like I've said something terrible."

"In a way you have."

"What are you talking about?"

"Let's sit down, and I'll tell you," I said, leading him off the dance floor.

Everyone from our table was dancing, so we had a few minutes of relative privacy. We sat down and I told him briefly about my choices.

"Well," he said when I was finished, "it seems obvious what you should do."

"Obvious," I repeated.

"From my point of view it is. You see, my family is going to be staying at Mount Snow over the holidays. That's not too far from where you'll be and I'm sure we can join forces."

"You're kidding!" I exclaimed. "That is a coincidence. But what about my mother's show and going to Aspen with my father?"

"Jill, it's not such a big deal. Just make a decision."

"I know you're right," I mumbled. "I don't know what's wrong with me."

"Nothing's wrong with you," Jimmy assured me, taking my hand. "And I didn't mean to send you into a tailspin just because I wanted to know what you were doing over Christmas."

"I know," I said, feeling foolish.

"C'mon, let's dance. They're actually playing something slow for once." He pulled me toward the dance floor.

"You're on," I said, and as he wrapped his arms around me and we swayed in rhythm to the music, nothing seemed to matter but the two of us.

Chapter Twenty-eight

Time sped by so fast that I couldn't believe it when Alex announced that he had to leave. He explained that he was filling in his father's doubles game first thing in the morning and he didn't want to "disgrace the old man" by being half asleep.

"They're playing at the ungodly hour of eight-thirty and if I don't get at least five hours sleep, I'm finished."

"What time is it?" I asked nervously.

"Almost two," he replied, pushing back his chair.

"You're kidding!" I exclaimed. "I've got to leave, too."

Then the others made noises about having to get home, and we all drifted out and went our separate ways. Jimmy walked me to my building and on the way confided to me that it was one of the best times he could remember.

"Me, too," I said.

"We'll go out again really soon," he promised.

"Hope so," I encouraged him.

"Like next Saturday?" he asked.

"I'd love to," I said.

The doorman was standing in the lobby of my building, so even if Jimmy had wanted to kiss me good night, it would have been too embarrassing. He held my hand tightly as I waited for the elevator and didn't let it go until the last second. Neither of us said anything as the elevator door closed, and I was in a daze as I pressed the button for my floor.

I was so caught up with the evening that I'd forgotten about dealing with my father. In the back of my mind, I trusted that he would be asleep. I opened the door to the apartment gently, not wanting to disturb him. But the lights were on in the living room and I knew my luck had run out. My father was in his bathrobe and slippers, pacing up and down.

"I was about to call the police," he said in an enraged tone.

"You knew I'd gone to the school play," I defended myself.

"The school play doesn't last till two in the morning," he barked.

"You might have guessed we'd go out after," I said, surprised at my own boldness.

"I don't guess about things. Where exactly were you all this time?"

"A bunch of us went to Out of Sight after the play. Nobody else had to report in."

"I don't care about 'nobody.' I care about

you. As far as I'm concerned you're still a little girl and while you're in my house you abide by my rules."

I couldn't help thinking that this never would have happened if I'd been living with Ronnie. She never gave me a curfew. Maybe that thought and my strong feelings for Jimmy gave me a new confidence. I'd never talked back to my father before, but a combination of anger and defiance made me stand up to him.

"I am not a little girl," I protested. "I'm almost sixteen, and besides, Ronnie *never* cares about what time I get home."

"I can't help what your mother does," he said angrily, "but I can help what you do. Now, if you don't mind, I'd like to get some sleep. When you start thinking straight, you can apologize to me." He stormed out of the living room and then slammed the door to his bedroom.

I was shaking by then, but it wasn't so much from fear as it was from anger. I'd just had a wonderful evening — as Jimmy had said, one of the best times I could remember. I honestly thought I was falling in love, and now my father had to ruin it all.

I took a hot bath, thinking that might calm me down, and then climbed into bed. But there were so many thoughts swirling around my head that I couldn't fall asleep. All my anxieties about the holiday, my mother's coolness, my father's anger, the double messages I received from my parents, and my own indecisiveness was driving me bananas.

I must have slept for a couple of hours, but when I looked at my watch it was only six o'clock. I knew I had to talk to Maggie, but it wouldn't be fair to call so early. I waited till nine and went into the kitchen to dial her number. She had her own phone in her room so I wouldn't be waking up the entire family.

She picked up after the third ring and said groggily, "Who is it?"

"Me," I said. "I have to see you."

"Jill, what's wrong?" She immediately sounded wide awake.

"Nothing and everything."

"Shall we meet at the zoo? I can be there in thirty minutes."

"Thanks," I said gratefully. "I'll meet you at the seals."

"Later," Maggie said, and hung up.

At least, I thought, as I poured some apple juice in a glass, I can count on Maggie.

I wasn't up to facing my father and wanted to get out of there before he woke up. I dressed quickly and was about to leave when I decided to write him a note. After all, even though I felt he was being unreasonable, I still loved him and didn't want him to think I'd run away.

I scribbled on a notepad in the kitchen: *Have gone to zoo with Maggie. Will return by noon. Jill.* I left the note next to the sink so that he would be sure to see it. Then I went into my room, dressed quickly, and quietly let myself out of the apartment.

It was a deliciously clear day, the kind that

makes you want to keep moving. In spite of myself, I could feel my spirits lifting and I walked briskly toward the zoo. *Everything in the cold light of day seemed less depressing,* I thought as I waited at the rail surrounding the seal pond.

When Maggie approached hurriedly toward me, a concerned look on her face, I waved and half-smiled.

"Are you okay?" she asked, breathlessly. "Except for a couple of dark circles under your eyes, you look fine."

"I didn't mean to sound hysterical. It's just that I'm more discombobulated than ever."

"Meaning?"

"Meaning I've got to get my act together."

Then I enumerated all the things that were bothering me and had kept me awake half the night. Maggie let me rattle on and didn't say much, just nodded her head. When I finally finished my list of resentments and confusions, and made it clear that I thought it was all my parents' fault, she looked thoughtful.

"You're blaming your parents for everything," she said. "Almost as though you have no say in the matter."

"Well, do I? They got me into this mess. I think what I'm suffering from is what's called 'conflicting loyalties.'"

"That's a good way of putting it," Maggie agreed. "But the only person who can solve that is you. Maybe the thing that's most important is to be loyal to yourself and your own feelings. I know that sounds corny, but I think it's true."

"You mean I should decide what I want to have happen and then take steps to make it happen. That's what Mrs. Carson told me when she found me crying in the darkroom because I couldn't make up my mind about anything."

"You were crying in the darkroom?" Maggie exclaimed in astonishment. "You never told me."

"Nothing serious. Just more of the same."

"Mrs. Carson is right, though, Jill. You have to decide what you want. And then you have to tell your mother and father how you feel."

"About everything?"

"Why not? How else are they supposed to know?"

"That makes sense," I said. "You make it seem so easy."

"Maybe it will be, once you decide to do it," Maggie said reassuringly.

"Well, one conclusion I've come to is that I definitely want to go to Vermont over the holiday. I think I knew that all along, but was afraid I'd hurt somebody's feelings."

"That's terrific for starters. Now let me ask a real tough one, but don't give me a fast answer."

"Shoot," I said, steeling myself.

"Would you rather that your parents didn't have joint custody, and that you lived with just one of them, which is what happens in most divorce cases?"

"I've thought about that, too," I said. "Sometimes I think it would be a lot simpler. The problem is that even though my father treats me like a three-year-old sometimes, I really do love him. He's one of the smartest people I know, and interesting, and even though he can be very serious, I like that, too."

"And your mother?"

"She's wonderful, and not nearly as strict, but she expects me to act like I'm thirty instead of fifteen. I'm crazy about her, though."

"What you're saying is, you like being a joint kid."

"I'm absolutely sure of that."

"Then *you* have to make it work."

I suddenly remembered what Mrs. Carson had said to me when I told her that I didn't want my father to see the paper I'd written on male chauvinism. *You have definite ideas. Why not share them with him?*

"What you're saying is it's up to me to make it work, not just them, and the only way for that to happen is to tell them what I'm thinking."

"Exactly."

"You know, once you said things would eventually fall into place. I think you were right about that, because everything seems so much clearer now. Even my love life seems to be straightening out."

"Meaning?"

"Meaning I sort of liked Jason, but he's honestly too far out for me; and Paul is the perfect gentleman, but he's too stuffy; and now there is Jimmy, and he's just right."

"You sound like the baby bear in *Goldilocks*," Maggie said laughing.

"Which reminds me, let's visit my favorite — the polar bears."

"Let's go," Maggie said, leading the way.

As we strolled over to the bears, I realized how much better I felt about life. I knew it wouldn't be easy telling Ronnie and my father what I wanted and believed. I risked hurting their feelings and not having their approval, but knowing what I had to do was half the battle. At last I was going to take a stand, and though part of me dreaded a confrontation I couldn't wait for it to happen.

Chapter Twenty-nine

On my way home I rehearsed in my mind all the things I wanted to say to my parents. I figured that since this was my father's month, it would be logical to start with him. My father, being a lawyer, could always out-argue me, but I also knew he would listen. He cared more about me than he did about making points. Ronnie, I knew, believed in "doing your own thing," and therefore she would understand my need for independence, even though it meant being less involved with her. These were the positive aspects of dealing with my parents. I tried not to think about the negatives, for fear that my recently bolstered confidence would begin to fade.

It was not quite noon when I returned home, let myself into the apartment, and was prepared to say, "Daddy, we've got to talk."

The minute I entered I sensed something was up. Then to my amazement I saw my father and Ronnie seated on chairs next to the fireplace, deep in conversation. They were so intent on what they were saying that for a few seconds they didn't notice me. Then I must have gasped, because they both looked up at the same time. Ronnie stood up, came to me, and threw her arms around me. My worry about her being cool toward me evaporated with the warmth of her hug. "Jill, sweetie, how are you?" she asked, not expecting an answer.

My father was still seated, a worried look on his face, but he no longer seemed angry. "Thank you for leaving me a note, Jill," he said.

"I didn't want you to worry," I told him, looking over Ronnie's shoulder. She still had her arms around me.

"Take off your jacket and come talk to us," Ronnie said, finally letting me go.

"Okay." I was slightly bewildered, but I slowly removed my jacket and hung it in the hall closet. Then I walked over to the sofa and sat down.

"You must be wondering what your mother's doing here," my father began.

"I was just about to ask," I said. "Why are you here, Ronnie?"

Ronnie took a deep breath before she spoke. "We might as well get to the point," she began. "I'm here because Tim asked me to come over."

"But why?" I persisted.

"Because we feel that living in two separate

homes, with two sets of rules, is an unfair burden for you," my father explained. "Last night, that became clear to me. I know I over-reacted to something that your mother would have taken for granted. I'm really sorry, Jill. I was unfair to you."

I was so surprised at what my father had just said that all I could do was nod my head.

"Anyhow," Ronnie continued, "we feel we're putting too much pressure on you from too many directions."

"That's why," my father said, his face sadder than I could ever remember, "we feel that you should choose which one of us you want to live with."

"And no matter what choice you make, we'll both try to understand," Ronnie added, her eyes tearing.

"What if I don't want to make a choice?" I said, finally pulling myself together.

"What do you mean?" they asked at the same time.

"I mean, I want to make joint custody work."

"You do?" Ronnie shouted, and clapped her hands together as though her prayers had been answered.

A wide smile spread over my father's face and he said slowly, "That's the best news I could have heard."

"The thing is, from the very beginning I said I could handle it. The truth is, I haven't been. I've been letting *you* handle it."

"What do you mean?" Ronnie asked.

"I've been trying to make everybody happy,

and not really saying what would make me happy."

"Like what?" my father asked, looking very puzzled.

I paused for a second and then forced myself to go on. "Like everything, from the way my room is furnished, to what I should do over vacation, to how you treat me with grown-ups."

Ronnie's jaw dropped and then she said, "I've always treated you like a contemporary."

"Maybe that's what's wrong. In a way it's very flattering, but I'm not in my thirties, and hearing about your friends' marital problems and stuff embarrasses me."

Ronnie put her hand on her forehead and said slowly, "Jill, I must confess, I never ever thought of that." Then she quickly asked, "But what's wrong with your room?"

"Nothing really," I answered. "But that dayglo poster gives me a headache." We all laughed at that, and the conversation didn't seem so deadly serious.

Then my father said, "I had a decorator do your room, Jill. I thought it was perfect."

"It is, Daddy, for a little girl who's still playing with dolls. And pink and white is not my favorite."

"I should have asked you first," he said thoughtfully. "I suppose you think I treat you as though you're still in the 'doll' stage."

"You do," I sighed. "Especially when your friends are around. It's as though I'm expected to turn off my ears, because I'm too young to understand."

"I've done you a great injustice." My father frowned and then added, "If anything's proven to me that you're *not* a little girl, it's this conversation."

"You might as well tell us what you want to do about your vacation." Ronnie was smiling resignedly.

"I worried a lot about that, because I didn't want to miss your opening and I didn't want to disappoint Daddy."

"But you do want to go to Vermont with your friends," my father surmised.

"I do," I said.

"I don't blame you," Ronnie said. "In a way it was selfish of me to want you to miss out on a trip just because of the opening. It's not as though the show won't be there for a few weeks."

"Oh, Ronnie," I exclaimed, feeling very relieved, "I'm so glad you understand."

"I understand, too," my father said. "When I was your age, I *only* wanted to be with my friends."

"You remember?" I asked.

"I'm not exactly senile," he answered, chuckling.

"Then I can go?"

"Not only can you, you should go," he said. "I've tried to protect you too much. I have to let you go in more ways than one."

"And I've got to stop expecting you to be a miniature me," Ronnie admitted. "You've got to be you."

"That's exactly the conclusion I've come to," I said.

We sat together in the quiet living room for quite a while, each thinking our own thoughts. I knew it wasn't going to be easy, that there would be battles and hurt feelings on all sides at times, but I also knew we would all try, and that finally they were going to help me be me.

PRAISE FOR *JUSTICE IS SERVED*

"People I talk to mention the Steele case all the time. It's still very much alive in Cleveland."
—Les Roberts, author of *The Cleveland Connection* and *The Lake Effect*

"Justice was served, but it was late in coming, this true crime story reveals. That it arrived at all was because of Ressler, who refused to give up on the case."
—*Minneapolis Star-Tribune*

"A litany of details spiced with pinches of bravado."
—*Kirkus Reviews*

"Due to Ressler's in-depth knowledge of the case and his skillful presentation of the events, this book is an excellent choice for the true-crime collection."
—*Library Journal*

"The book is a tribute to dogged police work."
—*Publishers Weekly*

St. Martin's Paperbacks Titles
by Robert K. Ressler and Tom Shachtman

WHOEVER FIGHTS MONSTERS
JUSTICE IS SERVED

JUSTICE
IS
SERVED

**ROBERT K. RESSLER
& TOM SHACHTMAN**

St. Martin's Paperbacks

JUSTICE IS SERVED

Copyright © 1994 by Robert K. Ressler and Tom Shachtman.

Cover photographs from the Cleveland State University Archives.

Library of Congress Catalog Card Number: 94-18328

ISBN: 0-312-95615-0

Printed in the United States of America

St. Martin's Press hardcover edition/September 1994
St. Martin's Paperbacks edition/January 1996

10 9 8 7 6 5 4 3 2 1

Judge not, that ye be not judged.
With what measure ye mete, it
shall be measured to you again.
—*Matthew, 7:1–2*

To the memory of Marlene Steele

Acknowledgments

This book was written to put to rest a case that I pursued during most of my career in the FBI and that followed me when I retired from the FBI. Although the murder of Marlene Steele mainly affected her family and in particular her sons Brett and Kevin, it also touched and affected the lives of many other people, some named in this book and others who remain anonymous. The purpose of this note is to do more than acknowledge assistance in the writing of this book. It is to thank formally and cite many who contributed to the solution of the murder of Marlene Steele and to bringing the murderers to justice. Chief among them is Major Louis C. Kulis, who retired recently as chief of operations of the Cuyahoga County Sheriff's office after more than fifty years of exemplary service in law enforcement; his outstanding detective work, including his detailed, probing interview of Judge Robert Steele just six weeks after the murder of Marlene Steele, created a firm foundation for all that followed.

I also wish to thank Cuyahoga County prosecutors Al Lipold and Carmen Marino, who oversaw the Steele trial, and the many men in local law enforcement in the Greater Cleveland area who worked on the case or associated cases, among them Mike Cannon, Warren Goodwin, Earl Gordon, Edward Kovacic, Pat Newkirk, Ted Shafer, Andy Vanyo, Chester Zembala, and John E. Walsh.

My former supervisor in the Cleveland office of the FBI, Martin P. McCann, Jr., helped to keep the cases

ACKNOWLEDGMENTS

associated with the murder active when they might otherwise have been closed, and provided my investigations with enduring, patient guidance. Among the special agents, John Dunn and Joe Harpold were particularly involved with the case, and I also wish to thank Bob Alvord, Jim Aschenbrenner, Dick Artin, Dick Ault, Fred Fehl, Pat Foran, George Grotz, Ted Jackson, John J. Jurey, Roy McKinnon, and Dave Witchen, along with David Margolis, who as chief of the Cleveland Federal Strike Force was supportive in a matter involving little that was under federal jurisdiction. While I was assigned to Quantico, Larry Monroe, Jim O'Connor, and Jim McKenzie supported my work on the case there.

I should also like to cite the efforts of Cleveland journalists Doris O'Donnell and Bill Miller, whose "crime beat" reporting assisted the investigations, and to acknowledge Jeffry Snyder, "Dianne," "Maxi," "Tex," and many others who must still remain pseudonymous.

My coauthor, Tom Shachtman, joins me in thanking the archivists of various Cleveland city and county agencies for their assistance to our research, and the many people in the law enforcement community who gave us interviews to supplement old memories and documents. Finally, I am eternally grateful to my wife Helen and my children Allison, Betsy, and Aaron, whose unfailing support sustained me during the many years spent unravelling the mystery and bringing the culprits to final justice.

—Robert K. Ressler
September 1994

Contents

CONTENTS

Part One

MURDERS AND PROSTITUTION

Prologue

On the morning of January 9, 1969, people in the Indian Hills section of Euclid, Ohio, a suburban town nine miles east of downtown Cleveland on the shores of Lake Erie, woke to find police cars outside the home at 2070 Miami Road. That's where the Steeles lived, municipal court judge Robert L. Steele, his wife Marlene, and their two sons, eight-year-old Kevin and four-year-old Brett. The Steeles were longtime Euclid residents; Bob graduated from Euclid Shore High in 1948, Marlene in 1949. Marlene's parents, Frank and Agnes Gallitto, lived five doors up the street, at 2054 Miami Road. The Steeles had been in the Indian Hills home for a dozen years. Two years ago, they had added a second floor to the home so the boys could sleep upstairs. The family had become quite active in the community: the judge was president of the Euclid Day Care Center, while his wife was vice president of the Women's Junior Board at Euclid General Hospital, an active PTA member, and a campaigner for the March of

Dimes. Both Steeles were Sunday school teachers at Collinwood Christian Church. "They were very agreeable people," a neighbor told a reporter who had come out along with the police cars. "They appeared to be an ideal American couple."

Police and reporters were on Miami Road because thirty-seven-year-old Marlene Steele was dead, shot twice in the head the night before as she slept in the downstairs bedroom, evidently by someone who had entered the house after midnight. The rear living room of the house overlooked a ravine that bordered a railroad track, the neighbors knew, and they pointed out to reporters that it would have been easy for a burglar to enter the yard of the house, unseen, from that ravine.

Late at night, the judge told the police, he had been in his den on the first floor, going over legal briefs, when he'd heard a noise and gone upstairs to see whether the boys were okay. There were two bedrooms up there, but both boys slept in one and the second was used as a spare room. While upstairs, Steele said, he heard a couple of sounds: "Pop, pop!" Coming down to investigate, he thought he heard some footsteps going outside and the front door slamming, but nothing beyond that, no car noise or anything. In the downstairs bedroom he found his wife, still and with blood on her head. Certain she was dead, he called the police.

Tom Keay, a police dispatcher whom Steele knew, had taken the judge's call at 2:11 A.M.: "Tom, for God's sake, get someone up here; Marlene's been shot." Keay had recognized the voice, and asked if the judge was at home. "Yes," Steele responded, "and call Captain Willocks." Orville ("Orly") Willocks had been at home, and Keay called him while he sent Sgt. William Donner and Warren Goodwin, in separate cars, toward the house.

There had been some freezing rain that night, and it was a misty, cold morning, with plenty of snow still on the ground; ice formed by the frigid rain made everything rather slick. Indian Hills was an upper-middle-class neighborhood where the homes were valued at forty to fifty thousand dollars each in 1969. A park on one side, Lake Erie on the other, and all within easy commuting distance of downtown Cleveland: these houses were considered desirable.

The first vehicle to arrive at Steele's home was the station wagon of Patrolmen Stanford McKibben and Larry Downing. No wet spots from the snow on the floor, McKibben noted as he entered the house at 2:15 A.M. through the front door, which was slightly ajar.

Steele, clad in a bathrobe, undershorts, and knee-high black socks, but no shirt, was visibly upset, trembling and crying. "I don't know what happened," Steele said to McKibben. Shortly, the judge lit a cigarette. He was known as a chain-smoker, a cigarette never far from his hand or lips, except when he sat on the bench.

They trooped into the first-floor bedroom, where McKibben found Mrs. Steele "lying in bed with her head to one side on the pillow as if she had been sleeping when shot," in the words he later used to tell reporters. There were two holes in her head, one above the right eye, the second an inch farther over toward her right ear, and blood had ceased flowing, although there was dried blood on the head and on the surrounding bedding. Her bloodied head was an awful sight. She wore red-white-and-blue-striped pajamas and a hair net. Her body was mainly under the covers, with one arm out. McKibben took her pulse; there was none.

Steele's father and mother arrived; Otto F. Steele was a well-known Cleveland probate attorney, instantly recognizable in downtown Cleveland legal circles by his uniform of old-fashioned bow tie and jacket. Capt. Orville Willocks showed up and ordered the street sealed off and the house, grounds, and surrounding area searched. No murder weapon was found.

Knowing that Steele was close to Willocks, Euclid's police chief, Frank Payne, wanted independent investigators on this murder case, and so the next to arrive on the scene was the new Cuyahoga County captain of detectives, Lou Kulis, whose superior had been called by Payne. Kulis and his associates, detectives Chester Zembala and his partner Casimir Lubobanski, had been given one clear instruction: remember Sam Sheppard. That case was burned into the minds of local law enforcement men. In the 1950s, Dr. Sheppard, an osteopath, had been convicted of murdering his wife, though he'd protested that the deed was done by an unknown assailant who had entered the house in the dead of night. In the 1960s, defense attorney F. Lee Bailey obtained a retrial for Sheppard, with enormous national publicity attendant upon it. For the first time, at that retrial, cameras were allowed in the courtroom, and

6

people from all over the country watched Cleveland squirm. The second time around, the state's circumstantial evidence was not considered enough to warrant a conviction. Sheppard had been freed. The notorious case became a blot on the escutcheon of Cleveland area law enforcement. And so on the morning of January 9, 1969, when Kulis and his men went to the Steele residence, already knowing that the call to the police had been a judge reporting that an unknown intruder had shot his wife, the investigators arrived having been strictly warned to be more than careful in obtaining the evidence on which a case might be built.

Entering the house, Kulis was amazed to see Otto Steele cleaning up ashtrays and in other inadvertent ways disturbing the crime scene; Kulis stopped such actions. Coroner Samuel T. Gerber called and asked Kulis who was in charge. Kulis suggested that if Gerber had any problems, he should come to the scene as well. Zembala and Lubobanski went outside to look at the footprints around the house and trace them as far as possible. The doors and windows in the house were closed and appeared locked, with the exception of the front door. Steele told the police that he was in the habit of locking that as his last act just before going to bed. Since he hadn't quite gotten ready for sleep that night, he hadn't locked it. There were no signs of forced entry, and nothing from the house was missing, so it didn't seem as though there had been any attempt at burglary. A canvass of the neighbors found that none of them had heard unusual or suspicious noises. Chip, the dachshund, hadn't barked all night, reported Guy Munt, the neighbor whose bedroom faced the Steeles'.

Zembala and Lubobanski, with flashlights, looked at the footprints outside the house. One set seemed to go toward the part of the grounds opposite the living-room window and back again toward the house, but another set, possibly from a different boot, led from the house toward the ravine. They followed the second set across the yard, down into the ravine, across some railroad tracks, up again on the other side, and onto a nearby road, where the prints disappeared; the assailant—if it was he who had made the tracks—seemed most likely to have been picked up there by a car. Kulis ordered casts taken of footprints in the snow bordering the Steele home.

While the investigators combed the house and environs, Euclid's law director, William T. Monroe, talked to the judge. They were longtime friends; Steele had been Euclid's police prosecutor for eight years before having been appointed to the bench in June of 1968. The law director wondered if his friend could have angered anyone by a recent decision on the bench and, if so, whether the killing had been done to take revenge on the judge. "If someone was after me, why did they shoot her?" Steele responded. Monroe didn't have an answer for that one.

Gerber arrived and preliminarily fixed the time of death at two in the morning. Marlene's body was photographed in the bed, then removed for an autopsy. Lou Kulis went upstairs to talk to Kevin Steele, the older boy, in the presence of his grandfather Otto. Kevin had heard something that he described as a buzzing or humming sound, not exactly like someone singing, but rhythmic. Other than that, Kevin remembered very little of note. Mom was usually the one to lock the door at night, he said, though Dad did do it occasionally. After the interview, both Steele boys were taken to the home of their maternal grandparents, the Gallittos, five houses away.

Before the judge himself left the house to go with the police to headquarters, he was asked directly whether he had shot his wife, and he said he did not know what had happened. He briefly recounted the events of the evening. The couple had watched the eleven o'clock local news together, and then he tuned in the Johnny Carson show, as he often did at that hour, while she prepared for bed. At about midnight Marlene had come into the den to kiss him goodnight. He had never seen his wife alive again. He dozed off during the Carson show, and when he awoke there was some sort of "cowboy movie" on. That was when he'd begun leafing through some legal papers, and then had gone upstairs to see the boys and had heard the popping sounds.

Deprived of Steele, the reporters fastened on Monroe, who told them, "The judge does not own a gun or have one in the house. He and his wife had a very happy relationship. If I am any judge of men, he had no part in this thing."

As Steele was driven to the Euclid police headquarters to make a voluntary formal statement and take a paraffin test to see whether he had recently fired a gun, reporters combed the neighborhood where the murder had taken place. Neighbors recalled that in better weather the Steeles used to go bicycle riding with their children. The family were devoted ice hockey fans; it was said that the Cleveland Barons wouldn't dare play a game without the Steeles in attendance. The minister at their Unitarian church, Rev. William R. Fortner, told the newsmen that Marlene was "Bob's biggest asset," a woman who was "interested in the religious development of her children" and for whom "everything centered around her family."

Marlene Gallitto Steele had been an attractive, quiet, brown-haired woman who seemed to one and all the epitome of a well-educated, community-minded suburban wife and mother. After high school she had gone to Lake Erie College, earning induction into an honors society. Married to her sweetheart while still in college, after graduation she taught in nearby Richmond Heights elementary schools while earning a master's degree at Case Western Reserve in Cleveland. As a volunteer at the hospital, she had done all sorts of jobs, such as recently chairing the committee for the annual charitable ball. She had moved quickly up the ladder of the organization, even though she'd only been in the hierarchy for six years; she was first vice president of the Junior Women's Board and had been scheduled to become president in 1970. One neighbor described her as "a great gal that's going to be so dearly missed." The adjectives others agreed upon to characterize her: marvelous, very kind, generous, thoughtful, quiet, pleasant, and articulate.

These same women recalled the minutiae of Marlene's daily suburban life, how the Steele boys had won prizes at Halloween parties for the costumes Marlene had made them, how she had cooked French dinners and been the class mother for Kevin's grade, how she enameled ashtrays and played in a volleyball league and tried to break 100 on the golf course. There had been monthly gatherings of a few of Bob's law school classmates and their wives, still a tight-knit group after fifteen years, a group that Marlene had helped keep intact. Now she wouldn't be the hostess at the post-hockey-game party she'd been planning; the Steeles had invited thirteen couples to go to the game and return to Miami Road for a social evening. In adjoining and surrounding homes people took tranquilizers, commiserated with one another, and planned to now begin to lock their doors and stay in at night, things they had never done before. If a prowler's gunshots could tear asunder "a model family," nobody in Indian Hills could consider themselves safe.

Judge Robert Steele remained at the Euclid police station until ten in the evening. Near the end of that time, he signed a statement, taken from his oral narration of events to Willocks and Kulis. A key section read:

I got up and just stood there and was looking at them [Kevin and Brett, in bed] and I heard this Pop! Pop! I headed out the door and down the stairs and as I was going down the stairs I heard a heavy noise of someone running and I heard the door just bang closed—the storm door. Then I ran into the bedroom. There was sufficient light in there that I could tell something had happened to Marlene. So I went over to her and I kneeled down on the floor and leaned over the bed. I know I pushed her, shook her, and held onto her hand and I talked to her and I don't know how long I was there. And then I went out and called the police.

Kulis and Willocks questioned Steele more closely on the open-or-shut conditions of the doors, on whether he had gone outside during the evening. They asked directly if he had killed his wife, and he formally denied it. As happens with most statements of this sort that are given to police, the subject was directed to read the transcript and amend it before signing it. "Rather than say I sort of hit her, it was more shoving at her, like trying to get some response." That comment was added to the narrative. After the statement was signed, Steele left in the company of his father, who had been with him during the questioning.

Euclid safety director Ralph O. Dunker had been in the FBI for thirty years before assuming his position in Euclid, but although he'd spent time in J. Edgar Hoover's public relations department, he wasn't prepared for the rapid-fire questions of inquiring reporters who rushed at him after Steele and his father had left. Dunker did manage to tell them that the judge had not been charged, but that he was "cooperating 100 percent." Paraffin casts had been made and sent for analysis to the FBI laboratory in Washington, D.C. The judge might take a lie-detector test soon, but not right away, because he was so emotionally distraught over the slaying that an immediate test would likely be flawed. Plaster casts had been taken of man-sized, widely spaced boot prints in the snow, and there were also tire impressions from the driveway to deal with, but there were currently no suspects in the murder, and the .38 caliber revolver that had fired shots into Mrs. Steele at close range had not been found. Until further notice, all days off were canceled for the eighty-five members of the Euclid police department. Forty-five officers combed the area around the Steele home, looking for clues. Fire department trucks helped police search the eaves and gutters of houses, possible hiding places for the murder weapon.

While attention had been focused on Steele at the police station, inside the Steele home coroner Samuel Gerber's top lab associate, Mrs. Mary E. Cowan, who specialized in blood analysis, took samples from stains in the bedroom. Experts from other law enforcement jurisdictions were also on the scene. "We are a close family out here," Chief Payne told reporters. "One of our family has lost his wife. . . . That is why we called in outside help."

Reportorial and neighborhood speculation about the murder centered on the idea that someone or a group might have been trying to exact revenge for one of Judge Steele's rulings; he was described as a tough man on the bench. One cluster of "hippies" who had taken over a Euclid apartment had drawn his ire. Steele had been threatened directly in the past week by a member of a motorcycle gang who had been arrested on a traffic charge; "I'm going to get you," the cyclist had reportedly said. Other possible suspects included a man to whom Steele had given thirty days in jail; on his way out of the courtroom, the man had muttered something nasty, and Steele had called him back and upped the sentence to sixty days. There was a black nationalist who had voiced antisocial thoughts in Steele's courtroom. There was a male baby-sitter who had taken care of Brett and Kevin but who had become disgruntled. Steele himself mentioned to police that a distant relative of Marlene's, who had spent some time in a mental hospital, had at one point threatened the couple with a knife. All of these leads were pursued initially by the police, but none yielded any significant clues to the identity of the murderer.

Two cars in the Steele garage were towed carefully away in case they contained bombs; they didn't. Tests on the body of Mrs. Steele continued. The conclusions: no sexual attack had been made, and there were no alcohol, no narcotics, no tranquilizers or other drugs in any significant quantity in her blood. The time of death of what the coroner termed "an apparently healthy person" was fixed at two in the morning, but not because of internal evidence, Coroner Gerber explained: that time was based on the fact that the judge had called the dispatchers at 2:11.

Since no one had seen any intruders, there was newspaper speculation that the judge might have had something to do with the killing. To squash the innuendos, Steele agreed to an interview with three reporters at his father's apartment and then took

Doris O'Donnell of the Cleveland *Plain Dealer* to his own home for an exclusive session. The major news: "Whoever came into our house knew someone in the house and knew the house," Steele told O'Donnell. The judge did not elaborate very much, but his surmise seemed to be based on the idea that the killer appeared to have known the location of the Steeles' bedroom.

Steele provided homey details of the early evening before the murder: he had taken off his suit and shirt and put on a bathrobe over his shorts; the boys did the same, and Marlene had teased them by asking if they wanted her to paint their chests so they'd look as hairy as their father. O'Donnell pushed him for the more difficult stuff, and he offered answers in a voice shattered with sobs and while his eyes were closed, as though recalling the scene. When he had come into the downstairs bedroom after hearing the shots, "I really can't say what I did. I kneeled or leaned, and got a closer look. I pushed her shoulders. I held her hand by the wrist, and let it go. It fell. I didn't know just what had happened. I couldn't believe something like this happened." After phoning the police dispatcher—in his frenzy, Steele called Keay by his father's name, he thought—the judge phoned Otto Steele, but not Marlene's parents, because "they're so highly emotional." He did not leave the house to look in the yard or elsewhere for traces of the intruder; yes, the killer might still have been hiding in the garage or basement, though it didn't occur to him to look in those places.

Once this whole terrible ordeal was over, Steele

planned to go back to the bench and run for election for the post in the fall. "I may seem rather cold in light of what's happened," he told O'Donnell, "but I'm devoted to public service." He also had two sons "to make a life for." .

Rumors had surfaced that the marriage of Bob and Marlene Steele had been on the rocks. Even the police had broached the matter to Steele in the hours of questioning at the station. According to Steele's father, Otto, there were many women who would have liked to throw themselves at his son's feet. The senior Steele told reporters that Bob had informed the police about a woman from Wickliffe with whom he'd had lunch recently; Otto couldn't believe that Bob's marriage was seriously in trouble, however, because if it had been, Marlene, to whom he had been very close, "would have called me over for a talk." Otto Steele was of the opinion that his son's political enemies (whom the newspapers did not name) were "out to crucify him." Both Steeles were Republicans, and Bob was thought to have a great future in the state of Ohio once Richard Nixon took office in a few days, because then the GOP would control both the White House and the Ohio state house.

Roy Martin, Ohio governor James A. Rhodes's chief of patronage, couldn't recall whether the governor actually knew that he'd appointed Robert Steele; more likely, the governor had just accepted the recommendation of the Cuyahoga County GOP organization and its leader, chairman Robert Hughes, and signed a piece of paper put in front of him by an assistant. Martin himself did remember

Steele—"I was impressed by his education and his experience as a prosecutor," he recalled—and there had been no reason not to go along with the county organization's choice.

Bob Steele had always been a comer. Like Richard Nixon, Steele had made his school football team more through doggedness than through skill. Valedictorian of his graduating class, co-editor of the yearbook and the newspaper, president of the student council, Steele went on to Ohio Wesleyan University on a small scholarship. There he majored in English and education and joined the Sigma Chi fraternity. He started at Case Western Reserve Graduate School, partly to get out of the draft for the Korean War, and aiming to obtain a master's degree in education. While finishing his first graduate year, he taught English at Euclid High. Students there remembered him as a good teacher and a good actor, one who could express the proper emotions while reading poetry to his class. After a year, however, he quit teaching and transferred to Case Western Reserve Law School. He entered a special navy program upon graduating from law school in 1955, serving until 1957 at the Great Lakes Naval Base. After that, he joined his father in a law practice and in 1959 became the Euclid police prosecutor. This position, as with many similar ones in small towns, permitted him to continue his private law practice, first in conjunction with his father and later on his own. He served in the prosecutorial post for eight years, receiving such awards as the Junior Chamber of Commerce's distinguished service honor. The town's police liked him: if a cop wanted a particular bad guy nailed, Detective John Walsh later remembered, Steele would work hard to obtain that result; if someone on the force needed some legal advice, even some minor legal work, Steele would do it graciously and, most often, wouldn't charge for the service. An active Republican since childhood, Steele was elected president of a local nonpartisan club at age thirty-one. Before becoming the police prosecutor he had been assistant law director for Euclid and won some notoriety for enforcing a Sunday-closing law and, when it was challenged, going successfully to the Ohio Supreme Court to defend it. He'd done so even though he disagreed with the statute, because he believed laws should be either enforced or changed, not ignored.

In July of 1968, at the time Steele succeeded a retiring judge on the municipal court, he issued strong statements about respect for law and order and backed up his statements with tough sentences for minor infractions: ten days in jail for two boys who'd been involved in drag racing; ten days for two others who had been drinking and fighting while in a car; fifty-dollar fines (the maximum permitted) for throwing firecrackers from a moving car; six-month sentences for rowdy, beer-guzzling motorcyclists who disturbed the peace. Inside the court system, other judges considered Steele reasonably well suited to the bench, though as a prosecutor he had sometimes been overanxious and too willing to cut corners. There were strong rumors that when Mayor Kenneth Sims of Euclid retired after forty years in office, as was expected shortly, Steele, who had been Sims's protégé, would be his logical successor.

Both reporters and the police, already investigating the notion that the Steele marriage had been on the rocks, soon found Barbara Swartz, who lived in the neighboring suburb of Wickliffe. She, too, was a married woman, of thirty-eight, and her hair was dark red and she wore it short, as had Marlene Steele; in many ways the two women seemed physically similar. Barbara was the mother of three sons; one from her first marriage was currently serving in the armed forces in Vietnam. There were two smaller boys from her second marriage, to contractor Orville ("Jay") Swartz; the couple had separated, and to earn money Barbara had started work in December for the Euclid Municipal Court in the area of trusteeships, a position obtained for her by Steele. She and the judge had met in July of 1968, introduced by a mutual friend after the Swartzes had filed for a separation. She admitted that she and the judge had shared lunches and dinners, but nothing more. Steele now told reporters that there had been problems in his marriage in the early years, but none lately, except those related to his long work hours; he was making many speeches at night, and the prospect of more evenings out as the election neared had been dismaying to his late wife.

Marlene was laid to rest in the Lake View Cemetery by the Steeles, the Gallittos, and four hundred other relatives and friends, and a group of friends offered a $25,000 reward for information leading to the conviction of the killer. Police were mystified by what clues and leads they had. Some of the footprints in the snow were one puzzle: they ended ten feet from the house. A motorcyclist had made wild threats against the judge after being arrested in Steele's courtroom while carrying a knife, but the cyclist, who had been free on bond, appeared voluntarily at the police station, and his alibi for the night of the murder was firm. Police took statements from Orville Swartz and from two "party girls" in their twenties who had lived in Euclid but who moved out of their apartment around the time of the murder. "No one would comment on the significance of quizzing the girls," the *Plain Dealer* observed. As he did when a public prosecutor, Steele maintained a private law practice in addition to his work for the town. Chief Payne and others were aware that Steele had at least once represented these party girls when they had been busted.

Party girls was a euphemism; one of them, Carol Braun, admitted in her interview with the Euclid police that she was a prostitute. Braun and her colleague, whom we will refer to as Nancy Mason, were not street hookers, but relatively high-priced call girls. Steele's direct client, however, was the man who admitted to police in his own interview that he was their pimp, Owen James Kilbane. Steele had become his attorney, the twenty-two-year-old Kilbane told the police, in April of 1968 (at the time of the arrest of the two women), and he had used Steele's services sporadically since that time. Occasionally they had lunch together, the last time on Tuesday, January 7, two days before the early morning murder of the ninth when they "discussed a legal matter." Had Steele ever been "set up with one of your girls?" No, Kilbane said, though he did admit that Steele could have gone to one of the prostitutes without Kilbane knowing about it. No, he had never been to Steele's home, though he had talked to Marlene Steele once on the phone when he'd called to ask for Bob. Sure, Kilbane said, he'd take a lie-detector test if they wanted him to.

The police didn't ask just then, and Kilbane left the station. The details of this interview were not provided to the reporters, not even leaked to them, but the reporters didn't mind because something else big had come up. In trying to get more information about "the other woman," Barbara Swartz, they had hit pay dirt: the petition for divorce that Mrs. Swartz said had been filed a year ago had actually only been filed in mid-December, around the time she started working at the municipal court. Another apparent discrepancy jumped out as they reviewed the reports of the first men at the bedside of the murdered woman. Patrolman McKibben's written record said that the body had been cool to the touch and that the blood on Mrs. Steele's face "seemed to be dry."

Mounting hints that the judge had been having an affair and that there were problems with reconciling all the evidence apparently spurred the judge to accept the invitation of a grandmotherly local television figure to publicly tell his story. Dorothy Fuldheim was sympathetic to Steele, as was most of the public. It was unfortunate that a murder had occurred when the respected judge was in the middle of a difficult marital situation, people concluded, but there was little doubt about the judge's sincerity.

The next day, headlines screamed that Steele's affair with Barbara Swartz had consisted of much more than lunches and dinners. Motel registers from as far away as Detroit showed that they had signed in together as man and wife virtually every weekend since October. Reporters cornered Steele at the home of his in-laws; they found him in his pajamas, hair mussed and unshaven. Braced, he verified the affair with Mrs. Swartz, adding that the police knew all about it and that he had also told his in-laws, the Gallittos. He was adamant that his wife had never known of the affair. He believed his father-in-law, Frank "Midge" Gallitto, a service-station operator, understood Steele's difficult position but that Agnes, Marlene's mother, "was hurt and crushed." Agnes and Marlene had been particularly close, more like sisters than mother and daughter.

The reporters then located Mrs. Swartz at her office in the municipal court building and told her that Steele had confirmed the affair. "What can I say?" she cried, and ran from her desk.

The revelation of the affair seemed to give to the crime what it had sorely lacked: a possible motive. Now police pressed Barbara Swartz and Judge Steele closely. Mrs. Swartz submitted to a lie-detector test and passed with flying colors. Steele's statements were checked with the other evidence. For instance, he had said that he and Marlene had eaten spaghetti together at around 8:15 P.M. If that were so, then the spaghetti would have been completely digested by two in the morning. But the coroner found traces of spaghetti still only partially digested in Marlene's stomach. That could mean an earlier time of death—say, at one A.M., rather than at two— but it could also be innocuous, the result of her sneaking a bite of the leftovers at ten in the evening, while cleaning up the dishes. The coroner's office was unable to pinpoint the time with great accuracy, however. Another instance: the judge had said he'd heard the front storm door slam; detectives had checked to learn whether the door actually made such a sound and whether the shuffling sound the judge said he'd heard on the stairs from the boys' bedroom upstairs could actually have been audible from that point if it had been made in the downstairs rooms.

On the evening of January 16, 1969, Judge Robert Steele submitted to a lie-detector test administered by "fully qualified polygraph examiners" on the Cleveland force, while reporters and photographers waited outside the Central Police Station. Steele was hooked up to three electrodes. One measured his blood pressure, a second his breathing, and a third his "galvanic skin response," that is, the electrical potential generated mainly by his sweat. The test was preceded by a control session in which Steele was asked to deliberately lie, in order to establish the parameters, and then he was asked the hard questions—did he commit the crime, did he know who did, did he hire or conspire with anyone to commit it? Steele looked haggard when he left the examination but expressed his belief that he had passed with flying colors. The next day, at a press conference, Euclid safety director Ralph Dunker made the "unanimous" findings of the experts public: There had been no evidence obtained in the lie-detector test that Steele had been "attempting deception." Rather, the test had been at best inconclusive, neither impugning nor proving his innocence.

Steele, on the other hand, crowed to reporters, "I'm glad it's over. This [the lie-detector test] shows I didn't do it." The Euclid police had no objections, he said, so he was making plans to take his two sons out of town for the weekend. He would be back on the bench by midweek, he predicted.

While Steele and his sons were sharing a weekend out of town, Barbara Swartz moved out of the house she had previously been sharing with her husband all during the months they'd been separated. The arrangement had been maintained in order to conserve money. Now she left, and her two boys stayed behind with their father. She had not shown up for work at the Euclid courthouse for several days, and no one knew where she might be.

While Steele was gone, police guarded his home. They permitted the Gallittos to enter, however, and to remove china, silverware, and everything that had belonged to Marlene or was a reminder of Marlene.

Before Steele returned, the Cleveland Bar Association began to consider whether to take action against him. The American Bar Association's canon of ethics stated (Canon Number Four) that a judge's conduct should be "free of impropriety and above reproach," and Steele's admitted affair with Mrs. Swartz, a clerk in his court, was certainly questionable. Should the Cleveland Bar Association or the Cuyahoga County Bar Association find him to have violated the canons, either group could refer the matter to the state supreme court, which could institute removal proceedings. There were a few calls for Steele's resignation from the bench. Otto Steele said his son would resign if the bar association asked him to do so.

Upon arriving back in Cleveland, Robert Steele disagreed with his father's pronouncement. He intended to resume his municipal court position, and if any bar association went to the state supreme court to try to get him removed over his affair with Barbara, he would fight that all the way. He felt that his admission of the extramarital affair was "a reflection of my honesty and integrity," he told reporters. "I'm weak, yes, like many people."

Father-in-law Midge Gallitto echoed Steele's sentiments, suggesting that while he and his wife, Agnes, did not condone the judge's conduct, he believed that the vast majority of men strayed now and then. Gallitto expressed complete confidence in Steele, who had loved Marlene and would always be welcome in the Gallitto house.

The man whom Steele had appointed to take his place temporarily on the bench, Paul Daugherty, resigned in protest, saying that he couldn't condone Steele's adulterous conduct; Daugherty and his family had been targets of criticism for his association with Steele. The Cleveland Bar Association asked Steele to stay off the bench until after he had met with their grievance committee in early February. A group of private citizens tried to invoke an 1871 law that allowed a probate judge to remove a municipal judge if charges of impropriety were proved; the same committee was concurrently involved in an attempt to have Cleveland mayor Carl Stokes removed from office for his actions after racial disturbances in Cleveland in the summer of 1968.

Community pressure mounted, and before any of the bar association committees could forward any formal recommendations to anyone, Steele agreed to resign from his Euclid judgeship. Concurrently, Barbara Swartz resigned from her clerkship at the Euclid courthouse and from her position with the Wickliffe school board.

While his home was still being occasionally combed by police for evidence, Steele and Barbara fled to Florida for a vacation, and came back, appearing to reporters to be tanned and happy.

Six weeks after the murder, on February 26, 1969, Cuyahoga detective captain Lou Kulis was ready to talk seriously to Steele. In the company of Sgt. Charles Miller of the Euclid police department, Kulis picked up Steele, brought him to an office, apprised him of his rights—he said he'd talk without the presence of an attorney—and began an interview that lasted for more than nine hours.

In the interim between the early morning of January 9, 1969, and February 26, Kulis and his associates had learned a great deal about Steele, Mrs. Swartz, and the circumstances surrounding the murder. For instance, David Lombardo, an attorney whom Steele had recommended for a job with the Euclid prosecutor's office, had come forward with an unsettling story. In September of 1968, Lombardo had met with Steele to thank him for his help in obtaining the job, and had said that if he could ever do anything for Steele, the judge should ask. Steele immediately asked if Lombardo "could find somebody to kill my wife for me." Lombardo initially took this request as a joke, but Steele had pressed on, intimating that Lombardo's law partner, a man with an Italian name, might be of service in this matter.

For another instance, tests conducted by Zembala and Lubobanski on the morning after the murder showed that the front storm door was restrained by a pneumatic arm and could not have "slammed" shut. For a third instance, the television station that had been showing the "cowboy movie" had taken the half-hour "Zane Grey Theater" off the air at 1:33 in the morning, so if the pop-pop sounds had been heard shortly after that, there was a discrepancy between the probable time of the murder and the moment, a half hour later, when Steele had called Tom Keay. There were many other disparities between Steele's version of events and those offered by other people or suggested by the facts, and in this long and grueling interview Steele was unable to resolve the inconsistencies. "I don't know," he answered repeatedly, or, "I can't explain that."

"I must say this, Mr. Steele," Kulis stated about halfway through the second reel of tape. "We have taken extensive tests at your home. I say this [the murder] could not have happened in the manner in which you describe. I think you're lying, Mr. Steele."

"I can only tell you what I saw and heard," Steele replied.

"I can only tell you that it doesn't fit. Did you ever ask someone about putting you in touch with someone to get rid of your wife? Your answer to that is 'no,' you never spoke with anyone about putting you in touch with someone to get rid of your wife?"

"No."

"Isn't it a fact that you did?"

"No."

"Did you make this statement or request in any form of any kind to anybody?" Charles Miller put in.

"Maybe in jest," Steele said.

Miller tried to help Steele by covering ground that might exculpate the former judge, for instance, asking whether Steele had had "a loss of memory at any time during this period from the time you found Marlene till you called the police."

"I'm saying that I don't think so," Steele replied.

Kulis was relentless. Why, if Steele had leaned over and touched his wife, possibly even kissed her, wasn't there any blood on him?

"If I had blood on me I made no conscious effort to remove it."

A bit later, Kulis asked, "Outside of yourself, who had better motive to kill Marlene?"

"I don't know; I wish I knew."

"This has not bothered you?"

"Has it bothered me? Yes, it's bothered me."

"How is it that we have not heard from you in the interval [between the death and the time of this interview, six weeks later]? You haven't come to us with one bit of information. I'm sure that if you didn't know who killed her, you would have been mentally searching constantly—"

"I have been mentally searching."

"—and by this time you would have come up with some idea, no matter how remote, and called it to the attention of the police."

Steele had conveyed several notions about the unknown murderer to the police through his father but had been deterred from doing more because "you guys have zeroed in on me and I just have a feeling that there was no point in my attempting to communicate ..."

"Can you tell me a better person to zero in on?" Kulis challenged.

In this long interview, Steele made no important admissions beyond the now-obvious one that he had been deeply involved with Barbara Swartz months before Marlene's demise and he and Marlene had had some discussions about a divorce.

After Steele had been questioned for nine and a half hours on February 26, there could have been no doubt in his mind that the police believed him responsible for the murder of his wife. Kulis had certainly become convinced that Steele had contracted to have his wife killed. So had Zembala. In fact, strong suspicions of Steele's guilt were now held by many other law enforcement people, both in and out of Euclid, even though they wanted to believe their friend was innocent. The evidence, including the Kulis interview transcript and other particulars, were submitted to Cuyahoga County prosecutor John T. Corrigan, who considered it all carefully. There was still no gun, no shooter, no person to connect Steele directly with the death of his wife. Circumstantial evidence had damned the prosecution of Sam Sheppard, and there seemed no sense in beginning what could turn out to be another fiasco. In the post-Sheppard climate, a Cleveland-area jury would not be likely to convict Steele without a good deal more evidence than was currently in hand. Unless a conviction could be practically assured, Corrigan seems to have reasoned, he would not attempt to have the judge indicted for the murder of his wife.

So Kulis put his interview tapes away in the files, and no one from the Steele or Gallitto families was apprised of their contents. The case technically was still open, but now more than ever the main suspect was free to get on with his life.

In Ohio in the spring of 1969, an uncontested divorce could be granted in a very short time after papers were filed by the two parties. That April, less than three months after Marlene Steele had been murdered, Barbara and Jay Swartz were divorced, and three days later, in a Chicago municipal court judge's chambers, Barbara married Robert Steele.

Custody of the Swartz children was awarded to Mr. Swartz. Brett and Kevin were brought back from the Gallitto home to stay with their father and new stepmother in the Miami Road home, which had already been put up for sale.

When reporters learned of the remarriage, they hastened to Steele for a comment. He told them that he had written to bar associations in Arizona, Nevada, California, and Florida about how he might meet the requirements to practice law in those jurisdictions, and hoped to move away soon, but he didn't say where he and his family might relocate. Reporters then ran up the street to the Gallitto home and found the former in-laws sad, not about Steele's remarriage, but about whether they would be unable to see their grandchildren regularly; aside from that, Agnes Gallitto said, "The only thing I'm interested in now is finding the killer of my daughter."

One

THE "OLD DOG" CASE

As a relatively new Special Agent of the FBI, though a fairly experienced detective and law enforcement official, I arrived in Cleveland in October of 1971. As readers of my earlier memoir, *Whoever Fights Monsters*, already know, for ten years before joining the FBI I had worked in the army's Criminal Investigation Division—the CID—and had commanded uniformed military police and plainclothes investigative units all over the world. In the late 1960s, based in Illinois, I was the ranking officer in charge of dozens of investigators who covered a five-state area. For some time before agreeing to come on board, I had been courted by friends in the FBI with whom I'd worked on cooperative cases; in addition to my army experience, I also held a master's degree in criminology from Michigan State, and that sort of schooling was beginning to be well regarded in the Bureau in J. Edgar Hoover's last years.

When you entered the FBI in those years, no matter what your background or age—I was thirty-three, older than the average new agent—you were treated as a green recruit and sent from field office to field office to learn the business of being a G-man. After stints in New Orleans and Chicago I was moved, with my wife and two daughters, to Cleveland in the fall of 1971. I wasn't too crazy about the city—it seemed a rather ho-hum town, not as interesting or as cosmopolitan as New Orleans—but at least we were now closer to our relatives in Chicago.

Those were the days when all FBI agents, including me, wore white shirts, dark suits, fedoras, and clunky cop shoes and had a clean-cut image; it was also the era when the Special Agent in Charge (SAC) of whatever office you were assigned to had likely been in the Bureau since Director Hoover's heyday in the 1930s and 1940s. Fred Fehl, who became Cleveland's SAC shortly after I arrived, was one of these, a legendary Bureau "headhunter." This was not a term of endearment. Fehl was regularly sent around the country by headquarters to clean up messes made by other agents; generally, in the cleanup, heads rolled. Those readers who saw the movie *Dog Day Afternoon* saw Fred Fehl in action; in that picture, an actor replicated a role Fred had played in the real-life drama that underlay the movie. He was the FBI agent who came on the scene, took over from the New York City police, then went into the bank where the Al Pacino character and his cohort were holding hostages. Inside the bank the FBI man looked at what was going on, got the lay of the land, said very little, and went back out, but you knew that all hell was going to break loose later at his command. Fehl was known as a difficult man to work for, feared, if not wholly respected, within the Bureau. He had come into the organization as a stenographer, long ago, and knew all the big shots in Washington, although it was said of him that he had no friends. If you were producing for him, you didn't have to be concerned; if you made a mistake, however, you had plenty of worries, for he would likely come down on you very hard.

Was I concerned? Here's an example. There had been a series of bank robberies in Cleveland, and a couple of Bureau agents had the misfortune to spot the perpetrators on the expressway on a Friday afternoon, and gave chase. It was an agent's worst fear that something important would go down at the end of a week, for it would invariably mean a weekend lost to paperwork. Learning of the chase, Fehl pulled out all the stops, sending out word over our radio channels that every available agent should get into the act. Perhaps visions of another Dillinger shoot-out danced in his head, with the heroic SAC giving the *coup de grâce*. It would have made a great movie scene, because the chase led into a rail yard dead end. The two agents and the two perpetrators, the good guys and the bad guys, got out their guns and started blasting away at each other. Lots of bullets were expended, but since everyone was hiding behind railroad cars and other barriers, none of the good guys and none of the bad guys were hit.

Fehl arrived at the edge of the yard and clambered on top of an automobile to hold a conference of backup agents, of whom I was one. During that confab I realized with a sinking feeling that in my rush to get to the scene, I had left my service revolver at the office. And no one around me had a spare gun to lend. Fehl gave the order to infiltrate through the yards and find the bad guys. I was presented with a terrible choice. I could go out and face death at the hands of armed desperadoes, or I could tell Mr. Fehl that I had forgotten my gun. You know it: unarmed, I went after the bad guys. Fortunately, the chase ended well and no one found out that I had been without benefit of my service revolver in the line of duty.

Fehl assigned me to a relatively new squad established to conduct surveillance of organized crime figures, a squad under the direction of a veteran agent, Marty McCann. In nearly every way, McCann was the opposite of Fehl. Marty was a moxie guy, a cocky Irishman who was known as an informant man, that is, as someone who could develop and talk regularly to informants. Being an informant man requires one to be personable, easygoing, and approachable, the sort of guy who makes jokes well and laughs at other people's jokes. Fehl had none of those qualities; Marty embodied them. He had a way of getting you to do work for him without making you annoyed in the process. Every new agent should be lucky enough to have a supervisor like Marty.

McCann had been in counterintelligence in New York City and had been in Cleveland nine years before he was tapped to start an organized crime surveillance squad. Putting Marty in charge of this squad was a good idea, because inside the Bureau only the counterintelligence guys had any real experience with surveillance. This was just at the beginning of the era in which the Bureau started going after organized crime; heretofore, there had been no special effort made against the various Italian and Irish mafias in Cleveland or elsewhere. So we began, as every good operation should, with the gathering of intelligence. For six months or so I worked on surveillance, collecting information by the usual methods, taking down license plate numbers and finding out who owned the cars, seeing which guys associated with known mobsters, learning the extent and the territories of the various Italian and Irish crowds, listening to wiretaps, et cetera.

We had a head start in this area because of McCann's skill with informants. McCann was obviously Irish, and he had used that fact to convince a man named Danny Greene to be an informant for him. Danny Greene was an amazing character who was so Irish that everything he wore was green, down to the crucifix around his neck; the labor shakedown company that he headed was called Emerald Industrial Relations. They specialized in pouring acid on the equipment of trash haulers who didn't see things Greene's way. Born in the Collinwood area in 1939, he had worked his way up to head of the dockworkers' union on the shore of Lake Erie before taking over the Cleveland Trade Solid Waste Guild, a predominantly Irish union. Greene was extremely well connected among the top Irish mobsters. He wouldn't tell tales about his bosses; rather, he'd regale Marty McCann with information about what the top Italians were up to. The Italian gangsters had had the run of the city from the 1920s to the 1950s, when they had mostly pulled up stakes and moved their operations to Las Vegas, but there was still plenty of mob in Cleveland in the sixties and seventies.

As an aside, I must tell you how Danny Greene met his maker. Greene was in the habit of appearing on television now and then, and taunting the Italians, saying that he wasn't hiding, that anybody could find him. According to *Cleveland Magazine*, Greene had been "the object of more assassination attempts than a South American dictator" but had survived all tries at killing him. Greene knew that the Cleveland mobsters favored the setting of car bombs to execute their enemies; in fact, the Greater Cleveland area had become the nation's bombing capital, with about two hundred reported explosions per year. So before Greene would get into a car, he'd always check underneath it to see whether there were any wires protruding, which, if present, would mean the car had been readied to detonate when the engine started. One day Greene went to the dentist, then came back out into a parking lot to check beneath his car. No wires. But the mob had draped a green blanket over a door of the car next to his and filled the door with a bomb, which they set off by remote control, killing Greene by means of shrapnel that bounced back and forth between that car and his own. Parts of his body were found a hundred feet away. Before Greene's untimely end, though, he was able to do me a small favor, and the reader will come upon that story a bit later in this chronicle.

JUSTICE IS SERVED

* * *

It was June of 1972, shortly after the death of J. Edgar
Hoover. After eight months on surveillance, I was
mighty restless—surveillance can be incredibly bor-
ing and doesn't really utilize the full talents of an
FBI agent. Today that notion has been officially recognized: much of the FBI's current surveillance is
handled by nonagents who are several grades lower
in rank than Special Agents. I figured it was one
thing to idle my motor in Cleveland, but quite
another to have the battery being drained by the
endless idling. I wanted to investigate my own cases
but for months had been told: "Just be patient." I
was so annoyed at this lack of progress that I actually
filled out an application to join the organization
that was the predecessor of the Drug Enforcement
Agency, the Federal Bureau of Narcotics and Dangerous Drugs (FBNDD); people there had enticed
me with an offer to jump me up two entire grades,
which meant a nice increase in salary, and wanted
me to be involved in worldwide training activities—
a lot of overseas travel, and so on. Top management
at the Bureau would have blown gaskets had I left
the FBI for such a good job in another law enforcement agency, but push didn't come to shove. I made
enough noise so that in June of 1972 I was handed
about twenty-five to thirty of my own cases, the
approximate usual number for an agent. They were
all more or less in the area of organized crime, but
they weren't very good cases; in fact, that was just
the point. When a new agent arrived in town, the
supervisor would ask his old hands whether they
had any cases they'd like to get rid of. Every agent

37

had a few that he particularly disliked, because they were ones that the agent might work and work at, and still come up with nothing. To rise in the Bureau, you had to be able to "make" your cases, that is, to turn them into indictments and convictions—in the parlance of the Bureau, to "get a stat," a statistic that headquarters could use when asking Congress for more money in the next round of appropriations hearings. If you got a stat—even a single stat—you were a hero, received a commendation letter, and could look forward to a promotion, transfer to a better location, and so on. Please understand: the "old dog" cases handed to new agents were not inconsiderable cases; they could be big or small, but that wasn't the prime consideration for a veteran agent who wanted to get rid of them. Rather, the old dogs were cases that seemed to require a tremendous amount of work in order to be turned into stats. The Bureau hierarchy wasn't dumb, and knew that the veterans loved to shuck off work in this manner, but the hierarchy allowed it to happen for a very positive reason: they hoped that the new men, bright-eyed and willing to work hard, would reinvigorate these old dogs, find ways to make them into better cases, and bring them to successful conclusions.

One such old dog case that landed in my lap that June was an "ITAR-Prostitution" matter. (ITAR is Interstate Transportation in Aid of Racketeering.) The central figure in it was a young Irish pimp named Owen James Kilbane. Now the FBI generally didn't interest itself in prostitution *per se*; that was a local police matter. But when there was any attempt to move women across state lines, it became a matter that fell within our jurisdiction. Even then, we usually dealt with prostitution at arm's length. There was a tradition in the Bureau, probably relating to Hoover's need to protect women from this sordid world: we presumed that women could only be the victims of crimes, not the perpetrators. So it was not the prostitutes themselves who became the occasional targets of FBI scrutiny, but rather their pimps and managers. You could see the dichotomy between male and female roles reflected in the title block of an FBI report, the space on the cover page in which one listed the suspects of an investigation. The pimps would be named as targets of the investigation and their crimes specified, while the prostitutes would be listed as victims.

I found Mr. Owen Kilbane's old dog case to be of more than mild interest. Kilbane was an up-and-coming Danny Greene. Owen had been born in 1947 to a lower-middle-class family in a Cleveland suburb. His father was a polio victim who worked sporadically as a court clerk. In later years, when Owen came up for trial, a series of papers would be filed with the court in which he described his upbringing rather precisely. The court was told that Owen's father was frequently abusive when under the influence of alcohol. The children were mostly raised by the grandparents; Owen's grandmother was "the strongest influence" in his life. A plaintive note was struck by the assertion that Kilbane "has not been close to his mother and father because they have not been physically or emotionally strong enough to provide him with any parental care or guidance since early in his life." Owen had a younger brother, Marty, who always tagged along with him, and an older sister who had become pregnant as a teenager and run away to get married. Unruly by the time they reached puberty, Owen and his brother were sent to a military school by their grandparents, who scrimped and saved in order to pay their tuitions. Owen endured reasonably well, but Marty was traumatized by the overly harsh environment.

After some early brushes with the law for stealing cars, which earned Owen probationary status, his first serious crime occurred when he was sixteen. He robbed and beat up the seventy-three-year-old owner of a neighborhood grocery store, then shoved him into the walk-in freezer. The man survived, but Kilbane was caught shortly thereafter. Had he been an adult, because of his prior probation the crime would have been treated as a felony and he would have been sent to prison. Instead, he was sentenced as a juvenile to eighteen months at Mansfield Reformatory, an Ohio facility for juvenile offenders.

As the reader may know from *Whoever Fights Monsters*, in later years I became an expert on serial killers and conducted extensive research into their family backgrounds and developmental patterns. Among the things I learned, applicable to many more criminals than just to killers, was that at the point in a potential offender's teenage years when things are starting to go wrong, if a juvenile offender can then be given positive role models and helped back onto the right path, there's a chance of his developing into an adult who will not turn to crime. In Owen Kilbane's case, the moment was lost. At a point at which he should have been given a lot of counseling, positive role models, and help to straighten himself out, he was sent to a very tough juvenile facility where the offenders ranged in age from teens up to midtwenties: a school for crime.

At Mansfield, Owen later told friends, he learned that if you were going to go into crime, you should do it in a way that wasn't high-risk. Only stupid criminals robbed grocery stores and banks, went the drill at this school for crime; smarter ones put their energy into prostitution, loan-sharking, and gambling. The reason was simple: in those enterprises, the cops could be paid off—which diminished the risk—and big and continuing profits could be realized. On getting out of Mansfield in mid-1965, Kilbane attended a private academy for a year. His grandfather died shortly after his release, and at eighteen Owen considered himself head of the family, with all of the responsibilities that entailed. Desultory work driving trucks and repairing electric motors wasn't enough for him; according to the above-mentioned court papers, he then "parlayed" some loans from his grandmother "into a succession of business ventures, including a barbershop sold in 1967, an industrial chemical supply business, closed in 1968, several beauty shops which were opened, put on a going basis and sold."

Nice try, Owen. After he came off probation in 1966, some of his business may have been legitimate, but his main occupations were that of pimp, loan shark, and receiver of stolen goods. Blue-eyed, of average height and weight, with reddish brown hair, sometimes with a beard and debonair mustache, he was a cocksure young man determined to make his mark. Owen Kilbane was eight years younger than Danny Greene and seemed to want to be like Greene, who had grown up in Collinwood, not far from the Kilbane home. For instance, Greene was quite vain and fancied himself as a good man with the ladies. Kilbane did the same, and went one step further by "turning out" young women to work for him as prostitutes.

Among these were two that Owen had known in his high school, Carol Braun and Nancy Mason. On his tax returns in the late 1960s Kilbane was audacious enough to list both these women as his dependents. Ambitious, entrepreneurial, and smart, Kilbane had set up his girls in apartments that were deliberately just outside the Cleveland city limits, to not only avoid the big-city police, but also to refrain from encroaching on the territory of various well-established mobsters. He cultivated the Irish higher-ups and put a relative of one of the Italian bigwigs on his payroll. Kilbane wore pimp outfits—for example, a purple suit, maroon shirt, white tie, and wide white belt. He obtained a small fleet of luxury cars, including a stretch limousine that supposedly had once belonged to the singer Tom Jones and included a bar and other interesting equipment. Kilbane's personal favorite seemed to be a white-over-green Cadillac, which had a radio-telephone, an unusual appliance in those days when car phones were few and far between. He designed a logo, an arrangement of geometric patterns that he used on his stationery, on his business cards, as a medallion for his automobiles, and as a motif woven into a rug mounted on his office wall.

Kilbane borrowed money from legitimate institutions on the basis of an inheritance that he would shortly obtain from his grandfather's will, and used this as capital. In his first several years, he did pretty well. Just as important, he made very few mistakes. The first one he did make was allowing his prostitutes to be busted in May 1968. Carol Braun and Nancy Mason were arrested for prostitution at the Statler Hilton in downtown Cleveland.

Steele had happened to go to the precinct where the police were holding the two women on "Jane Doe" warrants because they wouldn't give their right names. Taking over the matter on the spot, he worked out a deal so that the women would give their real names and addresses in exchange for the charge against them being reduced to loitering in a hotel lobby. Carol Braun thought that this was terrific legal work and introduced Steele to her pimp, Owen Kilbane. (Later, Carol would say in a sworn statement that she had met Steele even earlier, when he had been a prostitution customer of hers.) The working arrangement between the two men blossomed when Kilbane learned that Steele was also the police prosecutor for the town of Euclid and was obviously a man of influence in that community.

Shortly after the 1968 arrest, Kilbane moved his prostitutes into the eastern suburbs. He owned one seventeen-apartment building in a black neighborhood, inherited from his grandfather, and now began to pay the rent on apartments for his prostitutes in various large complexes, one of which was in Euclid, and considered buying a Euclid motel. In the summer of 1968, when Robert Steele became the judge of the Euclid court, Kilbane believed he was in clover. "I thought a judge was ten feet tall," he later recalled. He had rubbed his hands with glee at the thought of having such a powerful figure beholden to him.

In the wake of the Steele murder, though Kilbane was not a suspect, his activities were loosely monitored by local police units, but they were not shut down. Then as now, many people considered prostitution to be a "victimless crime," an activity that had plagued society since biblical times and was likely to do so until kingdom come; if the sex-for-money transaction occurred between consenting adults, this view held, it wasn't really so terrible, and law enforcement ought to devote its efforts to solving more heinous crimes. Many police departments kept themselves apprised of prostitution activities because there were often more serious crimes associated with them—burglaries, assaults, bribery—but if the prostitution didn't appear to bother anyone, the police would let it be.

In late 1969, Kilbane's name surfaced again in arrests of prostitutes in other towns for burglary and related small crimes. There were reports to the FBI that he hung out with several known mobsters. Kilbane had evidently profited enough from his operations to buy several racehorses and made an application to race the horses at a small track in Ohio. He showed the investigator for the racing association several bankbooks for various accounts, the apartment house he'd inherited from his grandfather, and other assets. His application was turned down because Kilbane had served time at Mansfield Reformatory. He appealed in 1969, and his appeal was handled for him by former Judge Robert Steele, who had not, as promised, left town after the death of his first wife, but rather had continued in business as a private attorney in the Cleveland area, with Owen as one of his major clients. Despite Steele's efforts, the state racing board in Columbus discouraged Owen's application, and it was withdrawn before it could be rejected formally.

The police in Lakewood had been conducting surveillance of the Kilbane prostitution activities off and on for about six months when, in April of 1970, they decided it had risen to an unacceptable level and raided an apartment that Owen and his women used, arresting all three. Within an hour of their arrest, Steele showed up to post a $500 bond and take Owen out of jail. Shortly thereafter, Steele told the prosecutor that his clients would be willing to plead guilty to the local prostitution ordinance, which carried a fine, rather than be charged under state law, where the penalty was jail time. They paid the fines in May and promptly went back to work, though in another jurisdiction. Kilbane's various enterprises made a lot of money; in 1967, he had told the IRS that he was worth about $12,000; by 1970, his net worth, as reported to the IRS, had risen to $183,000.

By this time, as well, he had attracted enough attention within the Bureau for a file to be opened on Owen James Kilbane and the matter assigned to one of the older agents in the Cleveland office,

Ambrose Burke, Jr. Contrary to public opinion, case files on citizens are not opened lightly by the FBI; the usual requirement is that there appears to be a danger to the public from such an individual, and Owen Kilbane already fit that bill. Over the next two years, although Burke found reason to suspect that Kilbane was providing prostitutes to houses in neighboring states—which was a federal offense—there was not enough evidence to come anywhere near consideration of bringing an indictment. The case file remained open, however. Burke was getting ready to retire when, on June 23, 1972, the old dog matter of Owen James Kilbane was reassigned to me.

The reader might think that the matter of Owen Kilbane, scarcely worth the time of a local police force, wasn't worth much of an FBI agent's attention; indeed, that was the attitude of many of the older and more experienced agents in the Cleveland FBI office in the summer of 1972. I thought differently. To me, Owen Kilbane was the very model of a young punk on the way up, ambitious to get in good with one mob or another—he was courting both the Italians and the Irish—and with a good head for business; someday he might well become an important organized crime figure, and if he did, well, it was my intention that by that time the FBI would have enough on him to put him away for a while.

Beyond my interest in Kilbane as a young mobster, though, lay the tantalizing suggestion that he and Judge Steele had somehow been involved together in the unsolved murder of Marlene Steele.

This provocative notion was already in the files I had inherited from Ambrose Burke, who had picked it up in conversation with local police authorities. In the summer of 1972, as I began working the Kilbane matter, cultivating informants of my own, talking to the various police departments about him and his operations, the word on the street, from both the cops and the people on the fringes of crime, was that the death of Marlene Steele had been a contract murder arranged by Kilbane for his friend and attorney, the judge.

When Andy Vanyo, chief of intelligence for the Cleveland police department, heard that I was working on Kilbane, he called me and said that his informants believed firmly that Kilbane had been connected to the Steele killing. Vanyo took me to meet a source, a man we'll call Hugo, in a safe house that the police maintained in Cleveland. Hugo was nervous, but confirmed that the Kilbanes, whom he knew personally, had been involved in the death of Marlene Steele.

"In what capacity?" I asked.

"Nobody knows for sure," Vanyo responded, but he thought it likely that Kilbane had been the middleman who had arranged for a shooter. The identity of the shooter was anybody's guess, though.

Similarly, Lou Kulis, the senior detective for the Cuyahoga County sheriff's department, believed that Steele might have arranged for the murder of his wife through Owen Kilbane. In the nine-and-a-half-hour interview with Steele, Kulis extracted information that led him to believe that for some time prior to the murder Steele had been sexually serviced regularly by Kilbane's prostitutes. Steele was now an officer of a couple of Kilbane's interlocking companies, as well as his lawyer.

The murder of Marlene Steele. It was a matter that wasn't really in my jurisdiction, but it got my juices going. Professionally, it was a crime that other law enforcement people hadn't brought to justice, and I wanted to break the case, to do something that nobody else had been able to do. There is frequently that sort of competitiveness among law enforcement people. Personally, I had very deep concern about this murder. It galled me in a central part of my being. I had been brought up with a very strong respect for law and order and had decided early to devote my life to that work, to the study of criminals, and to being a detective. That had been my interest in the army, where I'd worked for the CID, and that was the real motivation for my joining the FBI. The notion that a sitting judge might have contracted with a pimp to have the judge's wife killed—well, that was just anathema to me, an action contrary to everything I believed in. The victim was wholly innocent, by all reports a good woman and wife. I'm certain that she had her faults, as we all do, but whatever they were, they didn't warrant the early and violent death she had met. It also bothered me that the sanctity of the home had been violated, that the murder had been done in the judge's home, and while his children were asleep upstairs. Here was a deed that trashed the hearth, the family, the sanctity of marriage, the decency with which one human being ought to treat another—you name the social canon, this crime had offended it.

The deed bothered other people, too. Every January 9, Chester Zembala and his partner would take their county detective car and park it outside the new residence where Steele and Barbara lived. When Steele came out to go to the office, they'd follow the former judge from his home to the downtown building in which his business was located— just as a reminder of Marlene's death. Not once in the several years that they had been doing this had Steele come over to them to ask them whether there were any new leads or to thank them for this reminder that the authorities still hadn't given up on the case. And Detective John Walsh, who as a Euclid patrolman had been the recipient of free legal help from Steele, would look at Steele a bit askance when his former friend would now and then have to meet a client in the Euclid police department headquarters. "Come to turn yourself in?" Walsh once asked Steele during such an encounter. Moments later, he saw the former judge in a dark corner, trembling and crying to himself. Walsh's dig in the ribs may have been a harsh one, but after the nonindictment of Steele for the murder of Marlene, Euclid had come to have a reputation in the Cleveland area law enforcement community as a department that was "out to lunch." That rep had made it harder for Walsh and his colleagues to do their already-difficult jobs.

In the places where the area's law enforcement authorities gathered for an after-work beer, there was general agreement that if Kilbane had contracted to murder Marlene Steele, he must have done so in order henceforth to have control over the judge.

Blackmail is frequently a part of a prostitution operation, and Kilbane ran prostitutes, so he would have understood that once the deed was done, he could continue to hold the murder over Steele's head and command the judge's compliance. What Kilbane had probably not figured on was that Judge Steele's affair with Barbara Swartz would surface quite so quickly after Marlene's death and would result in Steele's forced resignation from the bench. That had lessened Steele's usefulness to Kilbane.

That summer, I received other information that also helped me both to target Kilbane and to understand some of the complex reasons why he might possibly have contracted for the murder of Marlene Steele. Through interviews with people on the fringes of Kilbane's operations, I learned that he and a man named Arnie Prunella had been rival pimps and that Kilbane was suspected of having had a hand in Prunella's disappearance in 1968. Word on the street was that Arnie had been shot dead on a boat, covered with chicken wire and tied to a cement sewer cover, then dropped into Lake Erie. Although bad blood between the two men had been documented, the belief among the elbow benders at police hangouts was that Kilbane might have had Prunella killed in order to prove himself as a provider of contract killers to the mob.

It was possible, then, that Kilbane had contracted for both murders as a way of showing his mettle to the large mob organizations, part of climbing the ladder to success in criminal activities. That fitted with information I was developing on Kilbane's expanding empire—ownership of two motels, prostitution operations at three or four sites, contacts with mob nightclub owners and with mob-run gambling, and attempts to provide prostitutes to mob-touched houses in other cities. Nonetheless, and even though I was building support for the notion that Owen Kilbane was on the path to becoming an important criminal, the guys in my office ragged me continuously about spending time on this matter. "Oh, sure, Ressler," they'd say, "you're going to solve the Steele murder any day now," and were heard to observe, "That Owen Kilbane is one big, bad man."

In the fall of 1972, the Bureau inspectors came to the Cleveland FBI office. These auditors came from headquarters and looked into every single thing that anybody in the office was doing. No field agent liked to see the inspectors coming, but it was something that we had to endure; we grudgingly understood that the audits were a good idea, a way of ensuring that the field was following the directives of headquarters. To be an inspector was to be part of the FBI headquarters hierarchy; everyone who wanted to rise higher in the ranks than a Special Agent had to put in a stint as an inspector—but nobody in the field liked the inspectors' nosing about. Full inspection audits of field offices occurred every year or so, though not regularly, in order that they couldn't be anticipated and the place sanitized before their arrival. Inspectors would go over every case being handled by every agent. Oftentimes the inspector would recommend that a case be closed for lack of interest or that one be swiftly brought to a conclusion or dropped. Only in a relatively small number of instances would an inspector suggest that more, rather than less, attention be paid to a case.

On that visit, the inspectors completely agreed with my assessment of Owen Kilbane as an up-and-coming figure in the Cleveland underworld, a guy who had all the earmarks of becoming a big shot someday, and said that Kilbane should definitely be targeted by the Bureau for vigorous investigation—as we would do, say, with a lieutenant in an organized crime family.

I could hardly wait for the inspection team to leave and the office to return to normal functioning. Now I had the blessing of headquarters to go after Owen Kilbane with the full resources of the Bureau, and the justification for spending a lot of my time in that endeavor.

Two

PROPRIETOR OF THE X-RATED MOTEL

Tracking an unknown killer is one of the greatest challenges a detective can have, and I've had my share of them in my years of helping local police hunt serial killers. The theme is a staple of detective stories. Unfortunately, most fictional detective stories are off the mark because they feature and emphasize the lone hero trying to figure out the identity of the unknown killer. Maybe halfway through the plot, the detective discovers the identity of the person he thinks is the killer. Then the detective goes after the killer, perhaps confronts the killer. And in half of the books and movies, the killer confesses when confronted. In most of the rest of the fictional accounts, there's a plot switch down near the end, where the detective's first guess is revealed to be wrong and the true villain is established. The fictional account usually ends with the villain being carted off to jail to stand trial. Or maybe with a satisfying shoot-out in which the killer gets what's coming to him or her.

Would that in real life the scenario were that simple! Most often, it's not. The first thing I want people to know is that in the vast majority of murders, there's very little mystery about the killer's identity. About 25,000 murders a year are committed in the United States, and about 20,000 of them are solved within a year of the victim's death. The high solution rate shows that the identity of the killer is often easy to establish. Most perpetrators turn out to be relatives or associates of the victim, and routine police questioning reveals their identities. The truth about detective work is that the preponderance of the cases have to do with instances in which the killer is known or a particular person is reasonably suspected of having had a hand in the murder. Learning the murderer's identity, that linchpin of fictional plots, isn't the end of the game in real life. What if you know the identity from Day One? There's still a lot of chasing to do. Once the identity of the probable killer is known, the question then becomes: how can the investigators (and the prosecution) prove the case? That is the *real* challenge of most investigative work, and that's at the heart of this particular, though extraordinary, detective story.

Putting the killers of Marlene Steele away and keeping them in prison took almost twenty years. When I entered the case in 1972, three years after the murder, it was fairly well established who the likely killers were. Plenty of information about this matter was held by the various police authorities in the area, from Euclid to Cuyahoga County to downtown Cleveland to other suburbs such as

Cleveland Heights and Lakewood. Today I am convinced that if in 1969 all those jurisdictions had gotten together and pooled their information about several crimes that involved associates of Owen Kilbane and Robert Steele, the murder of Marlene might well have been solved in short order, before I ever entered the picture. But it wasn't. In 1972, as an FBI man with a "new" matter in hand, I began to act like a bee, and go from flower to flower, picking up a bit from this local law enforcement agency, something else from that one, and to put all of this information together.

Often, the more time that has elapsed after a murder, the more difficult it is to solve, because the trail is presumed to have gone cold. In this instance, however, the three years that had gone by since the death of Marlene Steele had actually clarified certain aspects of the case. The story of an unknown, unseen assailant who took nothing from the house yet who coolly executed his victim—that story didn't wash. For instance, some of the boot prints outside the Steele home appeared to have been made deliberately to confuse the police pursuit, which looked like evidence that this part of the crime had been staged, for making two sets of boot prints in the snow was not something likely to have been done by some chance burglar or would-be rapist who on a whim pumped two slugs into a sleeping woman. It was also unlikely that Mrs. Steele's murder had been a professional hit, although Steele had dropped hints that some enemies of his Italian in-laws might have been working out vengeance against Marlene to punish Midge Gallitto, the Italian gas-station owner. But there were no tales circulating in the underworld about it, as there would be if this hit had been done by hired guns from, say, some crime family fiefdom. The police had tried to check out this possibility anyway, and had come up with nothing. The inescapable conclusion was that the murder had to have been done, as Judge Steele had told a reporter just days after the event, by someone with a knowledge of the Miami Road house and its inhabitants.

One of the key ingredients in a murder is the motive for it. Who could have and would have wanted this murder done? The most compelling fact in any discussion of motive was an incontrovertible and very public one: the judge's hurried remarriage to Barbara Swartz. Wanting to marry Barbara, Steele might have wished to get rid of a first wife he no longer loved and who had probably been unwilling to let him go without making a fight or imposing conditions he deemed too harsh. A second necessary ingredient in a murder is the means, access to a deadly weapon or to people not adverse to using such weapons. Most observers agreed that the judge was not the type to have shot his wife himself, but that his association with Kilbane could have provided the judge with both a shooter and a weapon. Kilbane was known to own several weapons—he'd listed them in that interview with the Euclid police, just days after the murder—and he was often seen hanging around with unsavory characters. Steele and Kilbane were linked together as officers of the corporation that was in the process of buying a rather run-down motel on the western end of Euclid, just at the border of the city of Cleveland. Such continued dealings between Steele and Kilbane in the years after the murder gave observers a basis for believing that the two men could well have conspired together.

Despite the suspicions of the law enforcement authorities, no one in that community knew precisely how the murder had been accomplished. We still had no murder weapon and no trigger puller. Where to begin?

To crack the case, I reasoned, I must go after a weak link, and the more vulnerable of the two men was Kilbane, whose operations were clearly and continuously criminal. Here again, though, the problem was how to prove that crimes were taking place.

In July of 1972, Owen Kilbane purchased the Hillcrest motel in Euclid and turned it into an X-rated destination, complete with waterbeds and pornographic movies that could be piped into the rooms via closed-circuit television. In those days, the showing of such films in such circumstances was novel, and Kilbane bragged about it to the newspapers. "Young people don't want to stay in a fossil of a place," he told the Cleveland *Plain Dealer*, and said he was trying to appeal to a "young and liberal clientele." Some of the suites had black walls, white ceilings, and scarlet carpeting and drapes, all illuminated by soft lighting, and Kilbane agreed that these were not for families; he said there were signs all around the check-in lobby about the X-rated films, and families that wanted to stay at the motel could request that the circuit between the projector and their rooms be cut. Others could watch six times a day during the week, three times on Sunday. Kilbane was adamant that the setup was legal and said he'd checked it out first with lawyers; moreover, "these are the same films you can see in a theater." Some time later, when *Playboy* printed a letter saying that the first X-rated motels had been tried in California, Kilbane proudly wrote a letter to the editor claiming he'd done it in staid old Cleveland before anyone else had the great idea. And he bragged.

> Since then, I've come up with closed-circuit, X-rated TV shows in the customized El Dorado limousine I offer for rent and I make a video-tape camera available for a fee, to guests who want to create their own shows. Until I move to California, Ohio will continue to lead the nation.

The publicity that he cultivated to advertise the X-rated motel was an indication that Kilbane had become very brazen in his operations. Soon he had another motel, across the street from the first, and had installed two of his prostitutes in an apartment in a large high-rise complex within sight of the two motels; he could look out his office window and see all three of these properties. The police knew that a shady operator was at work in their neighborhood—he was so insistent upon flaunting his operations that they would have to have been blind to miss them. Did Danny Greene cavort on television and tell the Italian mob that they knew where to find him? Owen Kilbane openly taunted powerful forces, too, but the ones he twitted were on the side of the law; his operation seemed now to demand investigation.

Although in those days I wanted to spend a good amount of time on Kilbane, I had to continue to investigate other cases and assist in the general work of the FBI office. A crackdown on illegal gambling had been decreed, and we spent some time shadowing a movable gambling enterprise run by organized crime. One week they'd hold their party in an abandoned warehouse; the next they might rent an unused store at a shopping center for their roulette wheels and card and dice tables. The number of fancy cars parked outside a grimy warehouse or shuttered factory was almost comical to behold. At a shopping center one weekend, in a place called Chateau La Cave, we crashed down doors and broke up one of these gambling operations. Although it was not a crime to gamble, it was a crime to set up and run the operation, so we just briefly questioned most of the guests and then let them go. In the recent past, a local chief of police had been caught in one of these raids and had tried to say that he was actually there doing undercover work. During this raid, while I was searching an attic crawl space above the party center, John Jury of our office called up to me that he had Owen Kilbane and thought I might be interested in seeing him.

I came down and took over the task of briefly interviewing and photographing Kilbane. Up close he wasn't terribly imposing, but he did seem cool and collected in his flamboyant clothes, and it was clear that he was sizing me up. He was just a customer, not one of those who was running the game, and I took down his answers to the routine questions—name, address, phone number, and the like—and tried not to overplay my hand. I certainly wasn't going to tell Kilbane why this particular FBI agent was interested in him. Not yet, anyway.

Outside observation of a prostitution business, even one as sophisticated as Kilbane's, can be done—you can conduct discreet surveillance to chart the comings and goings of people in a specific place and establish some patterns—but mere surveillance is usually unable to definitively establish the basis for a prosecution. To get inside the operation, you need information, and for information the FBI has always gone to what we call informants.

In the months after I got the Kilbane case, I started developing some of my own informants. Before I describe them and what I was able to learn from them, let me first define the term *informant* as the FBI uses it, since in common usage it has come to mean a fink who rats on his companions in crime, or who turns traitor to an in-group and causes a good man to be hurt, as in *The Informer*, the John Ford film about the troubles in Ireland.

The Bureau had several levels of people on whom we relied for information. Confidential sources could be those who verified that a neighbor had lived at a certain address for a number of years, that sort of routine thing. Beyond that were criminal informants, usually people involved peripherally in some nefarious enterprise who would give us information in exchange for our leniency in prosecutions.

Above that were top-echelon informants, men such as Danny Greene or Jackie Presser, men who were accused of being criminals, but who were considered important to major investigations being conducted by the Bureau. We were often forced to rely heavily on such sources of information.

Hoover's FBI had always placed undue reliance on informants and had eschewed undercover work. The two concepts went hand in hand. The director had watched the old Federal Bureau of Narcotics and Dangerous Drugs get burned badly when it permitted its men to go undercover to obtain information. Regularly, FBNDD undercover people would be lured into crime by the narcotics and money associated with the criminals, and Hoover determined that he couldn't run the same risks with his "untouchables." So he placed his agents beyond seduction by decreeing that they should obtain all their information from informants, that is, by cultivating people on the inside of a criminal operation and talking to them. Rather than having one of his own men inside, Hoover preferred his agents to work at a remove. You developed informants and then let one informant check on the veracity of the others. In this system, the agent would not be sullied by direct contact with the worst elements of the criminal world and therefore would be much less likely to be corrupted by its offerings. If need be, agents could work in conjunction with other agencies or cooperative business entities to obtain information in other discreet ways—through the phone company for lists of frequently called numbers, through the courts for wiretaps, through the post office for "mail covers," that is, the scrutinizing of envelopes before they were delivered to the addressee, and so on. Nowadays these latter techniques are still used but are arranged only through a court order.

I had no problem in working live informants, and in the first six months of the case against Kilbane, the latter part of 1972 and early 1973, I developed a fair number of them.

Now when an upstanding member of society is approached by an FBI agent for a piece of information, that person has little to fear; when the person approached is "dirty," and the FBI has an inkling of that, the dance changes. While such information sources as apartment complex managers and uninvolved neighbors of the Kilbane operations were quite clean, the people I approached to provide the most important information on Kilbane were at least slightly smudged. When dealing with a potential informant who is part of a criminal enterprise, the agent has more than a bland request on his side in his search for information; he also bears with him the threat of prosecution—sometimes expressed, sometimes only hinted at—if the source doesn't cooperate.

I like the term *develop* as it applies to working with an informant, because it accurately reflects the process that must be gone through to obtain and fine-tune a good source. A certain amount of trust has to grow between the agent and the source. When another agent and I first approached one of the men who worked around the Kilbane motel, a man whom we'll call Tex, we took care to do so off the premises, when he was at home, sitting on his front porch. We stood on the stoop, in full view of the neighborhood, and chatted. Tex was so nervous at the possibility of his neighbors seeing what were obviously law enforcement agents on his doorstep that he invited us inside. His hands were shaking as he talked to us, even though it wasn't a cold day. I already knew a lot about this guy. He was every mother's nightmare, an overgrown boy unable to hold a legitimate job, and with weaknesses—gambling, liquor, fancy clothes—that a savvy "user" of people like Kilbane would salivate to exploit.

I leaned on Tex, told him that I knew he was involved in prostitution activities, and that he could well go to jail unless he started giving us some information about the Kilbane operation. I told him he'd be able to inform without jeopardizing himself, as we were not yet ready to move on Kilbane. He took to the idea of meeting me in off-hours, usually in the dimly lit back of some bar that Kilbane wouldn't frequent, where we'd sit at a secluded table and I'd order a pitcher of beer and whatever food he wanted; he liked cadging "free" meals from the FBI, and, as with many small-time criminals, he liked being duplicitous to his boss. Owen Kilbane had lured him, as he'd done with a dozen or so other people, both male and female, by the promise that if they worked with him, they'd get rich. However, once they were in his employ, he'd pay his help the minimum wage and toss them a twenty- or a fifty-dollar bill now and again to make them think this was the good life. Even the thickest of employee skulls was soon penetrated by the understanding that Owen was driving a Cadillac, but the employee was still pushing a mop.

I didn't want to depend just on Tex, who sometimes lied to me, so I went after others in the Kilbane operation.

Here I must tell a few tales out of school, relate matters to which I would never had admitted when I was still in the Bureau. (I retired in 1990.)

To get close to any of the prostitutes working out of Owen's apartments in those large complexes was a challenge. You couldn't just show up at the guarded front door of the complex and ask for admission. Only guests cleared by the apartment dwellers could enter that way. And outside surveillance of the apartments couldn't produce much information beyond descriptions of the johns and the cars they drove. So I decided to cross the line from surveillance into what I characterize as light undercover work.

In every organization in the world, there are people who completely abide by the rules and get very little real work done, and there are those who bend and go around or sometimes even break the rules and get something accomplished. As I've indicated, headquarters had historically frowned on undercover work for its agents, but in the early 1970s some undercover assignments were just beginning to be done in the Bureau. I remember one perhaps apocryphal story about four Bureau agents who had grown their hair long and were going out west to infiltrate some sort of New Left outfit that reputedly had been planning to bomb a military facility. The four longhairs traveled by air, but they were such novices at undercover work that they didn't think to check their weapons through in their baggage; rather, when metal detectors located their shoulder-holstered guns, they told the pilot of the plane that they were FBI agents and were allowed to carry their weapons on board. What a breach of the sort of compartmented security that is paramount to any good undercover operation! Didn't those guys realize that the pilot might have told his friends and that word could easily have filtered through to the targets of the operation? My point is that the Bureau was still not very comfortable with undercover operations, and you weren't supposed to try one unless it was absolutely necessary, and then only when you'd prepared the paperwork and been sanctioned in advance to go undercover. It would have taken months to get permission to go even a tiny bit undercover, and I wasn't going to wait for that. No aggressive agent ever does. It was time to bend a rule and do the light undercover work that I deemed to be crucial to getting inside the Kilbane empire.

So, dressed in my army uniform, one day I checked into Kilbane's motel and walked around, to get an up-close feeling for the place. You might think that an army uniform makes a person stand out, but it didn't at that time; moreover, many servicemen on limited budgets stayed at small motels when they were traveling. I wandered into the lobby, the length and breadth of the parking lot. No prostitution was going on at the motel, but it seemed to be a headquarters for many other Kilbane endeavors. Some of the workmen looked more like toughs than they should have. In my room—no waterbed, thank you—I changed into my suit. Then I went downtown to work at the FBI office, returned at the end of the day, changed back into casual clothes, and hung around some more. Of course I hadn't advised my boss of where I planned to spend the night, another instance of not telling him what he didn't want to know. I was putting myself into the path of temptation, and headquarters might not have approved. In any event, I slept at the motel—no dirty movies, thank you—for a night or two, then moved on, having accomplished my modest mission of getting a firsthand feel for the place, where the records were kept, how many people were there, what time of the day or night registered the most activity. Now, if I had to plan a raid on the place, I knew it well enough to do so.

Next, something bolder. Dressed in a janitor's outfit or in work overalls or sporting a tool belt and carrying a rake or a shovel or a bucket, I'd stand around a side door of one of the apartment complexes in which the actual prostitution was taking place and look busy. When a renter would approach, I'd let the person go through the door with his or her key and then say, "Oops, hold it, willya?" The obliging resident would then restrain the door and let in someone he or she thought was either an employee of the complex or of one of the contractors who tended the gardens or did repair jobs. Burglars use this ruse all the time. As an FBI agent, I made sure *not* to note on my report how it was that I managed to get inside. My supervisor didn't want to know that, anyway, and headquarters sure as heck didn't.

On one such trip through a side door, I spotted Carol Braun coming up from the basement with a basket of laundry that was too large for her to carry. I offered to help her, and she agreed. So, carrying her basket, I went up in the elevator and to her door; she didn't want me to come in, but I was able to gain some information that I hadn't wanted to request from the front desk: which apartment was being used for the prostitution operation. Casual chatter with other residents confirmed that Carol's apartment received an inordinate number of visitors. There was so much traffic, people said, that it could have been a doctor's office.

I knew from other informants that a second young lady inside, whom I'll call Diane, had been unhappy of late, feeling as though she were a slave in this apartment, not permitted by Kilbane to go out except in the company of Carol Braun. I hung around on Diane's floor and watched for a while. I'd take a light bulb out, then put it back in. I'd remove a piece of molding from a wall, then replace it. Residents hardly gave me a second glance. When the corridor was busy, I'd stand inside the door where the garbage chute was located. When I saw that the coast was clear, I knocked on Diane's door, and she came to answer it. I used her name, and because she was inured to having unknown men show up at her door for the purpose of prostitution, she opened right up.

"Hi, I'm Bob Ressler and I'm with the FBI," I said to the short young brunette with the southern drawl. "Like to talk to you."

"What about?" The door wasn't opening very much.

"Well, we know you're involved in a prostitution operation using this apartment, and I'd like to discuss it with you."

"I don't know nothing about that."

"Look, we can do it quietly and keep it unofficial—"

"Uh-uh."

"—or we can do it officially, get a warrant, have you arrested, and we can talk that way. If you don't want to talk now, we can do it some other time, Diane," I said quickly, knowing my welcome was fading fast. "But don't tell Owen about this visit, and I won't tell anyone either. I mean it; don't tell him. Here's my card. Some other time, you might want to call me and talk. But if you do tell Owen, I'll find out about it, and then we'll have to come down on you all hard, and you'll do time; count on it. So keep this quiet, and maybe we'll do it later on."

The apartment door was slammed in my face, but my card remained in Diane's possession.

Some weeks later, Diane called and left the message that she'd like to see me. I called back. When? Three in the morning, after the last "trick" of the day.

Backup agent Ted Jackson and I went up to Diane's apartment at the appointed hour, just as though we were another pair of johns arriving for a session. The people at the desk downstairs had no problem with us; they called up to inquire whether we should be given access, and Diane told them to buzz us in. In the apartment, we talked for a while. This was a young woman, scared about what she was doing but firm in her belief that she could not escape from "the life." A small-town southern girl, she'd sought a good time in the big city, had gotten into using drugs, and went into prostitution as a way of making money to obtain the drugs. Now she was off drugs but was afraid of her pimp and felt she had no choice but to continue working as a call girl. I didn't get much information on this visit, but that wasn't the task as I saw it, anyhow: the first necessity was to establish trust.

In time, I gained the trust of several different prostitutes in the employ of Owen Kilbane, and these became my informants. In fact, in time, Owen Kilbane's organization was leaking so much information to me from so many sources that I thought of it almost as a sieve.

These informants provided me with more than information about Kilbane. One of them, whom I'll call Maxie, fairly articulate as well as full-sized and attractive, told me something important about what happens when a lawman deals with a prostitute. One night, while chatting with her in her apartment, I walked into her kitchen to get myself a cold drink and saw a pair of women's bikini underpants taped to an unusual place.

"What are these doing hanging on the refrigerator?"

"Well, those are underpants that I wore a couple years ago—I used to be a lot thinner, when I had a straight job—and my goal is to get back into those underpants. Of course, you can get into them any time you want."

She gave me a big smile, and I was nonplussed. There are some obvious dangers to a law enforcement officer trying to obtain information from a prostitute. The last thing you want is to put yourself into a position so that the young lady could one day turn on you and say that she's been servicing you. At one time or another, several of the women I talked to in Kilbane's stable offered to have sex with me. I declined all the offers, including Maxie's. This one, however, I took as an opportunity to explore with an intelligent woman the general subject of cops and prostitutes.

"Y'know, one thing you gotta watch," she told me. "Every girl, every hooker, wants to take a cop to bed."

"Why is that?"

"We look at men—across the boards—as just johns," she said. "To a hooker, even the president of the United States is just a john. Men are all the same; they'll jump into bed with you if the occasion arises. Hookers believe that all men are driven by sexual urges that they have difficulty controlling— so the thing is, if a hooker can get a cop in bed, it shows her that he's just another john, even if he is wearing a badge." By the same token, Maxie contended, if the cop refused the hooker's offer of free sex, then there was the possibility of a healthy respect developing between them. In my mind, such a respectful relationship could produce good information for the law enforcer and might provide the prostitute with an eventual avenue out of the life.

JUSTICE IS SERVED

From talking to the prostitutes, to the lieutenant, and to other people on the fringes of the Kilbane operation, I soon understood that the women for the most part operated under the first-level command of one of their own, Carol Braun, who in addition to being a prostitute was Owen's most special girl-friend. Braun often gave directions to the other women and collected money from them. The operation was being run in a meticulous way. Owen had promulgated three basic rules. First, the women were to spend no more than thirty minutes with a male customer. Second, they were not to perform any sex acts until the male was undressed and had also handed over the payment. Third, in the event that the man managed to skip out without paying, the prostitute would still owe Owen half of the expected payment anyway. There were two tele-phones in the prostitution apartments, a white one kept exclusively for dates, a beige one kept exclu-sively for other business. The women would be charged for excess use of the liquor and linens and for any long-distance calls.

On slow nights, Owen and Carol would have the girls make up several copies of the "trick books," written compilations that showed a customer's name, his sexual preferences, the date of service, and the price he paid. Generally, it was about thirty dollars for usual things and more for unusual ones. A few of the notations had to do with preferences for whips and fetishes, games in which the johns' wives and girlfriends evidently would not agree to participate. The variety of sexual experimentation was less amazing than the fact that a substantial number of these johns would pay by check, often by company check, and that quite a few would give the women their business cards and provide other sorts of identification. Were the men so stupid as not to realize that this information, which went right into the trick books, might someday be used against them? Kilbane knew how to use this data, all right. When a customer hadn't been by to utilize the prostitution services recently enough, Owen would have one of the girls use the information to call him up at the address on his business card or check.

"Hello, this is Miss Diane from ABC Supplies, calling for our production manager, Mr. Jones. Is Mr. Smith there? Mr. Jones would like to speak with him." They'd use this or a similar ruse—XYZ Cleaning Service—in order to get past the secretary and have the call forwarded to the former customer whose name and affiliation were in the trick book. When they got through, they'd brace the man directly. "Hello, Mr. Johnson? This is Diane from ABC Supplies. You remember me from a couple of weeks ago? Good! Well, this week, we're offering a special discount for repeat purchasers." Or a two-for-one special. Or some other offer that could readily be understood as a come-on for prostitution services. If the proposition didn't sound attractive this time, that didn't really matter, for the customer could hardly avoid listening between the lines and comprehending the implied blackmail threat behind the call. Contacted at his place of employment, the man whose name was in the trick book was coerced to comply, to become a repeat, steady customer. An enterprising young businessman, Owen Kilbane.

* * *

In the latter part of 1972, there were rumblings of trouble between Kilbane and Carol Braun; the other girls reported that she was moody and sullen. Pretty soon, though, her mood perked up again, as a brand-new all-white Lincoln Continental appeared in her parking slot at the apartment complex. Her relationship to Owen Kilbane was a roller coaster, and it headed down into another trough after the first of the year.

Toward the end of January, a somewhat unusual scenario shaped up for Carol Braun and Diane. A pair of johns, two visiting businessmen from Atlanta, wanted a blonde and a brunette to party with them exclusively all through a long weekend, and had contacted Owen. Both men were shady characters themselves, with some businesses that were legitimate and others that skirted the law. Owen agreed to the arrangement, and the women partied with the johns in Carol's apartment for several days and nights, going out to Chinese restaurants and cocktail lounges when they got tired of spending all their time cooped up in one place. During this time, they all became more closely acquainted than they might have in other circumstances. Learning of the women's dissatisfaction with their situation, the businessmen made an offer: come with us to Atlanta and continue the party.

At the moment, the idea sounded very good to Carol and Diane, who were both angry at Kilbane. Diane was dissatisfied with the life of a prostitute and wanted out, but Carol's reasons for needing to escape Kilbane went much deeper: Owen had forced her to give up an infant daughter, whom she had borne when she was seventeen, in order to be his main squeeze. At the end of the party, the women packed up their belongings and wrecked Carol's apartment, Diane taking particular pleasure in kicking in the front of a television set and Carol in writing on the wall, "Bob Steele killed his wife." Then the women drove in the white Lincoln to Kilbane's empty home and took with them some of his trick books as insurance against his trying to stop their getaway. Should they show the trick books to the police. Owen could be hauled in for being a pimp. They abandoned the Lincoln Continental at the Hopkins Airport, where they met the men, and flew with them to Atlanta. Upon arrival, the women were put up in a motel in an outlying suburb.

Carol then called Owen with the intention of telling him off, once and for all. She began the conversation in fine fettle, warning him about the trick books they'd taken and screaming at him about all the terrible things Owen had done in the past. But Owen didn't hang up, and neither did Carol, and the conversation dragged on for hours, during which both Carol and Diane took turns speaking to Owen on the telephone. Kilbane admitted some past problems and promised the women that he would treat them better in the future. He told Carol that he would now formally marry her, but that she must come back to him, because he was afraid that he was dying of cancer. Carol said she'd think about it. Diane was annoyed at this but didn't quite know what to do about it.

When the women did not immediately return,

Kilbane sent his brother, Marty, and an employee named John Schillar in Kilbane's distinctive white-over-green Cadillac down to Atlanta. These goons were dressed for the occasion in standard George Raft–type gangster clothes—striped suits, dark shirts, light ties. Marty Kilbane, who was in his early twenties, was often thought to be a very tough guy, but that was an impression conveyed by his appearance, which, like that of some Hollywood actors, was far nastier than his personality. Schillar was a somewhat burly guy who liked guns: another of the losers corralled by Kilbane.

It was a scene that Kilbane had orchestrated, even if he wasn't there in person. In that impossible-to-miss car with Kilbane's logo on it, the two flashily dressed goons wheeled up to the office of one of the businessmen, who had a drywall concern. The owner was not there, but an associate was, and the goons gave the associate one of Owen's logo-embossed business cards and told him that the boss had better call Owen within an hour or two, if he knew what was good for him. Their mission accomplished, Martin Kilbane and John Schillar turned right around and drove back to Cleveland.

The drywall business associate was a smart guy. He managed to note down the Ohio license plate number of the Cadillac before he passed the goons' message on to his boss. The boss rounded up the second businessman who had been on the wild weekend with him and brought along the associate to witness the dutiful call he then made to Kilbane. On the telephone, Kilbane was somewhat elliptic but kept saying that the Atlanta businessmen had some "valuable property of his," which he later on in the conversation identified as being a book and some rings. The businessman was thoroughly intimidated and promised to send them back.

Shortly thereafter, Diane and Carol (and the trick books and the rings) were hustled onto a plane in Atlanta and returned to Cleveland, where they went right back into the Kilbane prostitution operation.

A week later, the Atlanta businessman called Kilbane, hoping now that he had closed the books on this episode of his life. No such luck. Kilbane said that his property had been located, but that he wanted the businessman to come to Cleveland so they could meet and straighten out their differences. The businessman had another trip to make to Cleveland and, while there, got in touch with Kilbane once again, and Kilbane reiterated that he had better come in for a personal chat so they could settle what was still outstanding between them. The businessman felt certain that Kilbane's only purpose in arranging the meeting was to extort money from him, and he didn't go to see Kilbane; rather, he fled back to Atlanta.

Another week or so went by, and the businessman received a letter from attorney Robert L. Steele that said Kilbane was going to sue the businessman for "alienation of affection" in regard to Kilbane's wife, Carol Braun, and that he would seek $100,000 in damages "for the injuries he sustained as a result of your activities with his wife."

Sending the goons was a great grandstand gesture on Kilbane's part, but it was also a stupid mistake, compounded by the phone calls and letter to the businessman. When I learned of the women's flight from Andy Vanyo—and the details from my informants and from the Atlanta FBI agents' interviews of the businessmen—I cheered. This was a godsend. Now the government could legitimately contend that Kilbane had operated across state lines with his women for hire, and also that he had attempted interstate extortion—more charges to add to those we were already piling up for the government to lodge against the erstwhile proprietor of the X-rated motel.

Three

"CRIMINAL CONVERSATION"

To former judge Bob Steele and his second wife, Barbara, in the late winter and early spring of 1973 it must have seemed that they had successfully put the past behind them. They had moved from the Miami Road home to another residence in suburban Cleveland, one adjoining a golf course, and felt confident enough about public opinion for Mrs. Steele to have her photograph as a participant in local flying school taken and published in the *Plain Dealer*. Shortly thereafter, however, something from the past came back to haunt them. In 1970, Barbara's former husband, Orville (Jay) Swartz, had brought suit against Steele for alienation of affection and adultery, and sought a total of $300,000 from Steele in punitive and compensatory damages. In the spring of 1973, the case finally reached the Court of Common Pleas, presided over by Judge James Kilbane (no relation to Owen). The suit charged that back in November of 1968 Steele had alienated the affections of Swartz's wife and that "criminal con-

versation" between Barbara and Steele—a term that
denoted the rarely used civil counterpart of adultery—had taken place between them at that time.
The suit had been pending when Steele had written
to that Atlanta businessman on behalf of Owen Kilbane, seeking "substantial redress" for "alienation
of affections and criminal conversation, both of
which are subsisting rights of action under the laws
of the State of Ohio."

When Steele took the stand in his own defense in
the Swartz case, he developed selective amnesia. He
testified that he didn't remember having an affair
with Barbara before his wife's death, even though
in 1969 he had admitted that affair both to newspapers and to the police; now, he insisted, it was a
blank period in his memory. Those motel registra-
tion cards of 1968, which he had signed, were no
longer in his mind, nor could he remember whether
he'd ever had dinner with Barbara before her
divorce. When Barbara took the stand, however, she
admitted that she'd had sexual relations with Steele
prior to her own divorce, in numerous motels and
other places of assignation; she testified that her
marriage to Swartz had been a bad one, and that
she had not had sexual relations with Swartz since
the time she saw him in a bowling alley with another
woman in mid-1968.

The jury of six men and two women rather quickly
found Steele guilty and ordered that he pay Swartz
$20,000 in compensative and $25,000 in punitive
damages. After the verdict Barbara ran out in the
hall and was heard to exclaim, "That man [Swartz].

He already has my house and my children, and now $45,000. It's so unfair!" Steele planned an appeal.

I started talking to johns. It was easy. We were keeping the prostitution apartments under surveillance, which revealed the regular visits of certain automobiles and their male occupants. I ran the license plates through the Ohio motor vehicles' registry and came up with names, addresses, and phone numbers. One man, for instance, was in real estate, and I simply made an appointment to see him. I told him that he'd been seen repeatedly entering and leaving an apartment that housed known prostitutes, and that while I wasn't going to charge him with anything, we might need him to testify that prostitution was indeed going on at that location. This particular guy saw nothing wrong in what he'd been doing; he was divorced, claimed that his business left him little time for dating, and admitted that he used the services of the women in a manner he considered therapeutic. His information, along with that obtained from dozens of other customers and observers, went into a file to document the patterns of activity; once we'd accumulated enough of it, we could go to the courts, ask for search warrants, and make some raids.

To add to the pattern documentation, we used an old green surveillance truck. In the early morning hours, dressed in work clothes, we'd drive up to Kilbane's residences and business locations, throw his garbage in the truck, and haul it away. Before getting rid of it in appropriate dumps, we'd comb through it. No single piece by itself provided much information, but looking through the piles could yield an index of where he shopped, what sort of creditors he had, how many bottles of liquor per week he (and the prostitution operation's customers) were consuming.

You don't put in a report that you've hijacked a suspect's garbage to find out what he's up to. Rather, the information so gathered would end up in a paragraph that began. "An informed source reports that . . ." We also used the van for another job: surveillance of Kilbane's new A-frame residence in the far suburbs. I'd driven by the place a few times and noticed that a house was going up a few hundred yards farther along the isolated road. The workmen there didn't seem to show up on the weekends, so we'd pull up on a Saturday or Sunday, take out some carpentry tools, and use them to conceal long-lens photography equipment. We established who came to visit the wolf in his lair, noting vehicles registered to some of the henchmen, to the prostitutes, and to various other hangers-on.

I also kept in close touch with Tex, one of Owen's lieutenants, and one evening brought another agent with me to talk to Tex in his home. My partner was nervous. "How do you know Tex is not setting us up?" the agent asked me when Tex went to the bathroom. "He could've disappeared so Kilbane could come out and kill us."

No such thing happened, and, a bit later in the conversation, I asked Tex what he would do in case things got rough. Tex went into a drawer, pulled out a large revolver, and turned to show it to me. My nervous partner jerked out his service revolver, and suddenly there were two men with weapons staring one another down in a living room. I screamed for calm, asked Tex to first put his weapon down, which he did, and then told my colleague to do the same. A jittery peace was thus restored. Clearly, though, things were approaching the boiling point.

On Owen's side of the fence, there was a lot of heartache. His prostitutes were, as might be expected, emotionally fragile. According to some of my sources within the Kilbane organization, Nancy Mason had gone over the edge, spent some time in a mental institution, and then moved into the Hillcrest motel and ceased turning tricks for a while. Maxie was frequently on the verge of tears. Carol Braun had volatile ups and downs, often threatening to get out of the business, and Diane had made similar protestations. Accordingly, Owen had been recruiting more prostitutes, setting them up in outlying apartments, and sometimes delegating authority over them to his lieutenants.

I spent some time talking with Diane and with other sources, trying to get the facts right about the trip she and Carol had made to Atlanta, which I had first learned about from a source of Andy Vanyo's. Our late-night conversations were becoming very fruitful. Diane had stolen the trick books once, and I figured she could take them again. From time to time, she'd be able to do so, and to give them to me. I'd receive them from her at two or three in the morning, rush down to the FBI office and copy them, then return them to her before dawn. The list of names and phone numbers was quite extensive. The difficulties of being a prostitute were suggested by many of the notations about the johns: "troublemaker," "big mouth when drunk," "only take by himself," "don't mess with," "sprayed Mace by accident, he's OK." Every time I copied a trick book and returned it, I was not only building the base for our prosecution, but I was also demonstrating to Diane that I was as good as my word, because I didn't arrest her and I prevented any harm to her by returning the books before anyone knew they were missing. Though still in Owen's employ, Diane had become very willing to help destroy his operation.

An aside about these trick books and the copies I made: They were of overweening interest to the local police jurisdictions and to many newspaper and other media reporters in the Cleveland area, all of whom clamored to be permitted to look at and/or copy them. In this instance, the FBI's insistence on keeping information private when it doesn't directly impact on a prosecution prevented the list of names from getting out and embarrassing the "thousands" of customers of the Kilbane prostitution enterprise, some of whom were respected doctors, lawyers, city officials, and businessmen. Some agents in my FBI office wondered whether the newsmen and police wanted the books just for information or to compromise the men listed in them.

Those same agents were beginning to razz me again about the Kilbane case, saying that for all the time I spent on it, it wasn't going anywhere. I discussed the Atlanta episode with Marty McCann, and he helped me understand that we could now charge Kilbane with violating several more stat-utes—ITAR-Extortion and the White Slave Traffic Act (WSTA). These duly went into the title blocks, as we called them in our slang, of my newer reports and served to quiet down the critics.

In fact, every time the case seemed about to die, McCann revived it by finding new statutes that the Kilbanes had violated, thus giving me another few months in which to investigate it. Both he and I knew that the real interest lay beyond the prostitution, in solving the murder of Marlene Steele.

As we continued our surveillance and built the case against Kilbane, I kept up my late-night talk sessions with my best source, Diane. She had heard many stories about murders, some from Owen directly, others from his associates, principally Carol Braun. That Owen had had Arnie Prunella killed. That Owen had had a hand in killing Judge Steele's wife. That Owen had somehow hastened the death of his grandfather. All of these things were possible, and we moved to check them out. (Kilbane's grand-mother, when interviewed later by the IRS, believed that Owen and the judge were bilking her out of her late husband's estate but insisted that her hus-band had died of natural causes.)

We looked for Mrs. Prunella, trying to get her to tell what she knew about her own late husband's disappearance, and I kept trying to pry more infor-mation from Diane about the Steele murder. On another night, after all her tricks had gone home, as we sat talking I brought up to Diane the subject of Marlene's murder and Owen's probable involve-ment in it.

"Oh, Carol and me and him talked about that from Atlanta." During their long phone call, Carol had accused Owen of having a hand in the Steele murder. Also, in Diane's own conversation with Owen, he had as much as admitted his involvement in it, as well—perhaps in order to frighten the two prostitutes into returning to Cleveland and his employ.

This was terrific information, since it confirmed what people on the street had said—but it was still mostly secondhand. There had been no tape recording of the conversation between Diane and Owen, and if Owen were to be put on the witness stand, he could easily dismiss Diane's report as having been her interpretation of what he'd said.

It's an axiom in law enforcement circles that information doesn't come gushing out all at once, but in little drops. That's why good investigators keep going over and over the same territory with a witness or a source, trying to squeeze out those extra drops. On my next visit to Diane, I again steered the conversation around to the murder.

"Well, you know, Robinson did that," she said.

A younger agent might have jumped and said, "Robinson? Who's he? Give me his phone number!" Such a reaction, of course, would have blown everything by allowing the informant to learn the incredible value and stunning nature of the revelation—and possibly permitting the informant to fend off any further inquiries or even send the agent on a wild-goose chase. So, although my heart was pounding inside, I had to appear diffident about this breakthrough.

"Everybody knows that," I lied, and went on with the conversation, switching it to other subjects. After a few more minutes had gone by, I casually asked where Robinson was now.

"Oh, he's around," Diane said. A bit later in the conversation she referred to Robinson again, this time mentioning his first name, Rickey, and eventually she provided a rather hazy description of Robinson as a young white man of average height with sandy brown hair and beard.

When I left the prostitution apartment, I was elated—an insider to the Kilbane operation had provided me with the piece of the puzzle that had eluded the police for four years: the name of the probable shooter.

Except that it didn't wash. There was no Rickey Robinson, at least not in the files of the various law enforcement agencies or in the telephone books. I sought more information from Diane, from Tex, and from other informants, trying to remain as calm as possible while pursuing the matter. Yes, this Robinson was a man who hung around Kilbane, said one. Another advised that the guy had been paid $1,000 for the murder.

A lot of breaks happen in law enforcement because criminals are incapable of keeping their mouths shut about their nefarious deeds. Over the years Kilbane had bragged about the Steele murder to a fairly large number of people—probably in attempts to intimidate them—and some details about it were known by many different individuals. A third insider in the Kilbane circle indentified Robinson as a man who had a tall blonde wife and a small child. A fourth informant referred to the person who had done the shooting as "the Birdman." There were several people in and around the Kilbane operation who might have warranted such a nickname—for instance, two of the men had names that were the names of birds, and a third operated a pet shop in which Owen had an interest. Then there was a fourth man with a right-sounding name: he not only fit the physical description but also was named Rickey, Rickey Robbins.

Bingo.

As with so many people around Kilbane, Rickey Robbins was a certified loser. In 1973, Robbins was twenty-three and had a long record of troubles. The son of a former Cleveland police officer, Rickey evidently had suffered in his childhood from being in the orbit of this very tough guy. Later people would recall Rickey coming to junior high school with his face beaten black and blue. In eighth grade he started stealing things from school, and in ninth he shot himself in the leg with his father's service revolver. In tenth grade Rickey was involved in some firebombings in his neighborhood and was arrested for torturing a young boy with a cigarette lighter. Then Rickey stole a car and drove it to Florida; during a scuffle at the time of his arrest there, he was shot in the foot. Unlike Owen Kilbane, for Robbins's crime he was not sent to a hard-time youth prison, but he did go to a more moderate reform school. In the summer of 1968, two days after he turned eighteen, he was arrested for pouring gasoline on a neighbor's home and threatening to burn it down.

Faced with a possible adult conviction, Robbins

had taken the road that many a young man before him had trod. A judge permitted him to join the marines rather than go to jail. For many tough boys, this sort of deal can be a good thing; a stint in the service straightens them out. Not Rickey. He had gone through basic training but then went AWOL and screwed up in other ways. Finally, even though the war in Vietnam was at white heat, he had been chucked out of the service, though with an honorable discharge. One fact from his military career intrigued me: I had been very briefly at the Oakland Army Terminal in January of 1969, on my way back from a tour of duty with the military police in Thailand. Rickey had also been passing through Pendleton at that time—on his way home, AWOL. His AWOL dates began just before the night on which Marlene Steele had been shot.

After he had gotten out of the marines, in July of 1969, Robbins had been involved in another shooting incident, together with Marty Kilbane and Terry Ward, another young Vietnam vet who hung around Owen. The whole bunch had gotten into an altercation with someone equally young and tough, a motorcycle gang member. The fight had started with vehicles cutting one another off in a parking lot and had escalated to a point at which Ward had fired five shots into the chest and legs of Donald Phillipone. Robbins had also attempted to fire another weapon at the man, and both were indicted for attempted murder, along with Marty Kilbane and another young man. Bob Steele had gotten all of them off by showing that the gang member had sideswiped the Kilbane bunch's car and then had attacked them. This, Steele argued, had triggered Ward's Vietnam memories, provoking the veteran to automatically pick up a handy gun and fire it. Fortunately, Phillipone did not die, and all of the Kilbane bunch, including Rickey Robbins and Ward, were found not guilty.

The connection between Steele and Robbins had been there for a while, but though we now knew it, we didn't have enough evidence to arrest Rickey Robbins, nor even enough to form the basis of a successful interrogation. In the interim between 1969 and 1973, Robbins had settled down, a satellite to Kilbane. He evidently did so reluctantly. Robbins had married his girlfriend Sandy, who already had one child, and they then had a child of their own. So Rickey had four people to support, and Owen was his best source of money. That Rickey had these family ties made him less likely to leave town, and permitted us time to accumulate more information about him.

Tex had heard a story about an earlier murder that Robbins was believed to have committed. Tex hadn't been at the scene, he told us, but the story had made the rounds. In July of 1968, many black ghettos of the country had gone up in flames; there had been terrible troubles in Cleveland, and in headline-grabbing incidents several white policemen had been killed by blacks. Robbins, the son of a policeman, had brooded over that, and at a barbecue party, after a bout of drinking, Robbins took out a gun and announced that he was going to use it to shoot the first black person he saw. (In my opinion, Kilbane and his entire circle were quite racist, very nearly white supremacists.) To prove his intentions, Robbins carved the letter N into the head of a bullet, then left the party. Later on that night, a well-known and respected local black folksinger named Tedd Browne was found dead in his car, shot through the head at an intersection in Cleveland Heights not far from the site of the party. Still later that evening, questioned by friends, Robbins wouldn't admit to having killed Browne, but he wouldn't flatly deny it. Shortly after this incident Robbins had firebombed the house of his neighbor, made his deal with a judge, and joined the marines.

Tedd Browne had been an unusual and gifted man of forty-four, anything but a rabble-rousing black firebrand. Rather, he had earned his living as a folksinger in clubs whose clientele was predominantly white. During the Glenville riots, Browne had been in Cincinnati, where he had made a religious recording. The night of the murder, he and his wife had gone to a Catholic church in Collinwood to make a formal renewal of their marriage vows. The priest drove Browne's wife, Inez, home to stay with the couple's three boys, while Browne went to see his lawyer to firm up plans for opening a bar and nightclub of his own. It was while returning home from this meeting that Browne had stopped his station wagon at a traffic light, and had been accosted and shot.

I couldn't really pursue the Browne case further at this time, since all I had to go on was an informant's tip. The Prunella disappearance was in a somewhat different category, thought to be directly connected to my target, Owen Kilbane. So I looked into that.

Word on the streets told us that Marsha Prunella had a narcotics beef with the Cleveland police and would talk to the FBI in exchange for their getting her out of that predicament. Marty McCann and I promised that we'd put in a good word for her with the Cleveland authorities, and in the spring of 1973 she agreed to speak to us.

As with many of the other women in this story, Marsha was still a relatively young woman from a working-class background who had gotten into prostitution. Other members of the Prunella family were also on the fringes of the business, and Arnie, her husband, had been a pimp. Arnie and Owen had been both rivals and allies. Marsha recalled that in the spring of 1969, a few months after the murder of Marlene Steele, Arnie had been involved in a complicated scheme with Owen Kilbane. Arnie had devised a "special method" that he felt certain could "break the casinos" at Las Vegas, and convinced Owen to put up some front money for the attempt. Twice Owen gave Arnie money, and twice he dutifully went to Las Vegas and came back empty-handed. Arnie pleaded for another chance, and Owen gave him a third stake, and Arnie prepared to go to Las Vegas again. By this point, Marsha had had enough of Arnie and had skipped to New York City with a friend, even advising Owen where she was going. Marsha returned to the Cleveland area in May or June with her girlfriend, and the two women took up temporary residence in a suburban motel. Owen knew where they were, and came to visit them a few times, and expressed the notion that Arnie had beat him out of a considerable amount of money.

After that—boom—Arnie had disappeared, and that was all Marsha would say she knew. We tried to get from Marsha an admission that Kilbane had had something to do with her husband's disappearance, but for the record she would admit nothing more than she had had occasional contact with Owen in the intervening years and friends told her that he was still running a prostitution operation.

We had learned from other sources that Marsha's involvement with Owen since Arnie's disappearance hadn't been as casual as she painted it. These sources reported that some time after Arnie had vanished, Owen drove by Marsha's residence in one of his flashy cars, picked up Marsha and her young son, and took them for a drive. When they reached a highway along Lake Erie, Owen gathered up the young boy in his arms, pointed out into the lake, and told the boy that his father was out there, sleeping with the fishes.

The story recounts a crude and quite effective way of instructing Marsha to remain silent about the connection between Owen and Arnie. But how had word of the lakeside drive gotten on the street? It could only have been put there by Marsha herself or by Owen. Not much progress for us on the Prunella murder, either.

Kilbane's sidekick John Schillar got into a scrape in May of 1973, one that could have exposed the prostitution operation to undue scrutiny and ruined our own evolving case. On the grounds of the Hill-crest motel, Schillar took out a shotgun and winged a young man in the leg, for no other apparent reason than to assert his power around the place. Schillar was arrested by the police and taken to jail, but Robert Steele showed up and asked the prosecution to lower the charges against Schillar because the shooting had been both accidental and in defense of Schillar's employer's property. The deal was made, and Schillar, Kilbane, and company must have felt pretty good about it. In their view, they could now shoot people openly and not be prose-cuted for it.

One day in the late spring of 1973 I received a call at the FBI office from an old friend of mine, Ken Joseph. Ken had been the senior resident agent of the Lansing, Michigan, FBI office when we had met in the graduate program at Michigan State Univer-sity. He had completed a doctorate there and was now high up in the Bureau. A new and refurbished FBI Academy was shortly to be opened at Quantico. The function of the Academy was going to change; it was going to become a center for advanced research and information gathering, as well as a training facility for police from all over the country, and Ken wanted me to join the staff. I wasn't sure that this was what I ought to do, so Ken proposed an interesting test drive: come to the Academy for one term as a class counselor to a group of police officers attending the FBI National Academy. The FBINA offers a three-month course for midlevel managers in local police work; it is given four times a year, and is known throughout the world as the West Point of law enforcement. As a class counselor, I could try out the notion of being at Quantico, no strings attached; if I liked it, then perhaps I could transfer there on a more permanent basis.

The idea of going to Quantico intrigued me because my interests were in many ways rather academic. As I thought about it, I realized that I really did want to be at the heart of a growing enterprise in which the FBI would work seriously in the area of deciphering crime and its roots, not just in catching people who broke federal laws. And being at the Academy could lead to better things. I agreed to Ken's scheme—pending, of course, the approval of my SAC, Fred Fehl.

A few days later, Fehl summoned me into his office and said he'd just gotten off the phone with Joseph. "Do you want to go to Quantico?"

"Yes, sir."

"D'you mean to tell me, you're on *my* organized crime squad, Fred Fehl's squad—anybody would be thrilled to be on that squad; especially for a new agent, it's a plum assignment—and here you are, telling me you want to go and be a *schoolteacher?*"

I tried to explain that it was my understanding that being at the academy as a class counselor was an important step in the Bureau, a way of having your ticket punched to enter higher management, and that of course my ultimate goal was to be just like him, the SAC of an important office.

"So rather than train with me, you want to go and work for Jim Cotter?" Cotter was head of the

FBINA; rumor had it, he and Fehl didn't see eye to eye.

"Maybe just use the experience, sir."

Fehl dismissed me from the office, saying he'd take the request under advisement. A week or so later, he summoned me again. Ken Joseph's offer had been for me to be a counselor at the ninety-fifth session of the FBINA, in the fall of 1973. Fehl told me he had rejected that offer and asked what I thought of that. Knowing this to be one of Fehl's usual ploys to feel out an agent and test his loyalty and his response to authority, I responded that I'd wanted to go but would respect his decision.

"Okay," he said, and proceeded to outline a deal. If I was able to get an indictment on the Kilbanes, he would agree to allow me to go to Quantico to be a counselor at the ninety-sixth session of the FBINA, which started in the early months of 1974.

"Yes, sir!"

Obviously, now I had to work fast, and I gathered my material to put it in order to make raids and obtain indictments.

In early June 1973, Owen allowed Diane to take a brief trip out of town—and I decided that the time had come to get her statements down on the record. The question was where and how to do this. Normally, when one of his women went out of town, Owen carefully scrutinized their travel records, down to checking the ticket stubs and times of arrival and departure of the planes. We arranged with the former FBI agent who ran the security division of the airline to have Diane's travel records altered so that Owen couldn't tell that she'd returned a few days early, and when she arrived back in Cleveland we took her to a hotel near the airport and checked her in. Unfortunately for me, the woman behind the desk had recently worked at another hotel in the area, one at which my wife and I had stayed for a month when we first came to Cleveland; this woman recognized me and was chagrined to see me with "another woman." I'm sure she had dastardly thoughts about me, but I tried to ignore them as another agent and I debriefed Diane, typed up the notes, and asked her to sign a sworn statement reflecting what she'd told us. As in all such matters, we advised her of her rights and had her certify that she had completed enough schooling to be able to read and understand what was on the paper. In the statement, Diane admitted to being a prostitute, that she worked for Kilbane, that money had been collected from her by Carol Braun, and that the names of her customers were written down in the trick books. Diane went on to describe the Atlanta escapade in great detail, including what she had heard about the follow-up trip of Marty Kilbane and John Schillar.

Diane wanted desperately to leave prostitution and start a new life, but to defuse the Kilbane operation we needed to have her stay inside it just a bit longer. This was, of course, a terribly dangerous and difficult thing for her to do, but she courageously agreed to do it.

After we were finished obtaining the statement, we returned Diane to the airport and had her call Carol Braun from there to pick her up. With some trepidation, I watched Diane get in the Lincoln Continental and go back into the maelstrom. I couldn't allow her to stay in it much longer without bringing an indictment.

When the FBI has a case to make, that's the point at which we take it to the prosecutors—not before. So when we go, we try to be tremendously prepared and have an overwhelming amount of evidence on which to seek a prosecution. At this point in time, Owen Kilbane was the head of a prostitution operation that employed eight or ten women at four different locations; earlier in the year, one of the women told us, Steele and Kilbane had gone over the trick books and enumerated more than 3,000 customers. Kilbane was on the verge of making a move to take over the distribution of the X-rated movies that his motel featured; that may have been the source of the fight that led to Schillar's wounding of a young man on the premises of the motel. All signs pointed to the idea that Owen was expanding his criminal operations by leaps and bounds and was on the verge of becoming a big-time criminal.

A week after taking Diane's signed statement, we showed it, the corroborating statements taken from the Atlanta businessmen, the surveillance records, and all sorts of other documentary evidence to our Organized Crime Strike Force attorney, David Margolis. He agreed that we had excellent material to support charges of violations of the statutes against ITAR-Extortion and of the WSTA. On these grounds, the government could prosecute not only Owen, but also Carol Braun, Marty Kilbane, and John Schillar. Carol was in the title block because she'd functioned as a manager as well as as a prostitute. Marty Kilbane and Schillar had aided and abetted in the attempted extortion of the Atlanta businessmen.

In addition to arranging to present the matter to a federal grand jury on June 26, Margolis agreed to get Diane into the witness protection program in exchange for her testimony at the grand jury and her help in prosecuting Kilbane and his associates. Now we were ready to roll.

As the grand jury began hearing evidence presented by Margolis and his associates at the end of June, other sources in the Kilbane operation advised me that Owen was getting close to a Puerto Rican woman whom we'll call Fernandez, and that he was cozying up to Rickey Robbins and his wife, Sandy. Owen, Carol Braun, Rick, and Sandy had been seen at a restaurant; afterward, the foursome had gone out to Kilbane's A-frame house, where all four spent the night, and the next day the men had practiced firing pistols behind the house. My source thought that Kilbane, in concert with Robbins, might be getting ready to kill someone.

I had so many informants inside the Kilbane operation that it was becoming a problem to keep them all straight and—more important—to keep them compartmented, so that none of them knew that the other ones were also giving me information. While the grand jury was meeting in secret, I continued to juggle the various Kilbane informants quite successfully until July 5, 1973, when I made a mistake that could have been fatal, and to much more than the case.

Talking with Diane in the apartment, I happened to tell her about an arm of the operation that Kilbane was running in another suburb of Cleveland, a prostitution enterprise that centered around the Fernandez woman. Diane wanted to know all about this, and, like a dumb fool, I told her. Owen was permitting Fernandez to operate out of a different apartment and to act more or less as the manager of operations in that other suburb; and, of course, Owen was sleeping with Fernandez, too. I didn't think much of this exchange of information, and shortly left the apartment.

Then, at 9:30 on the night of July 6, 1973, Diane phoned me, in a panic and fearing for her life. She had told Carol Braun about Fernandez. That had sent Carol into a jealous tizzy, and Carol had confronted Owen—who had just moments ago called Diane and said, "After I have it out with Carol, I'm coming over to take care of you."

Four

"STRICTLY AN UNOFFICIAL
QUESTION"

Diane quickly filled me on the circumstances of the threat. Earlier in the day, she had casually dropped on Carol the information about the Fernandez woman. All steamed up, Carol dragged Diane into the Lincoln with her, and they went to see Fernandez.

Evidently, in Carol's mind it was okay for Owen to turn out other women as prostitutes, but not for him to sleep with them. Carol considered herself Kilbane's main squeeze and his second-in-command of the prostitution operations; in her view, the Fernandez matter was out of control. At the Fernandez digs, the three prostitutes had quite an argument. After dropping Diane at her apartment, Carol then went on alone to the Hillcrest motel to confront Owen with what she knew about his infidelities and indiscretions. She screamed at him, "You son of a bitch, you're keeping this woman Fernandez on the West Side and working her!," et cetera, et cetera.

"How do you know?" Owen coolly asked Carol.

She immediately told him that the information had come from Diane. That was when Owen had picked up the phone and called Diane. He'd asked Diane what she knew about the matter and how she knew it; when she didn't answer immediately, he said that she was in trouble. "I don't want you and Carol running off again like you did in January," Owen had said. There was something he had to do that evening and so he couldn't come right over, but Kilbane warned Diane that he'd arrive at eight the next morning, and that she'd better have some answers for him then.

On hearing Diane's story I immediately realized what a blunder I'd made by leaking to her the information about Fernandez. All I could do now was try to calm Diane down and rectify the mistake. "I'll be there soon. Don't do anything or phone anyone until I arrive."

With a few calls, even at that late hour I was able to assemble three other agents and our all-purpose green van, and with them I drove over to Diane's apartment complex and was buzzed in. She was crying and shaking. I told her that we weren't going to let any harm come to her. "Pack up everything you own," I ordered, "because we're moving."

"Right now?"

"You've gotta be out before Owen gets here. So let's get on with it!"

It was a half hour after midnight, and we were throwing things in boxes when the apartment phone rang. It was Carol Braun, who said she was on the way over and that Owen was not far behind her.

We agents retreated out of the apartment but

stayed close by in case of an emergency. Carol arrived, remained with Diane for more than two hours, and then left, carrying a small package.

As soon as Carol was out of sight, the other agents and I went back in. Diane told me that she and Carol had cried together about wanting to leave Owen, and that when Carol departed, she took the trick books with her and advised Diane not to do anything "foolish," for example, not to go to the police if she really intended to leave town and the prostitution business. Owen would arrive at eight in the morning, Carol had told Diane.

By four in the morning, the other agents and I, dressed in casual attire, had finished the packing and started carrying Diane's clothes and other personal belongings down the stairwell, through the lobby, and out to the van. Everything went smoothly until a Euclid patrol car and two policemen pulled up and the cops got out and braced us.

"Could we see some identification, gentlemen?"

I didn't want to give away the operation by proving to the police that we were FBI agents; I'd put too much time and energy into pursuing Kilbane to have some local cop with a big mouth blow it for me at the very moment when we were before a grand jury. So without hesitation I reached for my wallet and brought out a phony driver's license that I always carried, to go along with the phony license plate on the surveillance van, and handed it over to the policemen. (You'd be surprised how many times FBI agents have pulled such stunts on local police and vice versa.) I knew that the police had no way of checking my information before the opening of normal business hours, and that despite my activity at this time of night, I looked pretty clean and upstanding.

"What are you doing here at four in the morning?"

"Well, Officer, our lease is up at 8:00 A.M, and we have to get out of here before then. We have an attorney working to keep us from being evicted, but all that is taking a lot of time and paperwork, so we have to move now before they come to evict us in the morning."

"Well, all right. Try not to make any noise."

The cops weren't wholly convinced, so they parked their patrol car a block away and kept us under surveillance while they let us continue moving things up and down the stairs and into the van. Just before dawn, we finally had Diane out of there and drove her to a motel in another town.

With Diane safely hidden, we next had to defuse the situation so that Owen wouldn't hurriedly close up shop and destroy the evidence of his prostitution operation. In the motel, I asked Diane to make a call to Kilbane. She was shaking so much that I actually dialed the number myself and then handed the phone to her. She told Kilbane that she'd taken only her clothes, not any furniture, but that she had left because she was finished being a prostitute. She told him that Carol had taken the trick books and was also planning to leave. A wealthy boyfriend—a Cleveland attorney, Diane said—was going to take care of her in the future, in a new location. She wasn't going to the police, Diane advised, but just wanted to leave the game. Owen replied that he didn't need any police hassles since "the man watches me at all times as it is," and suggested that Diane call him after she had a few weeks' rest, because then she might be willing to resume working for him as a prostitute.

Reasoning that Owen would feel that if there were to be a raid, it would happen in the first day or two after Diane had vanished, we let ten days go by. Once the first few days had passed without incident, he resumed normal operations. That was what we wanted, to lull him back to inaction.

I used the intervening time to set up a military-style strike. As case officer, I was in charge of planning the raid, and as a man who'd spent ten years on active military service, I drafted it with a thoroughness that even surprised my boss, Marty McCann. We would have several teams of people and would all hit separate operations simultaneously, so that none of the targets would have a chance to call and alert any of the others that we might be on the way. I also wrote out what evidence we'd attempt to collect from each location and instructions for the places to which we would take our targets for questioning after we'd picked them up.

On July 17, when the raids were scheduled to take place, my wife went into labor for the birth of our third child. I drove her to the hospital. Once she was in good hands there, far more knowledgeable hands than mine, I turned to go to work. In pain, she begged me not to go on the raids just then, because she feared for my life. I won't say I ignored her plea, but wild horses weren't going to keep me from these raids, and we both knew it.

Starting at seven in the evening, a whole phalanx of FBI agents, search warrants in hand, raided several of the prostitution apartments, Kilbane's A-frame residence, and his business office at the Hillcrest motel. Seven o'clock might seem an odd time to begin a raid, but not a raid on a prostitution operation, which works principally through the evening hours. Only Marty Kilbane was home at the A-frame when agents pulled up in force and showed him the warrant. He told them there were guns in the house, several rifles, and a pistol, and that they were all registered weapons. The raiding party took the guns anyway, but their main haul was a great many records of the prostitution operation, records of loans, and a half-dozen different bank books for as many accounts. Some records were neat, orderly ledgers and trick books, while others were sloppy, newspaper clippings and odd bits of paper with phone numbers scribbled on them. The most absurd detail in the house: two fish tanks, one containing a piranha and the other converted to a terrarium that was home to a live tarantula.

At Carol Braun's residence, hit by another group of agents who were accompanied by Capt. Warren Goodwin of the Euclid police, the most important records were seized—address books, trick books, and other documentary proof of the prostitution operation. Carol didn't want to talk or even to sign a list of what was seized until she had talked to her lawyer. Bob Steele was called. Steele advised her to cooperate, but she still wouldn't sign the list. That didn't matter much, for we painstakingly inventoried everything. When the Bureau goes in, we do so in a thorough manner; part of the objective is not to make careless mistakes that could later be used by a defendant's legal counsel as grounds for throwing a case out of court or overturning a conviction.

I led the raid on Owen's office at the Hillcrest motel. The nattily dressed, red-bearded Kilbane was there, surprised and annoyed at us and our search warrants. He knew he had seen me before but couldn't quite figure out where or when. Braced in his office, Kilbane didn't raise too much of a fuss; as he was surrounded by a lot of agents, it would have been dumb of him to do so. More prostitution records and several more guns were found in and around the motel office. One of the guns was an unregistered, illegal weapon, a sawed-off .22 caliber rifle that looked like a hit man's weapon. Its presence would permit the adding of a gun charge to the racketeering and white slavery charges in the title block of my next report.

What a haul! We'd need some time to organize the material and get it in shape to present to the grand jury.

Before I was finished with the raid and its immediate sequels, the gathering and listing of evidence, it was the following day. Then I finally felt that I could relax my vigilance for a few moments and go and see my new child. By that time, my wife and newborn son had already returned home, and I had my first glimpse of my son. I'd missed the entire period they'd spent in the hospital. I can't really say that my wife forgave my absence at the moment of our son's birth, but as the sister of two Chicago police-men as well as the wife of an FBI agent, she knew all too well that some heartaches come with the territory.

FBI agents are sometimes depicted as cold and heartless, their efforts aimed only at rounding up criminals. In this instance, we were also spending our energy looking after several former prostitutes, whom we had sequestered in outlying motel rooms, young women who wanted out of the prostitution operation and out of the life. At Diane's request, we made plans not only for her testimony, but also for her return to her parents in another state. Maxie, too, was having difficulties; a day after the raid, she suffered terrible abdominal pains and had to be rushed to a hospital emergency room with a septic infection. Had we not intervened, it is likely that she would not have gotten adequate care in time, and she might have died. She was involved in a messy civil court case with her former husband and wanted nothing more than to start a new life for herself and her young child. It had been to support the child, in part, that she had agreed to become a prostitute for Kilbane.

Our care and feeding of these women were matters that did not get into the newspapers, though the raids themselves did make local headlines. From the affidavits that we had to file in order to get our warrants, reporters plucked good stories. They also did some digging of their own. As one report in the Cleveland *Press* concluded, "Apparently, business [at the X-rated motel] was good. Records at the Auto

Title Bureau show that in 1973 Kilbane purchased three new cars for $23,000, including the two cars allegedly used in call girl operations."

Toting up the value of Kilbane's assets, we found that his various cars, a boat, real estate, and other holdings were worth nearly $850,000, aside from whatever might be in his bank accounts. This amount of property was far in excess of his reported income for the past few years, and we advised the IRS of that, and they started investigating what he might owe them in the way of back taxes. The stories behind some of the property were also interesting. It seemed that the motel had been bought for an inflated price from a notorious old-time Cleveland gangster, Shondor Birns, known as an enforcer for the mobs. The price appeared to have been inflated to allow the mortgage to cover an outstanding tax lien; moreover, the bank that had given the mortgage was known to be rather shady itself. Kilbane's idol, Danny Greene, had started his career working for Birns and had perhaps been the intermediary in the transaction between the elder statesman of crime and the young would-be mobster.

In those days after the raid, I saw a good deal of my real adversary in all this, Bob Steele, who as Kilbane's lawyer had a lot of work to do. He first showed up at the Kilbane residence shortly after we had hit it, and Marty McCann remembers him there. Steele was exceedingly nervous, chain-smoking, hands trembling, as he watched the agents inventory the prostitution records. In the days following the raid, Steele was at our offices much of the time, looking over our lists of things taken from the various Kilbane premises. He acted in a professionally competent manner, but our thoroughness had left him little to do. Kilbane and Steele were entitled to look at the affidavits that we filed. From these documents, they were easily able to figure out that Diane was going to testify against the prostitution operation and part of the government's case was going to be based on the aborted trip to Atlanta of Diane and Carol. Articles about the raids mentioned the old connection between Kilbane and Steele, even repeating that they had had lunch two days before Marlene's murder. I'm sure that in those days of hanging around the FBI office Steele figured out that I was after him, but he said nothing about it.

If my interest in his wife's murder had at all sagged, it was revived just then because of the direct interest taken by Capt. Warren Goodwin of the Euclid police department, who had accompanied one of the prostitution raids. Goodwin told me that he'd been one of the first people at the Steele home on the morning of Marlene Steele's murder, arriving perhaps a half hour after Steele's first call to the police dispatcher. From the presence of dried blood and the absence of oozing wounds, it had been apparent to Goodwin and to other officers that Marlene had been dead for more than thirty to forty minutes.

Another person to come forward in the wake of the raids on the Kilbane prostitution operation was Betty Prunella, the mother of Arnie Prunella, who wanted to tell us that there was no doubt in her mind that Kilbane was behind the disappearance and presumed death of her son. She had recently bumped into a former prostitute who also had known Arnie and her daughter-in-law, Marsha; this woman had told Betty to forget about her son, because he was dead. Betty had asked how she knew, and the woman said, "I just know." We learned from other sources that this woman was a prostitute who worked directly for Kilbane.

When a fellow agent and I showed up at the Hillcrest motel again on August 2 to slap a subpoena on Kilbane, Owen was belligerent, cursing us out, telling us what anatomically difficult feats we could perform with the pieces of paper.

"It's just a subpoena for you to testify before the grand jury," I said, trying to calm him down. This wasn't an arrest, I explained, but I did need to deliver other subpoenas to Carol Braun and Nancy Mason.

Once we were inside Owen's office and it was clear that we weren't going to manhandle him, Owen started talking about the searches and I had to stop him and advise him of his rights. We carry an "Interrogation: Advice of Rights" form, and I showed one to him. He wouldn't sign it but did read it and say he understood it and wanted to continue our talk. To show me his good faith, he telephoned Nancy Mason, who was staying in another room at the motel, and advised her to come to the front desk and receive her subpoena. Carol Braun was away, Kilbane said, but he'd try to get in touch with her so she also could be served.

"Were you the guy who talked to me during that raid at Chateau La Cave?"

I told him I was, and also answered his questions as to whether I was the agent in charge of the ITAR-Prostitution matter pending against him, and whether that was my name on the affidavits. Yes, that was me.

Owen appeared flattered and fascinated at the wide-ranging efforts directed against him by the FBI. If the FBI was that interested in him, he seemed to reason, he must be someone important. Our pursuit evidently fed his fantasy of becoming a master criminal and joining with Danny Greene to take the leadership of the Irish mob in Cleveland. Perhaps that was why, in this office meeting, Owen acted as though our attention was a mark of distinction for him.

Nancy Mason came into the office, and we handed her the subpoena. She hung around as Owen continued to chat.

"The thing that took place at Atlanta," Kilbane began again. "You realize that telephone call was made from Atlanta to me, don't you?" His argument was that he hadn't phoned Braun, she had phoned him, and thus he had done nothing wrong. I didn't say anything, merely nodded to show that I'd heard what he'd said. He started to discuss the trip to Atlanta made by his brother, Marty, and John Schillar, then thought better of it and said he didn't want to talk about that just then.

Kilbane then rambled on about how impressed he'd been when he'd taken a tour of the FBI building in Washington, D.C. He wanted to know how many agents had been killed in the line of duty. "Not nearly as many as the pimps who've been killed in their line of duty," I retorted. He liked this response, and then realized that his question might be perceived as a threat; he advised that it had been "strictly an unofficial question" by which he'd meant nothing untoward. I guess he was so used to threatening people, he just did it automatically. By the time we left, Owen was starting to be downright friendly.

Just because the raids had been successful and had reaped large quantities of materials for the prosecutors, I wasn't going to sit back and let the legal system handle everything from then on. In the period between the raid and Owen's appearance before the grand jury, I regularly trawled among my informants for information on Kilbane and more evidence that could buttress our case. I learned that Owen had boasted to associates that we had seized his business records but had missed his hiding place for a fake driver's license and a stash of marijuana. He'd also bragged that if the FBI had waited a few more years to hit him, he would have been too big for anyone to bring down.

We didn't expect much out of the federal grand jury testimony of Owen Kilbane, Carol Braun, and Nancy Mason, but we had hopes that what Maxie and some of the other women had to say would prove more fruitful. Kilbane would have liked to prevent any of them from testifying. He couldn't get hold of Diane, since we were keeping her whereabouts a secret, but after the raid and her days in the hospital Maxie had returned to her old apartment, not to conduct prostitution operations but just to live while her civil court case was pending.

On August 4, a few days before Maxie was to testify to the federal grand jury on the Kilbane matter, she received a call from Owen telling her to keep quiet when she did testify. "I may have to do some time," he admitted to her, and "if I have to, I'll do it." He offered the opinion that the case was not a big deal. A short time later, Bob Steele phoned Maxie and told her that she ought to get out of the state to avoid a subpoena. When she explained to Steele that the subpoena had already been given to her, he advised Maxie that in front of the grand jury she should say as little as possible. Should she be offered immunity, however, she should "tell all."

Carol Braun called Maxie next, and wanted to visit her on August 8 in order to prepare her before the grand jury appearance scheduled for the next day. It was after Carol's call that Maxie phoned me. She was on the edge of panic and highly concerned that Carol would attempt to intimidate her and threaten her into refusing to testify.

"We'll protect you—but will you also let us tape the meeting?" I asked. Maxie said she would, and another agent and I hurried over with electronic monitoring devices and a consent form for Maxie to sign. In no time at all, we had her apartment wired with enough microphones so that if anyone breathed heavily, we'd capture it. We agents then retreated to a van parked just outside the building, where through the earphones we would be able to hear every word being said. We listened to this not only to obtain evidence, but also to be near enough to provide security for Maxie, should there be any problem.

Carol Braun arrived just after both she and Owen had testified. Each had carried into the grand jury room a paper typed up by Steele, which stated their constitutional grounds for their refusal to answer any questions other than to provide the grand jury with their correct names. "They're a bunch of idiots," Carol characterized the grand jurors to Maxie, "damn bunch of farmers who don't know nothing but picking corn and shit. Ya know? Owen calls 'em, what the hell does he call 'em, he calls them cattle. . . . You don't have to give your address or nothing else. Your age—nothing. Yeah. That's all you've got to say, ya know."

So far, there was nothing illegal about the advice that Carol Braun was giving to Maxie, but the tone of the conversation soon turned in that direction. Carol advised Maxie to "change your handwriting" in order to avoid giving a true sample, and admitted that she had done so: "I mean, I can write nice and neat if I want to, but I just scribbled."

Then my ears perked up. At the time that Carol had given the handwriting sample, she'd announced that she should be paid for doing so and (she told Maxie) "someone" had said to her, " 'Well now, walk right into Federal Bureau any day; we'd be glad to give you $2,000 for just being a witness.' "

"Who said that—the judge?" Maxie asked.

"No, this asshole FBI guy, Ressler. Fucker. He won't leave me alone for nothing."

In our listening post, my shoulder was punched.

"Maybe he likes you," Maxie teased.

"Shit! 'Likes me,' my ass. He'd like me to *talk*. That's what he'd like. Like me to sing a little."

"Are you sure you're not winking at him?"

"Oh, man, I hate that guy. Oh, I can't stand him."

What a pity.

Carol went on to reveal something of Kilbane's defense strategy: they would paint Diane as "nothing but a drug addict ... crazy ... nuts." Unfortunately, however, "she knew more than anyone knew, boy.... She not gonna get away with it, really."

Maxie was sophisticated enough to know a bell when she heard it rung, and she continued to press for details about what Owen was planning to do to Diane because Diane was testifying against him. Both women acknowledged that Diane would be put in some sort of relocation and change-of-identity program, where she would ostensibly remain protected by the government. Nonetheless, Maxie asked, "You mean she's had it?"

"You think that broad is gonna live the rest of her life? Are you kidding me? ... Shit, I'll get her myself if I can."

When I heard this line, I thought it was significant, because it meant that in the title block of my future reports I could now add another charge against Owen and Carol: obstruction of justice.

"That seems impossible," Maxie responded to Carol's pledge to "get" Diane. She reasoned: "If you moved to California and changed your name, how would I ever know?"

"You don't realize the people that Owen knows. Ya know what I'm saying? Like man, it might be five years, ten years, fifteen years from now, but somebody will run into her. She'll open her mouth the wrong way to the wrong person. It'll get back."

"I can't imagine Owen being violent, though, and actually—"

"Oh, he ain't gonna do it himself. Are you kidding me? There's more people right now to do it in a minute, to cover him in a minute, to come to him and say, 'Hey, Owen, if you want me to do something, just tell me, just say the word.'"

In another conversation that Maxie held on the phone with Kilbane himself—while I listened— Owen reiterated the theme that the FBI would only protect a witness up until the time of trial. "I dare anyone to stand on a witness stand and point their finger at me—they'll lose their hand."

Despite the presence of an FBI agent in the room, Maxie was so frightened that tears gushed from her eyes and she sobbed into the phone until the conversation was ended. It was all we could do to get her to testify a bit to the grand jury before hurrying her out of town and back into the bosom of her family. Kilbane—raided or not, on the edge of being indicted or not—was continuing to threaten those around him. He had to be put away, and soon.

Five

"MOVED TO THE TOP OF THE HIT LIST"

A period when you have witnesses before a grand jury is often a most fruitful one for investigation, because you've stirred up the hornets' nest and the insects' reactions may reveal even more about their activities and directions. Our sources told us that Owen Kilbane was losing control of his motels since he was now unable to make payments on his loans. Moreover, afraid that his telephones were being tapped and his residences were under surveillance—we *were* watching his home and motels, but we weren't tapping his phones, by the by—he was conducting his business warily, from pay phones. With his raided prostitution activities shut down, he tried to get money from other activities and to initiate out-of-town and hidden prostitution operations, but did so with little success. He "gave" several of his cars to former associates and to his brother-in-law in an attempt to keep the IRS from seizing them; similarly, he "sold" his A-frame to another friend.

On September 20, 1973, the federal grand jury returned a nine-count indictment against Owen and Marty Kilbane, Carol Braun, and John Schillar for violations of various statutes, among them those dealing with ITAR-Prostitution, the WSTA, and extortion. Should the accused be convicted on all counts, they could receive up to twenty years in jail and fines up to $30,000 apiece. Bench warrants were issued for the arrests of all four.

I had the satisfaction of arresting Owen Kilbane at his residence, advising him of his rights, and cuffing and carting him downtown to be photographed, fingerprinted, and otherwise processed into the criminal justice system. He'd known this was coming, and was calm. With Steele by his side, he pleaded not guilty, posted a $1,000 surety bond, and was able to go home again within a few hours, though not before an IRS agent informed him that a "jeopardy assessment" of more than $85,000 was being carried out against him for unreported activities and income dating back to 1968. That afternoon, other IRS agents seized Owen's boat and three cars and placed liens on all of his property and bank accounts. Schillar was arrested without incident a few days later, and Carol Braun surrendered; both pleaded in a similar fashion to Owen and were released on similar bonds. Marty Kilbane was in Phoenix, staying with a friend, John DiGravio; FBI agents arrested him there. On posting bond Marty, too, was released and told to appear in court in Cleveland on the first of October, along with the others. Later, Judge Robert P. Krupansky of the district court moved the trial date to October 16.

With everyone indicted, we next tried to pump our informants for information on what the Kilbanes and their lawyer, Bob Steele, might do. Remarkably, we found out a great deal, because the Kilbanes seemed congenitally incapable of keeping their mouths shut. We learned, for instance, that Kilbane was under a lot of pressure from his family to change his plea to guilty. Another set of informants told us that various mob characters in the Cleveland area were upset that Kilbane had let his prostitution records get into the hands of the FBI, and that they, too, wanted him to take a fall. Steele was also pushing Owen to plead guilty, other informants alleged, in order to keep the murder of Marlene from surfacing in the court proceedings.

I worked some of the time from the headquarters of the Organized Crime Strike Force in a downtown Cleveland building. One day, standing at the window, I looked out and up. There across the street in the window of his own office was Steele. He noticed me looking at him and stepped back. Thereafter, when I spent time at the strike force I'd make a point of planting myself by the window and gazing at his office. More often than not, I'd catch him coming to his window to peek over at us. Thus was the message conveyed: *We're watching you, Judge Steele.*

The most alarming thing that our informants told us during this period was that Owen had decided that Special Agent of the FBI Bob Ressler was responsible for all his troubles, and that Owen was telling his people, "Ressler has just moved to the top of the hit list."

Was this a credible threat? I knew that Kilbane had arranged the murder of Marlene Steele (though I couldn't yet prove it), and I had received information indicating that he had killed or had arranged the killing of Arnie Prunella. Other stories were circulating that he had organized the execution of a mob figure in Cleveland. On several occasions, when Kilbane's circle of friends used to sit with him and speculate on the many unsolved mob-related murders in the Cleveland area, Kilbane would chuckle and repeat the line: "This whole thing is a big puzzle and I'm the only one who knows where all the parts fit." Moreover, he was known to carry guns and to hang around people who carried guns. So this Special Agent took Kilbane's "top of the hit list" threat seriously.

One night, Carol Braun called me. This was quite a logical thing to have happen; I had pursued her for some time and had let her know—as recently as the handwriting sample incident—that if she wished to spill the beans about Owen, she might fare better in court. She didn't call to offer to turn state's evidence, but she did advise me that Owen had been discussing my assassination. Owen resented what he said was my harassment of him. (It was true that we were pressing hard; after the indictments, we continued to explore possible charges stemming from the illegal sawed-off .22 caliber rifle he owned, and in relation to the attempted blackmail of Maxie.) Owen had suggested to Carol that maybe one night he'd put Carol up to calling me on the pretext of cooperation, but really to lure me to a rendezvous from which I would not return alive. Carol told me she didn't want to have any-thing to do with such a plot, since she was in enough hot water as it was.

After thanking her for the warning, I wrote a memo to the files—in case I never made it home one night, people would know where to look for my killers—and told my boss what was up. Marty McCann immediately got in touch with Irish mob-ster Danny Greene.

"I told Greene that I was hearing things I didn't like," McCann recalls. "People making threats against the life of an agent. I told him I couldn't control what might happen if Owen Kilbane harmed an agent of the FBI."

That call from Carol inviting to me to a spurious rendezvous never materialized. To this day, I don't know whether or not Owen's assassination threat was real, or, if it was, whether Danny Greene quashed it—but nothing happened, and for that I am grateful.

During this time, we learned that another one of the DiGravios, a family who had known the Kil-banes since childhood, might be able to tell us some-thing about the Steele and Prunella murders. So, one night, Cleveland police lieutenant Andy Vanyo and I paid him a visit. He lived in a section known to be controlled by the mob, and we were at risk in such a neighborhood.

"Butch," I called in through a shut door of an apartment, "this is Bob Ressler of the FBI, and I think you know why I want to talk to you."

Andy and I heard an unmistakable sound: that of a shotgun shell being racked into a weapon. We could play that game, too. Rather noisily, I took out my Walther 9mm semiautomatic pistol—a weapon not sanctioned by the Bureau, incidentally—and loudly racked in a round of my own. No response. (Later, Andy would recall that in the hallway my weapon sounded more like a .50 caliber machine gun than a pistol.) Andy got out his own .38 and readied it, too.

We hung around the hallway for a while, but it made absolutely no sense to go in and provoke a gun battle, and Butch wasn't coming out. Eventually, we left. In the early hours of the next morning, we later learned, Butch threw suitcases into his Cadillac and headed for Florida. Several weeks later, off Miami, he and his boat were blown up. The assumption that Butch had been killed because he knew something about the murders that involved Owen Kilbane could not be proved, but it continued to trouble me.

Marty McCann did another favor for me in this period, one he never bothered telling me about until I began to write this book and interviewed him about long-ago events. Judge Krupansky had looked at the indictments, and wondered why an essentially local prostitution matter was cluttering up his federal district court calendar. He made known his displeasure and that he was thinking about throwing the case right out of court. McCann and David Margolis, the departmental prosecutor, hurried over to Judge Krupansky's chambers, where they explained to him that the Kilbane case was far more than a simple prostitution matter, that the real goals were to eventually solve the murders of Marlene Steele and Arnie Prunella. Learning this, Judge Krupansky agreed to let the indictments stand.

Steele, too, was active in this period. He represented a slew of other minor criminal figures beside Owen Kilbane, such as Louis J. "Lumpy Lou" Raffa, a passer of bad checks; Steele told the judge in the Raffa case that his client passed bad checks because he was depressed that his wife had been unfaithful. The judge was not amused, and Raffa went to jail.

There was pressure on Steele to remove himself from Kilbane's side in order to give Owen a better shake from the authorities. Steele resisted it. We figured that he wanted to be Owen's attorney here to control any possibility of Owen offering to turn state's evidence against Steele on other matters if the government dropped the prostitution charge. If that was Steele's strategy, it worked. On October 12, Steele stood by Owen Kilbane and Carol Braun as they showed up in Judge Krupansky's courtroom to plead guilty to one count of ITAR-Prostitution. There had been a bargain with the prosecutors, but it was only to plead to one count in exchange for not being tried on the other eight counts, and in exchange for letting Marty Kilbane and Schillar go free. Sentencing was set for early in December. The maximum penalty for one count was five years in jail and a $5,000 fine. Judge Krupansky wanted to have a probation report completed on Kilbane and Braun before imposing sentence.

My task was completed. Fred Fehl, SAC of the Cleveland office, still couldn't understand why I'd renew my request to leave the shores of Lake Erie and his bailiwick to go to Quantico as a lecturer, but I had done more than keep my side of the deal, having not only achieved an indictment of Kilbane, but a conviction as well, so now Fehl would have to let me go. I received a letter of commendation from the director of the FBI—always a good thing to have in one's personnel file—and a bonus of a few hundred dollars, an amount that loomed larger at the time than it does these days. To have gotten a "stat" was good for me and good for Fred Fehl. So Fehl allowed me to get myself reinvited to Ken Joseph's domain, to be a counselor for the ninety-sixth session of the FBINA, starting in January of 1974.

In late November 1973, lawyer Steele filed a "memorandum in aid of sentence" that was an argument to induce Krupansky to place Owen on probation and not in jail at all. This was the unusually revealing document that I've used earlier in this book to fill in the details of Owen's early years. In it Steele, obviously reflecting information fed to him by Owen, characterized Owen's father as a heavy drinker and his mother as having "intermittent periods of depression and mental illness." Steele's memorandum lauds Owen as a shrewd businessman who overcame a childhood of adversity to build up some legal businesses, and who slipped into prostitution as an attempt to provide a rather harmless community service:

> The Petitioner had accumulated over the years, a list of names of men who were interested in availing themselves of this service. In an effort to provide an outlet for these individuals, many of whom are

*well-known and distinguished residents of the
Cleveland community, and to capitalize in a financial way on this obvious community need, the Peti-
tioner recruited several women to join a joint-
venture with him wherein everyone would gain. . . .*

The argument was that Carol and Diane had gone
to Atlanta "in a jealous rage," that the women in
Kilbane's employ were "free to come and go as
[they] pleased," that the prostitution apartments
were "cleanly and discretely [sic] run," and that
"there was never any attempt to steal from [the
customers]." Vice President Spiro Agnew had
recently resigned under threat of prosecution, the
brief pointed out, and if such a notorious man were
not sent to jail, it was ludicrous to jail Owen Kilbane.
Steele concluded:

*I feel that an effort has been made to oversell the
allegedly sinister aspects of the Defendant's character. In fact, I have always been impressed with his
candor, his great efforts to establish himself in legitimate business endeavors, his loyalty to those associated with him, even to his detriment, and his sincere
desire to rise and advance himself as a business man
in the community.*

Accordingly, Steele offered to act as an unofficial
probation officer, to take upon himself the "moral
responsibility" of assuring Kilbane's compliance
with any conditions set by the court.

Steele didn't get to act as probation officer, but
his work on Kilbane's behalf did have some effect.

The government did drop the other eight charges against Owen and Carol and declined to indict them on the gun and blackmail matters. Judge Krupansky sentenced Owen and Carol each to a year in jail and a $5,000 fine and then, perhaps because of Steele's memorandum, suspended six months of the sentences. I was satisfied with that, even though six months was only a modest sentence, because thereafter Owen would have difficulty reestablishing a prostitution operation and, as a known criminal, would be subject to continued police scrutiny. Krupansky gave them both a month to arrange their affairs before they'd have to start serving their time.

While Owen and Carol were arranging their lives, I tried to tidy up some loose ends before I went to Quantico. Understand that at this point in time I could have walked away from the Steele matter entirely, and would have not been chastised for doing so by the Bureau. I'd done my job, nailed Owen Kilbane, and should have had no further interest in the murder of Marlene Steele, which was entirely a local police problem. But I had never pursued Kilbane just for his own sake and was certainly not going to leave for a new position without trying to put all the ghosts to rest.

So, in December and early January, and again three months later, when I briefly returned from Quantico to Cleveland to finish up some business before transferring permanently to the FBI Academy, I paid a few visits to some important people and called others in for chats.

Principal among my conversational partners was

Rickey Robbins. I left word at various places that I
wanted to see him. At that time, I had business cards
that carried only my name and a phone number—
no FBI identification at all. When Robbins didn't call
in, I took to leaving these cards around where he'd
be sure to see them, on his car windshield, for
instance, or at the houses of his friends. In the wake
of the shutting down of Owen's business activities,
Robbins had gone to work as an auto mechanic. Both
of his children had been diagnosed with physical
problems that were costing a lot of money to treat.
I finally persuaded Sandy, Robbins's wife, to have
her husband come to Cleveland FBI headquarters
to see me.

Andy Vanyo sat in on the session with me. Robbins was nervous, and we were very calm. In fact,
I didn't talk much about the cases at all, just made
chatter about his change of jobs, the raising of children, the fact that Owen was going to jail but would
be out in six months. Robbins's financial condition
had suffered because of Owen's arrest; unable to
find a job that paid him as well as Owen had, Robbins was in danger of losing his house to foreclosure.
As the conversation went on, and did not probe any
sensitive matters, he grew more and more nervous.

"What did you want to see me about?"

"Just touching bases, Rickey," I replied. "Talking
to all the people who worked for Owen." He knew
this was true, since word had gotten around that
I'd similarly spoken to several other employees and
former employees. I did refer to the Steele murder,
though in a roundabout way, by asking Robbins
about his time in the service. He was adamant that

he had reported to Camp Pendleton on January 5, 1969, and had not gone AWOL until January 22, a time sequence that would have placed him firmly out of town at the time of the murder. I told him that I had friends in the CID and could check those dates. That disturbed him a bit, but not enough to knock him offtrack. In answer to another query, he also said that he had been questioned by the police in connection with the case of Tedd Browne, the black man murdered in Cleveland Heights, but then, so had everyone else who'd hung around Farragher's Bar.

After more than an hour, the conversation wound down and it was time for Robbins to go. As he got ready to leave, I asked him rather casually, "By the way, Rickey—what size shoes do you wear?"

He sagged a bit and then responded, "Nine and a half." After that, he tried to hide his shoes under the chair. He knew that the footprints in the snow outside the Miami Road house were an issue in the still-unsolved murder of Marlene Steele, and now he thought I knew a lot about those footprints and that he had quite possibly made them. I didn't have nearly as much information as he thought I did, but he couldn't tell that. When he left, I was firm in my belief that I'd planted an important seed in his mind.

In this period, as well, I visited several groups of local law enforcement officials and let them in on some of what I'd found out about various murders in the area. As I've mentioned in my earlier book, in the 1970s the "one-way street" approach was still endemic in the Bureau: agents gathered information from all sources but usually gave it out to none.

What the public hasn't known is that back then the FBI habitually sat on a lot of collected information and didn't disseminate it. The rationale went like this: in the course of investigating a counterfeiting, let's say, FBI agents would come across information about drug trafficking; however, the Bureau wouldn't give this information to the federal agency that handled drug cases, unless and until we'd wrapped up the counterfeiting case, and possibly not even then. Our prosecutions came first, even if the ancillary charges—for instance, drug trafficking—were more serious and socially important than the counterfeiting, interstate commerce violations, or whatever it was that we were investigating. This misguided, miserly attitude has now changed, but back then, under Hoover and his immediate successors, whatever we collected was kept within, only reluctantly passed on to other agencies, and mainly when there was no chance of it jeopardizing the FBI's own investigations.

Even at the time I considered the one-way street an ill-advised policy, because of my experience in the CID, which frequently operates in conjunction with other law enforcement commands. Working together, army and civilian agencies had often done very well, and I knew that when law enforcement groups shared information freely with one another, fewer matters slipped through the cracks that exist between jurisdictions and more crimes were solved. So in Cleveland I worked around the one-way street as best I could, without stepping out of FBI bounds. My most important visit in early 1974 was to Earl Gordon, who had been the chief of detectives of

Cleveland Heights at the time of the murder of Tedd Browne in 1968. When Marty McCann and I dropped by his office, Earl had become deputy chief of the department.

Gordon was a fine policeman, detective and chief in his time. He had been enraged by the Browne murder, and his vow to Inez Browne that someday they'd find Tedd's killer was heartfelt and real. Since 1968, Gordon had stayed on the case, running down the leads that occasionally surfaced, and he still spoke regularly to Browne's widow to assure her that he'd never let the investigation die. The case continued to puzzle everyone, because there seemed no motive for the murder. In our conversation in early 1974, I told Gordon that several of my informants had heard and repeated to me that Browne had been shot by Kilbane's associate Rickey Robbins. Robbins had been at a party in the wake of the riots, the story went, and had gotten drunk and nasty; he'd expressed the wish to go out and "kill the first nigger" he saw, and had been waving around a pistol at the party. (Brandishing a pistol at a party was a frequent occurrence in the Kilbane crowd, as family photos would later show.) According to accounts from people who had not been at the party but who'd heard of the incident from friends, Robbins had left the festivities and later returned, not precisely admitting that he'd killed someone, but uttering phrases that led people to believe that he'd done so—especially after hearing police sirens cut through the night and reading the headlines the next morning.

My informants' story included two important

details that had not been released to the newspapers: the caliber of the gun and the notion that Robbins had carved an N into the head of the bullet to indicate his preferred target. Gordon respectfully listened to our information and said that the department had interrogated Robbins in 1968, as they had done with others who had been at that party, but could come to no conclusions about Robbins.

After I gave this information to Gordon, he and the Cleveland Heights police department did not then aggressively pursue it. Their reason has become obscured by time, and perhaps by a bit of embarrassment. Here's my guess as to what happened. Having been on the force since '48, Gordon had known Robbins and the Kilbanes as young troublemakers—and he'd been trying to get people in that crowd to talk about the Browne murder for nearly five years, with no success. There had been many rumors about the Browne case, and what I conveyed to Gordon was just one more rumor. Local police were usually inclined to be distrustful of federal agents, whose general MO was to act in a rather heavy-handed way, moving in on their jurisdictions and brooking no objections. A further irritant was our above-mentioned usual style of seeking information from the police and giving nothing back in return. It was often difficult for the FBI to tell local police anything, because it always seemed as if we were trying to run their cases. After all I was providing no informants' names, no physical evidence, and seemed to be just mucking about in old waters.

The man I most wanted to see on this Cleveland

trip was Steele, and I saved him for last. As I had done with Robbins, I left word around town that I wanted to talk to Steele, and he promptly called the FBI office.

"You want to talk to me?"

"Well, yes, I'd like to, but I'm packing up to go to Quantico, and I've got a lot of last-minute things to take care of, so I don't know when we could get together."

Steele was so anxious to find out what I had to say that he insisted on coming right over. No more than five minutes later, he appeared in our outer office, very nearly out of breath. He must have run all the way from his office, four blocks away.

I sat him down and took an approach similar to the one I'd pursued with Robbins, meandering all around the subject without really saying much of anything. Steele chain-smoked, as though he didn't know what else to do with his hands.

Finally, my casual chatter got to him, and in an exasperated voice he said, "Look: if the FBI has anything on Bob Steele, let's lay it on the table once and for all."

"If the FBI has anything on you, Mr. Steele, you know very well that we won't tell you until it's too late for you to do anything about it."

"I want to know why you're poking around in my life."

"I'm transferring to Quantico," I told Steele, "but I'm staying on this case." Bureau rules permitted an FBI agent to continue to pursue a case after transfer to another station, should he choose to do so, and I was going to do just that. "So I just wanted you to know, Mr. Steele, that when this is all over, I'll have the killers of your wife, Marlene. We know who those killers are, and we're closing in on them. I just thought you'd like to know that there's every hope that this case will be solved.''

Steele reached for his cigarettes in his shirt pocket, and was so nervous that in extracting the pack he tore the flap from his pocket. As the conversation continued on for some time, he tried repeatedly to push the now-torn material back up into position. I took this gesture to be an unconscious replication of his state of mind: his carefully constructed façade had been rent apart, and he was desperate to repair it.

I took some satisfaction from that. I hadn't cornered Steele yet, but I felt a break in the case was within reach, because I did have the suspects either in jail or mightily flustered.

Part Two

PURSUIT AND TRIALS

Six

"I HEARD THE MURDER PLANS BEING PUT TOGETHER"

The environment at Quantico was good for me, and after my initial three-month tryout I was transferred there permanently in the spring of 1974. My assignment was as a criminologist and instructor in the Behavioral Science Unit. This was the little-known unit that one day would be featured in the book and film *Silence of the Lambs*. Coming in on the ground floor of the growing discipline of profiling likely suspects in serious crimes against the person, I developed into an expert in this field. I continued to work in that unit and be based at Quantico until 1990, when I retired from the Bureau.

In 1974, intrigued and involved though I was in my new work, I did not forget my promise to Bob Steele to bring to justice the murderers of his wife. Toward that end, I kept in touch with the Cleveland authorities. Andy Vanyo came to Quantico as a student for three months, and we would sit in the campus beer hall and talk over the Steele case, postulating who might have done what to whom. It was as a result of these discussions, I think, that another FBI agent and I drove down to the prison in Alderson, West Virginia, to see Carol Braun. Our visit was unannounced, but she agreed to see us. Carol was in her late twenties, a young and attractive woman, even in drab prison garb. In fact, she looked better than she had when she was turning tricks— exercised, relaxed, and having put on a few pounds. I brought with me three gifts and presented them to her one by one. Candy and flowers were the first two, and this former prostitute seemed as pleased to receive them as any young girl about to go to the high school prom.

The third gift was a folder of gruesome color photographs of the head of a woman, taken as she lay in her bed with blood streaming over her face from the two gunshots that had killed her.

"Who's that?" Carol asked as I spread out the photos.

"Marlene Steele."

"You son of a bitch!" Carol screamed at me. "You have no right to do that to me!"

I put the shocking photos back in the folder. They had served their purpose quite well.

"Why did you show those to me?" Carol asked mournfully.

Her reaction made it clear that she had not simply been shocked by the bloody photos, and that her terror derived from her knowledge that her lover had indeed been involved with that particular murder.

When we had calmed Carol down, I told her that I had shown the photos to her for her own good.

When her prison sentence ended, in a few months' time, she might be thinking of going back to Owen Kilbane. I argued that if she did, she might one day end up just as Marlene Steele had, shot dead in her bed as she slept. After all, Carol knew a great deal about the nefarious activities of a violent man. To avoid Marlene Steele's fate, Carol should make plans to leave her former pimp.

This notion also upset her, because she had long been in love with Kilbane, even though she acknowledged that he had pushed her to do things that weren't good for her and had wronged her further by living simultaneously with Nancy Mason and her.

She comprehended what I was saying, but I could see that I wasn't convincing her to leave Owen, so the other agent and I left the prison in the evening and came back the next morning. I reiterated my theme: "When and if you ever decide to get away from him, you might need help. And if you do, you should call me." As I had done with Diane, I offered Carol my card. She thrust it back at me.

"Think of it as an insurance policy," I suggested. "You may not need it right away, but someday you may want to get in touch with me, and when that happens, you'll be able to find me."

Carol Braun took the card and promised nothing.

A year went by. Kilbane and Carol got out of jail and went back to Cleveland and picked up their lives where they had left off. And nothing happened on the Steele case. Nothing, for a whole year! At Quantico, I chewed on the carpet with annoyance, and called Marty McCann every month to ask about progress. He didn't have any real news for me and counseled a wait-for-the-break attitude. I thought that the Cleveland authorities would certainly have begun to move against Kilbane on the Prunella murder, or found some way to get at Rickey Robbins, or cracked Steele's façade—something. Couldn't anybody else in the world advance these cases? Even my good friend McCann became annoyed at my impatience.

In fact, what had happened to the Steele matter in the FBI's hands at this time was that it became— once again—an old dog case, assigned to another agent, who was probably intimidated by the twenty-five volumes of material that had been amassed during our investigation of Owen Kilbane and his associations and perhaps was not really interested in pursuing a murder that was still a local police matter, not something for which the agent could get a stat. Much to my chagrin, the Steele murder case lay dormant for some time. I did hear a bit about it now and then when friends sent me newspaper clippings, or in phone calls to and from the guys in local law enforcement who often gathered at the Hofbrauhaus, a German restaurant in downtown Cleveland that generally featured a police car or two in its parking lot and some uniformed elbows at its bar. My going-away-to-Quantico party had been held there.

The judgment against Steele in the Jay Swartz civil suit was reversed on appeal in the summer of 1974, so the former judge was released from the obligation to pay anything to Barbara's former husband. Word reached the police that the Steele boys had been mistreated in the home of Robert and Barbara Steele, made to feel inferior to Barbara's other children, directed to come straight home from school, and not permitted out of their rooms even to go to the bathroom, even subjected to abuse, though no charges were filed. Shortly after this information reached the ears of the law enforcement community, Steele completed an arrangement with the Gallittos by which the grandparents agreed to assume full custody of Brett and Kevin, and to move with the boys to Florida, in exchange for keeping them out of the public eye. Steele's parents had also become Florida residents, and they were to have visitation rights.

Steele and Barbara took pleasure trips to Spain and let it be known that they were thinking about moving to that country. There he would teach English at a school and write children's books that she would illustrate. They'd go just as soon as they were able to obtain a good price on their new home, which bordered a country club. Prices were somewhat depressed, just then, so they'd wait until the market recovered.

In the spring of 1975, John Walsh came to Quantico to be a student at a session of the FBINA, and before he arrived he reviewed the Euclid files of the Steele case. As a young detective on the Euclid force, Walsh had known Steele and liked him. The murder of Marlene had changed his view of Steele. Six years later, the unsolved case still bothered Walsh, who was now on his way to becoming a lieutenant. The failure to indict the judge for his wife's murder even though others in law enforcement knew that Steele had been involved had tarred the Euclid police department with a reputation of being a bit out to lunch. That wasn't justified, Walsh knew, and he decided that he'd study the Steele case again in the clear light of the FBINA. At the academy, he introduced himself to me and signed up for my course. I thought then that he resembled the perfect television detective: tall, straight, handsome, clipped mustache, a semitough manner that befitted the son of a police officer. We had several beers in the beer hall together, discussing the Steele case. Maybe someday there'd be a break in it.

On August 4, 1975, at 7:45 in the morning, I got a call at Quantico from Carol Braun. She was in Saint Louis, she said, hiding from Owen Kilbane. Crying, sobbing, near hysteria, she told me that she'd been having a lot of trouble with Owen and was in fear for her life. Owen had gone back into the prostitution business in Cleveland with Nancy Mason and other girls. Carol said that she was staying with a female friend whom she'd met at Alderson, a woman she trusted implicitly, but she needed help. She implied that she was willing to tell a lot of things about Owen and the murders.

"Hey, Carol, I'm having a lot of trouble with this connection—I can hardly hear you properly. I'll have to call you back. Can you give me the number there?" She read me the number and said she felt comfortable in taking a call from me, that night or the next morning.

There had been no trouble on my telephone line. I had heard her loud and clear and was jumping at the opportunity to hear more, but I wanted to record any future conversations. In the next few hours, I received permission from my supervisors to do so, and touched base with McCann in Cleveland and also with the FBI's office in Saint Louis. I also called Alderson for the records of Carol's friend.

The next morning, I telephoned Carol at her friend's apartment. She said she was feeling better and that she could stay in the apartment until she could get her head together. She'd called Owen. He wanted her to come back, but she claimed a need for rest; that was true enough, but her avowal of fatigue was also an attempt to avoid arousing his suspicions about why she had gone out of town.

Two things had brought her to the point of a break from Owen, Carol said: my visit to the prison and a recent phone call from Diane. Now resettled and out of the life, Diane had apologized to Carol for causing her to be jailed, and pleaded with her to get away from Owen while she had the chance. Carol had told Owen about my Alderson visit, but not about Diane's call. Carol now recognized, she said, that in order to be entirely free of Kilbane she would have to cooperate with the FBI, even if that meant testifying as to what she knew of several murders in which Owen had been involved. She'd been present during many Kilbane conversations about the Steele, Prunella, and Browne murders, and would relate what she knew. And, she added in a postscript that surprised me, she'd even submit to hypnotism or truth serum to dredge up all the details, if necessary.

Two days later, I phoned Carol again, this time with a tape recorder running. She said she was "a nervous wreck," trying to relax herself; Owen hadn't called for three days, and she was worried because "I think he might be hip to what I'm doing."

"I doubt that," I said. "You couldn't be much cooler. You're out in Saint Louis, for God's sakes. . . . Have you thought much more about getting out of that scene altogether?"

"I said I'm not going back there, Bob, and I meant that. . . . I'm just going through some real bad emotional changes in my head. . . . I'm fighting to stay away, y'know, because, like, y'know, he's got me so brainwashed for so long and my head, it just— sometimes I go at night, uh, I go to bed and I just fight my head, y'know?"

Kilbane had been operating prostitutes at various truck stops across Ohio, and Carol wanted no part of that. Moreover, she'd done a lot of thinking and had concluded that the "six months I did in jail I was free; ten years I've been with him is when I've been locked up."

Carol started telling me what she'd heard about the Prunella murder, and I realized that her version meshed extremely well with what I had been told by other informants. She began to ramble on about other matters, and I suggested that I meet her in Saint Louis within a few days to get the whole story, and also to "make some arrangements . . . plan for your withdrawal from that whole scene" in Cleveland. She readily agreed, and we spent some minutes establishing precisely where and when to meet. I cautioned Carol not to tell anyone that I was coming, not even family members, who'd also been urging her to leave Kilbane.

For another ten minutes she continued to vilify Kilbane and to plot her revenge on him; for instance, she was going to take down from his office wall the rug she'd crocheted for him, the one with his logo in it, and "put it over his casket when he dies and burn it with him." After she had vented her spleen, I steered her back to the Steele murder. She remembered that Owen had left the house on the night of the murder and had been waiting in a car on the street for a report that the deed had been done. Then "the man came home bragging—I can remember that—boy, him bragging his ass off how he did it, y'know, and how they did this and did that." Nonetheless, she believed it was going to take some time to recall all the details. She hated to do so but would, because "all I can see is what's-her-face's picture [Marlene's bloodied head] every day of my life, y'know?"

Initially, the FBI hierarchy wanted me to have an agent from the Saint Louis office take a statement from Carol, but she refused to speak with anyone other than me, so I was authorized to go. It would have been incorrect procedure for me to be there alone, so more wrangling had to be done to enable Marty McCann to fly to Saint Louis from Cleveland to witness my taking her statement. Sometimes the Bureau can become unreasonably recalcitrant and protocol-bound in these matters; it was obvious to Marty and me, and should have been obvious to anyone in management, that this potential witness trusted me and wouldn't trust someone she didn't already know. In any event, after a while permission was granted, and Marty readily agreed to come: this was the break we'd been waiting and working for, the single thing that could bust the Steele case wide open. Saint Louis is always terribly hot in August, but I'd never been happier to go there.

Carol had wanted me to bring along photos, documents, and other such items to jog her memory, but if I had done so, those might later have permitted an astute defense counsel to claim that I'd coached her on the details, so I brought nothing of that sort. Nor did I ever intend to use hypnosis or other such techniques, though I hadn't said no to her about them in our phone conversation. It was just me, Marty, and our pencils and notepads. FBI rules specified that such statements were never to be tape-recorded. Rather, agents were to keep notes, then type these up into a coherent statement, and then meticulously go over the statement with the witness until the witness had the document in such shape that he or she could stand by every word in it.

I did make some other important arrangements. Despite the extensive phone calls I'd held with Carol over the past week, we still couldn't be certain that we were not being set up by Owen Kilbane. No telling who might step out of an elevator with a gun in hand. So, from the airport, Marty and I called Carol and instructed her to come to one of the airport hotels. When she alit from her friend's car at the hotel, I went down to meet her alone, while Marty stayed out of sight. Once her friend had driven off, we took Carol to our waiting car and whisked her across town to another hotel in order to take her statement. She was hungry and before talking first wanted to eat. In the hotel restaurant, she grinned and said, "Wouldn't it be great if Owen walked in and saw me with you two guys?" That didn't help either Marty's or my appetite.

Upstairs, we three talked for several hours that first day; then Marty and I sent Carol home. The next day, we met her at the hotel but for security's sake immediately took her to another place, a Stouffer's hotel, downtown. This time it was Marty's turn to bring Carol up to a room, where I waited. And to be on the lookout for men in the shadows who might be bearing guns.

As he and Carol entered the elevator, Marty did recognize someone, a civilian he knew from Cleveland. This acquaintance was stunned to see McCann in Saint Louis with a young and attractive woman who was not the Mrs. McCann he knew. Marty couldn't very well tell his acquaintance what he was doing here or give away the identity of his companion, and so said nothing. Such are the vicissitudes of an FBI agent's life.

Carol, McCann, and I talked for many hours over two days. We used no aids except pads and pencils. After taking notes, Marty and I went to the Saint Louis FBI office, where I dictated to a stenotypist a distillation of what Carol had said, divided into two statements, one about the Steele murder and one about the Prunella murder. These documents I took back to Carol, and we went over them laboriously; in her own handwriting she crossed some things out and added others, noting all the changes by also affixing her signature and/or initials. I wanted her to attest to only those matters that she remembered with certainty. The sworn statement began with an acknowledgment that McCann and I had advised Carol of her rights and had given her a form about these that she had read and understood; having completed the eleventh grade in school, she was well able to read and understand this form.

I'll save what she said about the Prunella murder for a later chapter and, for the moment, concentrate only on her statement about the Steele case. Carol attested that she had originally met Steele as a prostitution customer, and had introduced him to Kilbane, whom she had known since she was eighteen and for whom she worked as a prostitute. Then we got to the heart of the statement, which is reprinted below as it later appeared in court records, complete with the usual FBI capitalizing of all proper names:

I knew from conversations with OWEN JAMES KILBANE that BOB STEELE was having trouble with his wife MARLENE. I had heard a number of conversations indicating that OWEN JAMES KILBANE was to arrange the killing of MARLENE STEELE for her husband, BOB STEELE. I had heard conversations between OWEN JAMES KILBANE and his brother, MARTIN KILBANE, concerning the murder of MARLENE STEELE either prior to or subsequent to her death. OWEN JAMES KILBANE had arranged for an alibi for himself on the evening of the murder and to the best of my knowledge MARTIN KILBANE and RICK ROBBINS were actually directly involved in the murder. It was OWEN JAMES KILBANE's idea that RICK ROBBINS wear shoes several sizes too large to confuse the police should any footprints be left on the grounds of the residence of Judge STEELE. RICK ROBBINS was to enter the STEELE residence and kill MARLENE STEELE upon a pre-arranged signal from Judge ROBERT STEELE who would be in the house at the time.

In another portion of the statement, Carol related what had happened when the police had asked her and Nancy Mason about their connections to Steele; in this particular section, Carol took pains to cross out what had originally been typed in and substitute her own characteristic phrasing: Kilbane and Steele, she wrote, "told us to 'be cool' and not to provide any information to the police concerning what we knew and told us to lie, which we did." In conclusion, Carol stated that while the information was as complete as she could make it,

I have lived under extremely trying circumstances over the past ten years and some of my recollections concerning the sequence of events that occurred in the killing of Mrs. MARLENE STEELE are hazy; however, in my own mind I know that I heard the murder plans being put together prior to the killing which did take place. I also heard the murder discussed after the killing by OWEN J. KILBANE and others, who's [sic] names I can't recall at this time.

When Carol had signed the statement and Marty and I had witnessed it, we all said good-bye and went our separate ways. Carol returned to her friend's apartment, McCann flew to Cleveland, and

I took the next plane back to Washington, D.C., and Quantico.

I thought that was it, end of story! The detective had cracked the case, obtained an important insider's account, and could now rest on his laurels. Fairly soon, I assumed, I'd get a call advising me that Carol had entered the federal witness protection program and Steele, the Kilbanes, and Rick Robbins had all been arrested and charged with Marlene's murder. Maybe, confronted with Carol's statement, one of them would even confess and give us more details.

Dream on, Ressler.

I heard absolutely nothing for more than a month, and then, quite concerned, I made my own call to McCann.

"We haven't heard from her," McCann said. "We think she's gone back to Owen."

Well, maybe she just went back in order to kiss him off and would shortly return to the FBI fold. Another month went by. And another. Along about this time, I heard from Andy Vanyo. Following a new lead, he had received permission from County Attorney Corrigan to go to California to reinterview the source we called Hugo. On this trip, Andy obtained information from Hugo to the effect that Rickey Robbins had been involved in both the Steele and Browne murders. Hugo didn't want to sign a statement or appear in court, but his recollections corroborated what we'd already heard from Carol Braun, and from other sources over the years.

McCann told me the Steele matter had been asigned to a relatively new agent, Joe Harpold. *Great*, I thought. *Now it's an even more ancient old dog case.*

But that wasn't quite so. Joe Harpold had come to the Bureau from extensive on-the-beat experience in the Kansas City, Missouri, police department and was—I discovered when he called to talk to me about Steele—a particularly polite, thoughtful, and thorough person. The previous agent who had the case had had no personal interest or investment in the matter, but Joe Harpold decided not only to read through the twenty-five volumes of files I'd assembled, but, in the wake of receiving the dynamite Braun statement, to work at better organizing it so that the material might one day be utilized in a prosecution. In short, he believed in the case, and that was a wonderful boost for me and for the investigation. I began to understand that McCann was craftier than even I had given him credit for: Joe Harpold, his choice to carry on the case, had taken some almost-dying coals and blown life into them.

But Harpold soon informed me that the Kilbanes were thinking about moving to Ireland and the Steele house was closer to being sold.

"Did you give out the Braun statement to the Euclid police?" I asked Marty in a phone call. "How about the stuff on Robbins and Browne, to Cleveland Heights?"

"We can't disseminate this sort of stuff so easily," McCann said. "These things take time, Bob. You know how it works around here."

My response was unprintable. By early 1976, and despite Joe Harpold's enthusiasm and diligence, I was almost certain that the people Carol Braun had sworn were the murderers of Marlene Steele were going to continue to get away with their crime forever.

Seven

"HELLO, BOBBIE. . . . I THINK YOU'RE IN TROUBLE"

It was 1976: seven years had passed since the murder of Marlene Steele. Although there is no statute of limitations on murder, the passage of the years dims people's memories, and we didn't want the participants to be able to slip away because someone could no longer remember a key detail.

I still had allies in the pursuit of justice in this case—in addition to Joe Harpold, there was Jack Walsh of the Euclid police department, now a senior detective; in my class at Quantico in the late spring of 1975, he and I had gone over the Steele matter. A year later, in early May of 1976, Walsh learned that Lou Kulis was about to resign his position with the sheriff's office of Cuyahoga County because of differences with the current sheriff, and asked Kulis if before he left the Euclid police he could listen to the nine-and-a-half-hour interrogation that he and Charles Miller had conducted with Steele in February of 1969. On Kulis's last day in his office—May 6, 1976, a date that remained clear in both men's memories—Kulis got the tapes out of a sealed package and listened to them for the first time in seven years, and in Walsh's presence. Hearing them, Walsh now had no further doubts whatsoever about the complicity of Steele and the Kilbanes in the murder of Steele's first wife. On one tape, for instance, Steele even admitted having two lunches the day before the murder, one with his paramour, Barbara Swartz, and afterward a second lunch—in the same restaurant—to discuss "legal matters" with Owen Kilbane.

Eighteen days after the tape session, near five o'clock on the afternoon of May 24, 1976, a young man who had recently been a mental hospital patient walked into the office of Cleveland Heights prosecutor Paul Greenberger, and sought some advice on how to deal with his father, who had been beating him up. According to later published reports, after Greenberger suggested to the young man that he move out and avoid the hassle, he announced that he wished to unburden himself of some long-held information. "I know who killed Tedd Browne," he said. Greenberger listened to the man spill some details, and hustled him into the offices of detectives Mike Cannon, Jr., and Richard Borowiak. Cannon's father was chief of detectives, having replaced Earl Gordon, who had moved up to deputy chief of the department. According to the reports, the young man then told the detectives what Charlie Rice, the host of the party on the night of the Browne murder, had told him: that Rickey Robbins was responsible for killing Browne and also for killing Marlene Steele.

When I first related the same information to Cleveland Heights in 1974, they had more or less dismissed it. In late May of 1976, when a man with a history of mental illness walked in off the street with a similar story, they decided to take action. While detectives were dispatched to find Charlie Rice, technicians ran Rickey Robbins's prints against those that had been found on Browne's car. Both sets were in the files. Later a story would circulate that the reason the prints had not been compared at the time of the murder in July of 1968 was that even though Robbins's name had surfaced as a suspect, he had then been seventeen, and as a juvenile he could not be fingerprinted. His prints first went on file, the authorities said, in August, after he turned eighteen and had been arrested for a firebombing. (It had been after that arrest that Robbins had made the deal to join the marines.)

Charlie Rice, hearing that he was wanted for questioning, surrendered to the police at the Heights station, and as he was being fingerprinted he said, "I don't know a thing about the murder. Why don't you check Rick Robbins's prints?" This was already being done, and the next day the comparison turned up a match, but it was only a partial match, one palm print and not several fingerprints. The match served in the mind of law enforcement to put Robbins at the scene of the murder, but in a court of law, they knew, a partial print was not considered sufficient evidence on which to obtain a conviction.

Lt. Mike Cannon, Sr., the chief of detectives, was almost ready to retire and wanted very much to bring to justice this case that for years had haunted

him, Earl Gordon, and everyone else in the department. That afternoon, when Charlie Rice sat down
with Cannon for additional questioning, Rice's two
public defender attorneys insisted that their client
be charged or let go, and advised him not to make
a statement.

Ex-marine Cannon knew that he had nothing on
which he could legally hold Rice, but he also knew
that if Rice did not cooperate, he couldn't nail Robbins. So Cannon bluffed. He admitted that he didn't
have enough to charge Rice with any aspect of the
murder right now but said that someday he might,
and that he'd eventually obtain a conviction, for
which Charlie would spend years in prison, break
up his family, etc. Cannon summed it up: "If Charlie
walks out of here now, something walks out with
him—immunity. We'll make a deal with the next
guy."

Against the advice of his lawyers, Rice then
agreed to give a statement to the effect that on the
night in question, Robbins had set out from Rice's
house to murder a black man. Rice added a significant detail that the police claimed they also had
never heard before this moment, though it was a
detail that my informants had told me and that I'd
also provided two years earlier to Cleveland
Heights: that Robbins had carved an *N* into the head
of the bullet. Rice also knew that the gun Robbins
had used was a .45—a detail the police had never
released to the public—and said that he had driven
Robbins away from the area after the murder, a
fact that actually could have made him liable for

prosecution as an accomplice to the murder of Tedd Browne.

This bluff of Mike Cannon's was one of the greatest ever pulled off in the annals of Cleveland law enforcement, and was the key to bringing the Tedd Browne case to trial, and all that followed out of that prosecution.

As soon as Rice's statement was signed, on the evening of May 26, 1976, Cannon got a warrant for the arrest of Robbins, and shortly thereafter Robbins was picked up by Cleveland Heights officers.

"I don't wanna talk about nothing," Rickey said when Cannon tried to question the young auto mechanic.

After midnight, Bob Steele came to the station as Robbins's lawyer and met deputy chief Earl Gordon in the hall. Gordon was in a good mood. He had always felt that if law enforcement hung on doggedly enough in its pursuit of this sort of "spontaneous" crime committed by young people, one among the group of youngsters would eventually talk. And that's what had finally happened. Gordon's vow to Inez Browne would soon be fulfilled. Gordon also knew beyond a doubt now that there was more to the Robbins-Steele connection than the lawyer-client relationship.

"Hello, Bobbie," Gordon remembers saying, deliberately using the diminutive to needle Steele. The lawyer mumbled something about his client, Robbins, being in deep trouble.

"I think *you're* in trouble," Gordon retorted.

"What do you mean?"

"I think you know what I mean."

Steele turned pale.

Robbins was arraigned, with Steele beside him, at first in juvenile court, because Robbins had been under the age of eighteen at the time of the Browne murder. Then the case was transferred to an adult venue.

No sooner was the arraignment made than the newspapers started linking Robbins to the Steele murder, and Robbins's family and friends—especially the Kilbanes—put pressure on Steele to withdraw as the attorney in the case. He did so and was replaced by Gerald S. Gold, an experienced courtroom defense lawyer.

Robbins was upset about his arrest. In many ways since 1968, his life had changed, and for the better. His wild days as a violent teenage thug were in the past, and, now in his midtwenties, he was more stable. His marriage and the need to maintain a family of four had settled him down; his abusive father had died in 1974, freeing him from that influence. And while he had not entirely broken free of the Kilbanes, he had reached a point where he was not so dependent on them as he had once been.

"All this recent publicity about Robbins and the stories that I have been part and parcel of Owen Kilbane's prostitution and pornographic empire are just untrue and unfair," Steele told the Cleveland *Press* as reporters caught up to him in the Cleveland Criminal Court building, where he was the attorney in another pending and unrelated case. "I am a criminal defense lawyer now. And if occasionally I have to represent an Owen Kilbane, well, that's just my job." He pointed out that Robbins might have a grudge against him because he had represented the young man in the 1969 Phillipone case and Rickey had been paying off his legal fees at five dollars and ten dollars a month since that time.

Steele characterized the continued pursuit of him by the Euclid police as a "vendetta" promulgated by Police Chief Frank W. Payne, in reaction to a letter that Steele had sent when Steele was the prosecutor of Euclid, a letter to the town's mayor requesting that Payne be fired. (Chief Payne denied the charge, or even knowledge of who had written that old letter; he was, however, intrigued to find out after all this time just who had sent it.) Steele complained to anyone who would listen that the police had never focused on any suspects in his wife's murder other than himself. "I am an intelligent person," he told the *Plain Dealer*. "I was a judge. If I were going to have it done, I would have made sure that I was out giving a speech, but I was in the house at the time."

"If I was going to run away," Steele told several newspapers, "I would have done it long ago." "Everyone" knew that for the past five years he and his wife had planned to move to Spain in June of 1977, after Barbara's child graduated from high school. Steele doubted that the "new evidence" would provide investigators with anything that would solve the murder of Marlene.

Reporters also called Owen Kilbane for comment and asked whether he or Marty had been involved in the Steele murder. "No way, there is no way," Owen had responded, and when asked if Robbins had been involved, Owen said, "No way. From what I understand he [Robbins] was in the army."

Reporters located Inez Browne shortly after she had been told of the arrest of a suspect in the slaying of her husband. Gratified at the turn of events, she told them, "I always thought justice would be done. I never married again because there just wasn't another man like him." She still lived in their former home, with her three boys, she told reporters and added, "I feel sorry for the mother of this boy [Robbins]."

Now that the cat was out of the bag on the Browne murder, Marty McCann, Joe Harpold, and I finally convinced the FBI hierarchy that it was essential for us to tell local law enforcement what we knew about the Browne and Steele cases. As I've discussed earlier, the FBI often holds on to information that it ought to give out, and the Carol Braun statement and associated materials about the Steele murder had been in our possession for too long. In June, after Harpold had done great work in getting ready the underlying information that would back up what was in the Braun statement, I reentered the case in a telephone hookup to representatives of the several Cleveland-area departments who had gathered in the Cleveland FBI office. From a telephone at Quantico I led the FBI in officially disseminating everything we knew about the Steele and Browne cases. This included Marty and Joe handing out copies of Carol Braun's statement, and other supporting information from the voluminous files. The statement itself would not have been of tremendous help to the police without the materials from the file, which corroborated Carol's close relationship with Kilbane.

In the meeting, a strategy developed: convict Rick Robbins on the Browne case, and then get him to roll over and provide state's evidence against the Kilbanes and the former judge in the Steele case. That proved easy to say, but not so easy to do.

For one thing, Robbins not only pleaded innocent, but was confident enough of his own position to let it be known that, if required, he would take the stand in his own defense. For another, the chief prosecution witness, Charlie Rice, was extremely nervous at the thought of testifying, and believed that certain people—he didn't identify them, but it was clear he was referring to the Kilbanes and their friends—might retaliate against him for doing so. Mike Cannon, Jr., the Cleveland Heights detective and son of the detective chief, was going to have to baby-sit Rice for five weeks, until the time came for Rice to testify at the trial. Cannon, Jr., and Rice were the same age and had grown up near one another in Cleveland; they developed a friendship that helped solidify the case.

Rice was willing to sing if granted immunity for himself. His ex-wife also knew what had happened and she had not done anything like drive a getaway car, so she needed no immunity. Robbins had told her in 1973 that he had shot Browne and that the death was hanging heavily upon him. In addition to the Rices' stories, strong physical evidence had been marshaled against Robbins. The *N* that Rice remembered having been carved in the bullet was actually discovered to be still present on the slug that had been removed from Browne's body; the carving, which was quite faint, had not been noted as significant when the bullet had been examined in 1968. This really was a stroke of luck, because most bullets fired into the head are deformed by impact with bone. That nicked slug, coupled with the palm print and the stories of the Rices, was deemed by the county attorney to be sufficient evidence on which to go to trial.

That trial began in late August 1976, and my cabal at the Hofbrauhaus sent the Cleveland papers' reports of it to me at Quantico. Several aspects of the trial were of interest. The first was the composition of the jury: all white. Did they have what it took to convict a white man of killing a black man? The second was that Marty Kilbane, Robbins's friend since childhood, was amassing witnesses for Robbins's defense. This seemed only more evidence to me that the Kilbanes had a lot at stake in whether Robbins went to prison or walked free.

The state's case was ably presented. Rice placed Robbins at the scene and recounted how Rick had run away from the site of the murder and what he had said to Rice as they drove away in the car. He said he'd kept quiet in the intervening years because he had always been afraid of Robbins. Rice's former wife, Sue, related how she had met Robbins in 1973, when he was a night clerk in Owen's motel; they both had been depressed, and had told each other why. Rick had given as his reason the Browne murder, which had been hanging over him—but not because he felt any guilt. Rather, he was annoyed that circumstances had worked against him. If the car had rolled down the hill instead of staying at the top, Browne would have been considered just another among the ten victims of the riot, Rick had opined. And, she testified, "He felt that if it had been an ordinary black person [instead of a local celebrity], the investigation would have been dropped."

The witnesses rounded up by Marty Kilbane included several guests at the party who swore that Robbins had never left the premises during it, another man who said that Robbins never owned a gun, and others who contended that both Charlie and Sue Rice were habitual liars, exaggerators and self-aggrandizers whose testimony could not be trusted.

Finally, Robbins took the stand in his own defense. Since his arrest, he had been in the county jail, unable to post the required $200,000 bond. Under questioning from his own attorney, Gerald Gold, Robbins denied even discussing the Glenville riots at the party, and denied that he'd ever owned a .45 pistol or even a bullet. He had never killed anyone, he testified.

After four days of testimony, jury deliberations began. There was some concern about a hung jury when the members could not complete their discussions on that first day and were sent home overnight. But at 2:30 in the afternoon of the following day they returned their verdict. The all-white jury declared Robbins guilty of first-degree murder. Sentenced to life imprisonment, Rickey Robbins was led away by deputy sheriffs while his sobbing mother, wife, and other relatives and friends ran out of the courthouse, trying to duck the television cameras and other members of the press.

"It's been a long week, the longest in my life," Browne's widow told the press in a quivering voice. She had sat in the courtroom throughout the trial, holding a prayer book; often her seat had been near that of Robbins's mother. "I'm just glad there is justice in the land," Mrs. Browne continued, "and that my children can grow up knowing there's justice in the world."

Euclid police authorities were chafing to get at the newly convicted Robbins in order to convince him to turn state's evidence, to speak out about the others involved in the murder of Marlene Steele, but at first they made no headway. Before the Browne trial, Cuyahoga County prosecuting attorney John T. Corrigan had had a conversation with Robbins in which the twenty-six-year-old refused to concede that he had been involved in that murder. Corrigan told Robbins that if he ever changed his mind and wanted to talk about it, Corrigan's door would be open.

In the state prison in Columbus, Ohio, Robbins was a target; the story of his having specifically shot Browne because he was black, and of carving an N into the bullet, was enough to enrage many black inmates. It did not aid Robbins that his language was full of racist expressions; in one letter to Marty Kilbane, he called the black inmates "cooties" as well as "fools." While he was standing in the chow line one day, an attempt was made to knife him to death. The prison authorities then removed him from the general population and placed him in isolation; this was done in order to save his life, but it also had the effect of severely limiting his social contacts and mobility, and of increasing his desperation.

About two months after Robbins had been incarcerated at Columbus, Lt. John Walsh and Capt. Warren Goodwin of the Euclid police department drove down to talk to Robbins about the Steele murder. On their first visit, he again denied that he had anything to do with it. He even said he'd been in the service when it happened.

"That's bullshit," Walsh exploded. By this time, he had my reports showing that Robbins had gone AWOL before the murder. "You decide which side of the table you'll be on in the next trial," he warned Robbins.

That approach didn't get anywhere right away, but Jack Walsh kept Robbins talking, eliciting stories about how close Rick had been to Marty Kilbane. Robbins was grateful to Marty for rounding up witnesses in his defense in the Browne trial, even though the verdict had gone against him. Both Walsh and Robbins were the sons of tough Cleveland police officers, and that helped the conversation along. To Walsh, Robbins seemed more intelligent than the marines had given him credit for: on his discharge papers, Robbins's IQ had been listed as 70. The killings had occurred when Robbins was a teenager, and he had matured since that time. Asked to recall the early days of his friendship with Marty Kilbane, Robbins told Walsh the following story.

Rick and Marty had been in Marty's Corvette,

heading toward Lake Erie and Owen's boat, and had gotten in a traffic altercation with an old woman who had baubles and other things dangling from her car mirror. The old lady cut the two boys off. They'd reciprocated and then, their vengeance taken, tried to drive away. But the woman followed them and they couldn't lose her, even at speeds of over 100 miles per hour. The boys threw oil cans out at her, hoping to deter her, but she kept on coming. She rammed the Corvette. They fired shots at her and eventually drew up their car next to that of a policeman and sought protection; only then did "the old lady from hell" drive off. What tough young guys!

On a second visit, Robbins grudgingly admitted to the detectives that he knew something about the murder of Marlene Steele—but said he had a wife and two children and would need protection for them as well as for himself if he talked, because he feared reprisals. Robbins asked the two detectives, "How do I know I can trust you?"

"You have to make a choice," Walsh pointed out. "Trust us, the Kilbanes, or yourself."

Robbins continued to maintain that he would only talk if his own life imprisonment sentence were somehow reduced. Otherwise, Robbins would remain silent, because no one in prison likes a "snitch."

In law enforcement, you are often faced with the need to use the testimony of one criminal to convict others of crimes—after all, it is unlikely that there will be many uninvolved witnesses on the spot when crimes of the seriousness of premeditated murder are committed. While it was important to condemn the shooter in the death of Marlene Steele, it was more imperative to bring the true instigators of the crime to justice, and that's why Walsh and Goodwin were willing to convey Robbins's requests to the authorities who might grant them.

In this instance, that meant John T. Corrigan. The county attorney advised the police officers to go back to the prison and obtain from Robbins an oral statement, since it was clear they weren't yet going to get a real written admission. With an oral statement in hand, Corrigan could ascertain whether Robbins's information was "worthwhile," and if he considered it to be so, they could then offer some help and return to obtain a full confession.

On a fourth visit, Walsh and Goodwin took along two persuaders. The first was Robbins's wife, Sandy, who urged Rickey to cooperate. The second was the information that Corrigan was asking Rhodes to commute the sentence and had met with the parole board and recommended that they give consideration to Robbins if he testified in the Steele case.

Robbins still hadn't definitively said yes, so on their fifth Saturday trip to Columbus, Walsh and Goodwin prepared to turn up the heat. "Take it or leave it," Walsh told Rickey about the tentative deal in place. Robbins wasn't at all convinced that Walsh understood what role he, Robbins, had played in the murder of Marlene.

It was an important moment. But Walsh knew something that Robbins didn't—namely, what Carol Braun had told us about this matter. So Walsh

Robbins had not answered Owen's pejorative and provocative question. Owen broke off the discussion, telling Rick to "think about it" and they would get back to him. There was no further discussion of the subject during the rest of December, and on January 4 or 5, 1969, Robbins's parents took him to the Cleveland airport and put him on a plane that would take him to Southern California and Camp Pendleton.

Since the previous summer, when he had joined up, Robbins had received the general training of a new recruit in the marines. Pendleton was his new duty station, and Robbins and every other marine who went there knew it was a temporary one that served as the jump-off point for Vietnam; in early 1969, before the inauguration of President Richard Nixon, the fighting in Southeast Asia was still heavy, and newly minted marines were almost all shipped to South Vietnam, where their casualty rate was extremely high. On the second day at Camp Pendleton, Robbins's statement said, he became "homesick."

Although the statement didn't mention anything about calling his parents, Robbins had not called home at that time, probably believing that his parents would advise him not to leave his post. (Later on in 1969, when he had been AWOL for some time, his father did indeed advise him to go back to Pendleton and face the music—do his time in the brig, if required—in order to honorably complete his obligations.) Robbins had but one thought: to call "the only person . . . who would be able to send me money to come home," Marty Kilbane. Robbins made a collect call, and Marty agreed to the request, saying he'd get the money from Owen and wire it to Robbins. Ironing out the details of where to send $100 required another call. The money was waiting for Rick at a Western Union office in Oceanside, California, just outside the base, on the seventh of January. From there, Robbins went AWOL. He took an expensive cab ride to the Los Angeles airport, where he bought a standby ticket; this meant he would be given a seat on the first plane to Cleveland that wasn't completely filled with passengers. That moment didn't come until the late afternoon, and even then his flight was delayed. He arrived in Cleveland near midnight with nothing in his possession but his uniform, his military records, and a few dollars left from the original $100. On landing, he called Marty at the Cedar Road home, and shortly thereafter the Kilbane brothers arrived in the Cadillac El Dorado to pick him up.

(The timing of the messages to and from California would turn out to be significant. Owen had his hastily called lunch with Steele on January 7. It seemed likely that he'd scheduled that lunch immediately after Marty had wired the money to Robbins, and knowing that they would later pick up the AWOL marine at the airport. At the lunch, Kilbane would have told Steele that the perfect shooter had been found, a man who would only be in Cleveland a short time before returning to California. Perhaps in the back of the minds of both Steele and Kilbane was the possibility that the shooter would then be sent to Vietnam and might die there and take the secret of the murder to his grave.)

It was on the early morning of January 8 when Robbins climbed into the backseat of Kilbane's El Dorado and the car sped away from the airport. Marty showed Rick a bag on the floor. In it were some clothes. Marty told him to put those on and stash his uniform in the bag. Owen asked him if he was "ready" and handed him a map of the Steele home and began to explain some of the details on it.

"Owen must have sensed that I was uneasy," Robbins told Walsh and Goodwin, because after a moment or two Owen took back the map, and then he waited until they were at his office to explain "the details and plans." These included street directions, a freehand drawing of the ravine and the location of the house, and its layout, "who was in the house and where they were at." The home was in a subdivision that Robbins did not know, and he had to be made familiar with the lay of the land. The diagram was sketchy but could be understood. Owen pointed to the part of the drawing representing where Mrs. Steele would be sleeping in a downstairs bedroom and said that Steele and the two children would be upstairs. Owen then "said that she was a heavy sleeper, and she wouldn't wake up." And Owen added a very important piece of information.

"Don't try to knock off a quick piece," Kilbane had instructed Robbins, because Mrs. Steele "was on the rag."

After dropping that tidbit, they completed their discussion of the plans—where Marty would drop off Rick, where he'd pick him up—and explained the "signals." Before they left the Kilbane home to commit the murder, Owen was supposed to call Steele "to let him know Marty and I were coming." Then, "to let me know that everything was 'go,' the upstairs lights would be on in the Steele home, and the front door was to be open approximately eight to ten inches."

Owen told Robbins he would pay him $15,000 for the "job" and handed him a .38 caliber "hammerless breaktop pistol" and said, "This is what you'll use." They put a bullet in it and otherwise readied the weapon, then put it away again. Owen wanted to know if Robbins could remember all the details.

"I think so."

They planned a dry run.

"Do you think you can do it?" Owen asked Rick.

"I don't know."

"You can do it, Rick," Marty insisted.

"You killed that nigger," Owen reiterated.

One more time, Robbins did not respond when the Browne murder was thrown up to him. The idea that Robbins had killed once before, and had bragged about it to the Kilbanes, was a refrain that would be played again and again by the Kilbanes, one that bore with it the implied threat to expose Robbins for that murder should he refuse to go along with the plan to kill Marlene Steele.

Later that day, at the small apartment building that Owen owned, the men burned Robbins's uniform and service records, and then they drove by the Steele house on a dry run. There was the ravine; there was the peculiar totem on the outside of the house, the one that distinguished the Steele residence from the others. Robbins was very nervous and asked for a drink, but Owen wouldn't give him any alcohol; he didn't want it in Robbins's system. Nearing the time for the murder, in the late evening, Robbins was asked to don some dark clothes and rubber gloves and to take the gun; Owen wiped his own fingerprints off the gun before giving it over into Robbins's charge. He also gave Rick pills, two green-and-black, two "medium blue." Robbins recognized the latter two as Librium, but he didn't know what the green-and-black ones were; nonetheless, he downed them all.

They got in the car sometime very late in the evening—Robbins had lost track of time and wasn't sure about the hour—and they made the trip, which took longer than expected because "Marty and I got caught at just about every traffic light on the way." The streets were deserted when Rick was dropped off near the Steele house and started approaching it on foot. As he got closer, Rick put a nylon stocking over his face and the rubber gloves on his hands. He was wearing Marty's shoes, which were a size and a half too small. When he saw that the front door of the Steele home was partly open and the "the indication was 'go,'" he told his interviewers, "I started to panic.

"Thoughts went through my mind. The fear of killing someone that never hurt a soul, and the fear of the other people if I didn't do it. I guess that the fear of the people that asked me to do it was greater than the fear of the crime I was about to commit. I guess you could say, kill, or get killed. That's how I felt." He walked in through the storm door, and didn't remember if it squeaked or not. "It probably didn't, 'cause if it did I would have shit myself."

He proceeded through to the bedroom, he said, and recited for the detectives the specifics of hallways passed through, lights on and off. "It was very quiet. All I could hear was my heart trying to jump out of my chest." Mrs. Steele was asleep, covers pulled up around her neck and "a shower cap or hair net" on her head. He shot her twice at close range. The noise wasn't very loud, and she did not move in the slightest or make any sounds.

After that, "I turned and ran out of the room. As I rounded the [corner?] heading for the front door, I tripped over the telephone cord, and knocked it off the stand and on the floor. The bells clanged, and the receiver bounced all over." He thought about picking it up, because Marty was "supposed to call Steele when we got back to the Cedar Road house," but decided that Steele would do it. As he went outside, the storm door didn't slam "as most of them do." He made his way out of the house, down and up the other side of the ravine—gun in hand, because Owen had told him to bring the gun back, so they could properly dispose of it. He noticed a flashing yellow light at a corner, which gave them clear sailing, a fact that registered with Rick because they'd been held up by red lights on the way to the murder.

Marty picked him up and, moments later, Owen drove up alongside in another car, with Larry DiGravio sitting next to him. Windows were rolled down by both Kilbanes. Owen asked "if everything went all right, and Marty said yes." Then the cars separated. On the return trip to the house, Rick noticed that even more lights had changed pattern; ones in front of a school that had previously operated "in a normal manner" were now flashing.

When they got back to Marty and Owen's home, they had drinks and stayed up for a while, until exhaustion caught up with them. Rick continued to live there with them for some time.

Several days after the murder, Owen handed Rick two bundles of money with the bank wrappers still on them, each containing $500 in $20 bills. Rick and Marty went out and "bought some clothes," and Rick gave his parents either $300 or $350, he couldn't remember precisely which amount, but did recall putting it in an envelope and putting it in his parents' mailbox. Owen had told him "there's more where that came from," but he'd never gotten another dime.

"What a nightmare that turned out to be," Robbins summed the matter up to Walsh and Goodwin. They nodded, for they now knew the dimensions of the nightmare.

Eight

"STEELE SAID TO ME 'GOOD JOB' AND WINKED"

When I learned what Rickey Robbins had said to Walsh and Goodwin, I was overjoyed. At last, the Steele case could be brought to trial. Later Rickey would tell me personally that the dirty trick I'd played on him in 1974—asking him what size shoes he wore—had rattled him. That question, and what it implied about my knowledge of his involvement in the Steele murder, preyed on his mind for two years and had been a factor influencing his decision to admit to having been the triggerman in the gunshot execution of Marlene Steele.

On the basis of the "oral" statement given to Walsh and Goodwin by Robbins, Cuyahoga County prosecutor John T. Corrigan felt he had enough to start the process that would culminate in a trial. Justice Department officials began work on relocating Sandy Robbins and the two children.

Corrigan and his assistants had reviewed the Browne case and thought that it had been done very well; that is, there were no errors that could be made the basis for an appeal that would assail or overturn Robbins's conviction and incarceration. The only way to change Rickey's life sentence was a gubernatorial commutation. Before recommending that to Gov. James A. Rhodes and the parole board, Corrigan first spoke to Inez Browne and in effect asked her permission to go ahead with a deal for Robbins's testimony in the Steele case. She assented, and he began the process.

To make a case, you really need two strong elements. Robbins as a witness was one element; Carol Braun's evidence would provide a second. But as November yielded to December of 1976, Carol Braun herself could no longer be counted on. She was seven months pregnant with Owen Kilbane's child. This would be her second child. Her first had been born out of wedlock eleven years earlier, when Carol was just seventeen. She had told me that one of her main heartaches with Owen stemmed from his forcing her to relinquish the care of that first child, who had a different father. Now Owen and Carol were having a baby of their own. That certainly might account for her staying out of touch with Marty McCann and others of the Cleveland office who had tried to call her in the year and a half since we'd taken her statement in Saint Louis in the summer of 1975.

Nonetheless, we had that sworn and witnessed statement and were confident that when the time for a trial came, even if Carol didn't want to retell her story on the stand, she would have to attest that she had given us the statement. That admission would permit its contents to be entered in evidence, and it would be the second element with which to nail Steele and the Kilbanes.

While we waited for Corrigan to bring Robbins before a grand jury so he could obtain an indictment, my successor in the FBI office in Cleveland, Joe Harpold, and his colleagues were busy interviewing many of the people peripheral to Owen Kilbane, some of whom had knowledge of the murder of Arnie Prunella. The thinking was to bring that case to court after the Steele case had been resolved.

On December 1, 1976, after Rickey Robbins's wife and children had been taken out of town and put into the witness protection and relocation program, he was brought from the county jail, under heavily armed guard and wearing a bulletproof vest beneath his red jail suit, to testify before a grand jury. For two hours he answered Corrigan's questions in a forthright way. Later Robbins was conveyed to the county attorney's office to reduce his testimony to a written statement. In that, he reiterated some of what he'd told the grand jury, adding a few new details to those he'd previously given to Walsh and Goodwin. The most important of these: "I was involved in a homicide relating to Tedd Browne," a phrase that was an admission of his guilt in that murder, culpability that he had steadfastly denied during his trial. Turning to the Steele murder, he described the byplay with the pistol that was to be used—it was so flimsy a gun that while he and the Kilbanes were manipulating it the firing pin had fallen out. Four years after the murder, in 1973, Robbins had an accidental meeting with Steele at the wedding of Owen's sister. Marty had brought

Rickey and Sandy over to meet Steele and Barbara, and "as my wife and I turned and walked away, Robert Steele said to me 'good job' and winked or patted me on the shoulder or something—I don't remember what it was—it was one of the two." Robbins viewed Steele's behavior in this incident as acknowledgment by the former judge of Robbins's role in the murder of Steele's first wife.

Reached by the press for a comment on the rumor of Robbins's testimony, Steele said, "If it implicates me, it's a lot of bull, and I have nothing else to say."

On December 2, 1976, the grand jury finished work and its judgment was handed down: Steele, Owen Kilbane and Marty Kilbane, and Rickey Robbins were all indicted for first-degree murder. Reporters went looking for reactions. They found Barbara Steele, who assured them that the "new" evidence against her husband was "manufactured" and asked rhetorically, "If you were this fellow [Robbins], wouldn't you say anything with the deal they offered? I just don't happen to buy it." Barbara Steele believed that Robbins had been promised a full commutation in the Browne case. The *Plain Dealer* suggested that the commutation would only be to reduce the charge from murder to manslaughter, and that Robbins would have to serve some time, since manslaughter carried a sentence of up to twenty-five years.

A crowd of reporters swarmed over Steele's office in downtown Cleveland, but he wouldn't talk to them. He did, however, respond to a request from an old ally, Channel 5's commentator Dorothy Fuldheim, who had been with WEWS for twenty-nine years. In 1969, just after the murder, Fuldheim had given Steele a sympathetic hearing, and Steele seemed of the opinion that she alone would give him one now. Despite attorney James S. Carnes's plea to him not to say anything to anybody in the media, Steele was determined to have his say before he was arrested, and went to the television station anyway.

The "octogenarian with flaming red hair," as one newspaper article described Fuldheim, sat down with Steele for the televised interview in the late afternoon. Steele, now forty-four, appeared haggard, with dark circles under his eyes; no makeup man was nearby to apply something that might conceal those circles. Fuldheim asked Steele to calm down, eat a sandwich, drink a cup of coffee; he could do none of these.

"It's a question of my word against that of a convicted murderer," Steele contended on the air, and recited the litany of how the police had always focused on him and had never looked in any other direction for the actual murderer. As Steele lit into Robbins's "fabricated story" and the notion that Robbins would have his sentence commuted in exchange for "accusing me of hiring someone to kill my first wife," the former judge broke down and sobbed.

Fuldheim patted his hand and said to him, "Any man who's innocent would react the same way." While waiting for him to quell his sobs, she went on, "Well, Judge Steele, I don't need to tell you that I have tremendous feeling for you. I understand how agitated you must be. I hope profoundly that the real murderer will be found, which will then completely free you."

"I love you so much," Steele offered in return.

Afterward, the television station was swamped with telephone calls castigating Fuldheim for lack of objectivity in the interview and for possibly prejudicing a fair trial—but some people continued to believe, as did Fuldheim, that Steele was innocent. Even Mrs. Gallitto, Marlene's mother, whom newspaper reporters reached at her home in Florida, said of her former son-in-law, "I still can't feel that he's guilty. He was always so good to her [Marlene]. I can't imagine what would make him change. They seemed to be a well-adjusted couple, very much in love." But, she added, "If he is guilty, he should be condemned." No, even after eight years, it wasn't possible to put the murder out of her mind, she sobbed. "I go to bed every night and I think about her."

I had flown in from Washington to take part in the arrests of the Kilbanes and Steele. Agent Ressler's presence had been requested by the Cleveland authorities because I was the only person who had had personal contact with each and every one of the suspects, as well as with Carol Braun and other people expected to be material witnesses. Thus, at 3:45 in the afternoon of a cold Friday, I had the satisfaction of being present at the new Steele home as two detectives and Capt. Warren Goodwin knocked on Steele's door. When Steele responded to the knock, he seemed surprised, and said, "I thought I was supposed to go in Monday." He believed that, like some underworld chieftain seeking to avoid the expected crowd, he was going to be permitted to surrender to custody through a side entrance in a courthouse.

The law enforcement people who had waited eight years for this moment allowed Steele to make a call to his lawyer and then took him in handcuffs to the county jail, knowing full well that it would not be possible for him to be arraigned before the weekend had passed. Barbara Steele yelled and screamed obscenities at us as we took him out, especially at me for continuing what she believed to be a vendetta against her husband. There was no vendetta. But Steele had vilified the Euclid police once too often—the Fuldheim interview was the last straw—and the timing of the arrest was payback. By five o'clock on Friday afternoon, as darkness fell, the former judge was in a cell, and he would remain there for the weekend. On Monday, the police knew, instead of being able to appear in a suit and tie for his arraignment and having bail already in hand so he could instantly walk out, Steele would have to arrive in court in a prison uniform, wearing handcuffs and shackled by leg irons to other prisoners due to be arraigned.

After we had Steele, we went to find the Kilbanes. Owen was gone, believed to be in California. However, Marty was at Owen's home and so was the very pregnant Carol Braun.

"Remember our meeting?" I asked Carol. She did but said that she also now wanted to retract what she'd attested to in 1975; she claimed that she had been very depressed then and felt differently now.

We left after making an arrangement for Marty to come in voluntarily and be arraigned on Monday morning.

Over the weekend, a ground swell of discontent rose against the possibility that Rickey Robbins would get a full commutation of his sentence for the murder of Tedd Browne. The idea that Robbins might be taken off the hook for the killing of a black man, in exchange for testimony that would convict others for the killing of a white woman, was anathema to many people. It was assumed by most people that the angry ones were in the black community, but they also included such white men as Earl Gordon and others on the Cleveland Heights force who had worked so hard on the Browne case for so many years. Congressional representative Louis Stokes and a dozen more prominent black leaders readied a letter to send to Gov. James A. Rhodes, protesting the deal reported in the newspapers, which would permit Robbins to go free after serving only four or five years of a manslaughter sentence. This sort of deal, their draft letter said, would "give validity" to the belief, already extant in the black community, "that a different standard of justice applies for a white man who kills a black as opposed to a black man who kills a white."

Their sentiments were irrefutable, but there was equivalent force in the state's reasoning for making some sort of deal. Robbins's testimony would not only solve the Steele case; it would also be critical in the conviction of three more men, those who had participated in what the state actually considered a more egregiously heinous crime, murder for hire.

On Monday, Marty Kilbane did come in under his own steam to be arraigned, while Steele was brought in from his cell. The former judge waived the reading of the indictment, pleaded not guilty, and was released on $75,000 bail. Marty's bail was set at $100,000, and there was some question as to whether he would be able to raise it. The week of Steele's arraignment, former Euclid police captain Orville Willocks died; "Orly" had been the last man on the Euclid force who had continued to believe in Steele's innocence. Shortly thereafter, a nationwide hunt for Owen ended in Las Vegas. Policemen checking license plate numbers in the parking lot of a motel noticed Owen's car, ran the plates, and learned that a warrant was out for his arrest. Going inside, they found him with a woman—and she was not Carol Braun. Jailed briefly in Las Vegas, Owen was released at Corrigan's behest to return to Cleveland for arraignment; the prosecuting attorney believed that extradition proceedings to get Owen out of a Nevada jail would have taken several months, and agreed to let Owen return voluntarily. Owen soon did just that, and was also released on bail, as was Marty when the cash amounts needed were lowered.

After speaking with Rickey Robbins in jail and helping the prosecutor's office prepare some materials, I returned to Quantico and my own work.

Awaiting trial, Steele returned to his law office and his practice; there wasn't much to do, now, except prepare for his own defense. Reporters who reached Barbara learned from her that the former judge was depressed, unable to eat. Christmas and

New Year's came and went. At about ten in the morning of January 3, 1977, Barbara walked into their bedroom and found Steele lying on his side, curled up, unable to speak and almost comatose. An empty bottle that had contained fifty Valium tablets was beside him. She called for an ambulance, and Steele was rushed to Hillcrest Hospital, where his stomach was pumped out and his condition was stabilized. He recovered but was very weak. Three days later, attorney James S. Carnes, who had been representing Steele on the murder indictment, said that he and his client had had "a parting of the ways" over payment of the attorney's bill, and other matters. To reporters who asked whether the suicide attempt had anything to do with his resigning, Carnes responded, "Perhaps."

The next day, recovering at home, Steele said that he'd fired Carnes because of the attorney's insistence on a $5,000 advance payment. "I have $300 in the bank, have two cars and owe on them, and I owe on the house," Steele explained to a reporter from the *Plain Dealer*. "If I could collect my accounts receivable, I could pay for my home and two more like it." But business was terrible, so he had no money to meet Carnes's demand. There had been two bottles in the medicine cabinet, side by side, one of aspirin and the other of Valium, and he had taken the latter "by mistake. I had no intent of doing away with myself at all: it was purely an accident."

On January 9, 1977, the anniversary of Marlene's death, Cuyahoga County detective Chester Zembala took up his post outside Steele's home, in his recognizable county sheriff's department car, as he had done on each of the previous seven anniversaries of the crime. This vigil, Zembala now had the satisfaction of believing, would be his last one, for very shortly Steele would be on trial for having set that crime in motion.

Nine

HOSTAGES

The trial had been set to begin on Valentine's Day, February 14, 1977, but was postponed to give Steele's new attorney a chance to familiarize himself with the case. Finally it was scheduled for March 7, and I received permission from the Bureau to go out to Cleveland for pretrial conferences with the prosecutors, as well as to testify at the trial itself, and traveled there the weekend before the opening of the trial.

As things turned out, my immediate presence was required not in the downtown courtroom, but across in suburban Warrensville Heights, where a serious hostage situation had developed. In the interim between leaving my post in the Cleveland FBI office and early 1977, I had become one of the FBI's leading experts and primary trainer in hostage negotiation, and for me to be on the scene when such a situation occurred was a great opportunity for me to get some on-site experience, and, I hoped, would also be of assistance to Chief Craig Merchant of the Warrensville Heights police department. Merchant had previously been a student of mine in a criminal psychology course at Quantico, and we had become good friends. Had I not already been in Cleveland, my presence as an expert negotiator would have been required in a potentially far more explosive situation that developed in Washington, D.C., two days later when a group of Hanafi Muslims killed one person, wounded a dozen others (including future D.C. mayor Marion Barry), and took nearly a hundred people hostage at three different locations in the capital.

Here's what had happened in Warrensville Heights before the call for help. In the early afternoon, a black former marine named Corey Moore had entered the Warrensville Heights police station with an overcoat draped over one arm, and had gone into the traffic ticket waiver office, where he'd begun an argument with a clerk, Shelley Kiggans. She was an attractive seventeen-year-old white girl who worked as a clerk for that department in the afternoons while completing her senior year in high school. In the course of the argument, Moore fired two shots into the ceiling. This caused the dispatcher to phone the police headquarters upstairs, and Capt. Leo Keglovic to come running downstairs to investigate. Moore got the drop on the captain, and then had two guns as well as two hostages. Shortly, Moore barricaded himself and the hostages within the traffic waiver area, and the drama began.

The Cleveland FBI office had its own expert on hostage negotiations, J. Bernard Thompson, who had taken part in two such headline-grabbing situations in the area in the previous two years, and I worked in concert with him, while across town jury selection began in the Steele murder trial. The first rule in all hostage cases is that the longer you keep the kidnapper talking, the better off you are; the second rule is that you try very hard to trade hostages for something that the kidnapper wants. There was a telephone in the traffic office, and Moore was willing to talk over it. Various black reporters for newspapers and television stations were his preferred conversational partners. We tried to get Moore to be specific about his demands, and also to permit someone to deliver food and insulin for Keglovic, who was a diabetic. It was a good sign when Moore allowed Chief Merchant, unarmed, to go in with assistance for Keglovic, his friend and colleague.

Merchant emerged with Moore's demands. They were these: "I must talk to President Carter personally," and, "All white people are to leave the planet within seven days." If the latter was not feasible, then whites were to show their good faith by "burning all of their money—the source of all evil." Now it was clear that, as we had suspected, we were dealing with someone not in his right mind. Moore's obvious derangement convinced me that we ought not to even attempt to let him talk to the president. I thought that this demand had arisen because—as reported in the Cleveland papers in the past few days—the newly elected president had been talking by telephone to people from all over the country in an attempt to be more accessible and responsive to the citizens. Carter's reaching out was good politics,

I supposed, but it fomented in the mind of a deranged man the possibility that the president should talk directly to him. (Later Moore would confirm that he had wanted to reach Carter on a call-in program a few days before the hostage taking but had missed the televised program.)

To my astonishment, a guy from the Secret Service, stationed in Cleveland, believed it was his duty to get through to his superiors in Washington with Moore's demands. Moments later, as we sat on siege outside the Warrensville Heights police station, I was handed a mobile telephone and informed that the White House was on the line. The caller was Jody Powell, President Jimmy Carter's press secretary, who told me that the president was willing to talk on the phone with "the terrorist."

First I told Powell that we had no terrorists in Cleveland at that moment. That was the truth. But then I lied to Powell, saying that we were trying to get the hostage taker on the phone, and would get back to him if the president's call was deemed necessary. Immediately after this exchange, I phoned Bureau headquarters in Washington and told my superiors to attempt to dissuade the White House from intervening. Presidential intervention, I believed, would screw up this situation and cause us more trouble in the future. Mental cases would then feel that by taking a hostage they would get the opportunity to dictate policy to the president of the United States. What a message to be sending out! Later on, I learned that Attorney General Griffin Bell had been apoplectic at the idea that the president would so readily agree to speak directly to a hostage taker.

After Powell's call, though, we just kept talking to Moore. Members of Moore's family were there, and childhood friends, who were extremely helpful to us. However, it was the reporters whose ears Moore really wanted to bend, and shortly after midnight Bill Jacocks, a newsman from a local station, convinced Moore to trade the young woman hostage for a television set. Jacocks had been selected to act as the negotiator in the absence of black police officers or FBI agents trained in hostage negotiation. Moore had demanded to talk to an "important black person" whom he would recognize. Jacocks was an anchorman for Channel 5. I gave Bill a short cram course in negotiation procedure and remained at his elbow during his telephone dealings with Corey Moore. I wasn't happy about rewarding Moore with a television set, because keeping the hostage taker isolated from feedback about what is happening outside is often essential to the successful resolution of the situation. But the promise had been made, and to go back on it would be counterproductive. A television set was brought to the police station and sent inside. As Shelley came out after the exchange, she was almost crushed by the horde of reporters; the new SAC of the Cleveland office had to rescue her, calm her down, and instruct her not to say anything to the reporters that would in any way ruffle Moore's feathers—since Moore now had a way of monitoring what was going on outside of the police station and would be sure to see her interview on television. She performed beautifully.

Despite such additional glitches as the TV reporters conveying to Moore by their coverage the precise location of police sharpshooters and other aspects of the siege that should have remained secret, we were doing just fine, on the verge of a complete breakthrough that would allow the situation to be resolved without bloodshed. Then a new wrinkle surfaced in Moore's demands. President Carter was due to have a news conference at ten that morning, and Moore—TV set at the ready—demanded that the president, in front of the *national* television audience, take note of Corey's demands and apologize for several centuries' worth of bad treatment of blacks by whites. I argued against the president doing this, because it would set a terrible precedent and embolden future hostage takers, but my outrage was in vain. At the news conference, Carter did take note of the gunman's demands; as soon as Corey Moore had seen that happen on television, he unloaded the two guns and handed them and himself over to Captain Keglovic. On emerging from the building, the former marine even got to be the star of his own press conference. After that, he did talk briefly to the president personally, by telephone. Within hours, in Washington, the Hanafi Muslims took over the B'nai B'rith headquarters and other buildings and all but held the entire nation's capital hostage for several days. Since their takeover had been in the planning for quite some time, I doubt that the Corey Moore incident had anything to do with its inception, but I believe to this day that the president's willingness to, in essence, cave in to the demands of a Cleveland hostage taker was a factor in the prolongation of the situation in Washington.

With a sigh of relief, I returned to the Steele case. This was a more orderly scene, though it exuded a similar sense of being under siege because of the number of lawyers all trying to direct the operation and the crush of lots of interested spectators. Judge Joseph J. Nahra of the Court of Common Pleas usually operated from a courtroom on the twenty-first floor of the Criminal Justice Center in downtown Cleveland, a modern building in which one room is much like another. Recognizing that there would be a larger than usual number of people attending the trial, he had transferred the proceedings to a top-floor courtroom that could seat sixty spectators in addition to the participants. The defense table was crowded. The most experienced attorney, Leonard W. Yelsky, represented Steele. Owen's lawyer was Ralph Sperli, another experienced hand who had formerly worked in Corrigan's office. Marty Kilbane was represented by James W. Burke, Jr. Reporters characterized Burke and Sperli as natty dressers and one-line joke tellers. Yelsky was more conservative in his attire and more serious in his mien. Steele was a lawyer, too, and the briefcase bulging with papers that he lugged to court every day made it seem likely that he was assisting in his own defense. On the prosecution side, a good pair of men were handling the case. Carmen Marino, thirty-four, was the more openly aggressive of the two, while Albin Lipold was the older, more assured and steady hand. During most of the trial, Jack

Walsh sat with Marino and Lipold at the prosecution table.

In criminal trials, each side must disclose to the other in advance their list of potential witnesses. Carmen and Al had persuaded Judge Nahra that three of the state's witnesses had to remain unnamed, because it was feared that the Kilbanes might try to take reprisals against them if they were known. One was Carol Braun. The other two were Larry DiGravio, who Robbins had said was present in Owen's car just after the murder, and the third was former Euclid police sergeant Charles Miller, who had assisted Lou Kulis in his long interrogation of Steele.

During jury selection, Nahra revealed himself as a strong jurist, one who kept a tight rein on all the attorneys and wouldn't easily let jurors out of their obligations. One woman claimed that her husband was on medication and needed her to administer it; the judge ruled that she must stay and serve, because other people could give her husband his pills. A peremptory challenge removed a man who said he was very nervous because he'd quit smoking recently and he was afraid he'd go back to cigarettes if he became upset during the trial. Out of a panel of fifty-nine potential jurors, not a single one could be found who had not heard of the case; however, enough of them were considered satisfactory by Judge Nahra and the opposing attorneys to allow the seating of a jury of eight men and four women by the end of the second day of the trial. The jurors included a graduate business student, a pipe fitter, an Ohio Bell supervisor, a production planner, a baker, a fashion sales representative, a housewife, and a grandmother. By the time they were seated, the focus of interest had shifted to something quite controversial: the arrest of Carol Braun as a material witness.

She was arrested at Owen's home on the afternoon of the second day of the trial, but not without an uproar. The problem was that about a month earlier she had brought home from the hospital baby Patrick Ryan Kilbane, and she was a nursing mother. "Kidnapping!" defense lawyers screamed to the press. Owen allowed that he was "amazed and angered by the arrest," and attorney Burke let reporters know that if the cops had tried something like this in his home, he would have killed someone. Marino countered by saying, "We had reason to believe if she was not arrested she would not be on hand for trial testimony." In the courtroom, Nahra ordered Carol taken out of jail, placed in a hotel or motel under guard, and reunited with her child pending her appearance in court the next day. On the spot, Owen hired attorney Thomas W. Shaughnessy to represent Carol.

Now the real issue was joined, and a trial within a trial began. Out of the hearing of the jury, the defense attorneys argued that Carol Braun was really Carol Kilbane, that the couple had a common-law marriage that dated back before the time of the murder, and as "proof" they cited the fact that Owen's 1968 federal income tax filing listed Carol as his dependent. Their tactic was clear: if they could say that Carol was Kilbane's wife, she could not be forced to testify against him, and the statement that

Carol had given me in 1975 would not be permitted in evidence—and the state's case would be seriously impaired. As someone on the prosecution side told reporters about this statement McCann and I had taken from Carol, it was "dynamite." The prosecution needed to prove that Carol had been a prostitute, not a wife, especially at the time she'd made her statement, and could therefore be compelled to testify about what she'd told me. So Al Lipold countered with the equally persuasive evidence that when Owen had been interviewed by the Euclid police right after the murder of Marlene Steele, he had told them that Carol Braun was his "employee," not his wife.

"The courtroom setting was as bizarre as the legal question," the Cleveland *Press* avowed as, the next day, Judge Nahra had the jury taken on a tour of the murder site, and continued this sidebar trial out of the jury's presence, but with reporters hanging on every word. A photo in the newspaper showed Carol Braun looking like a dimpled and lovely June Allyson, carrying her adorable, blanket-covered infant into the Criminal Justice Center. At one point during the proceedings, a recess was ordered so Carol could carry the baby into a side room for a breast-feeding session. When Carol returned to take the witness stand, she rocked back and forth on the swivel chair as little Patrick Ryan gurgled and moved about in his blanket. Carmen Marino ignored the baby and went right to the point:

Q: Weren't you arrested in Lakewood on April 9, 1970?

A: I don't remember.
Q: What was the charge?
A: I don't remember.
Q: Wasn't the charge prostitution?
A: I don't know what you call it.

Marino kept on, inquiring whether it was true that she had told the police at the time of that prostitution arrest in 1970, and had told the FBI in 1975—meaning me, but my name had not yet been made public—that her name was Carol Braun, not Carol Kilbane.

"Yes," she said, "but I was scared to tell them I was Carol Kilbane."

The lawyers cross-examined Marty Kilbane, who knew very well that Owen had also lived with other women from time to time during the period when he was supposedly married to Carol; Marty denied any such knowledge. Hadn't Owen lived in California for at least eighteen months during the ten-year period in which he and Carol were supposed to have been married? Nobody on the defense side would admit to knowing anything about that. It became clear to me that Carol herself was a hostage to Owen, and would remain so. I recalled her having told me that the only time she'd really been "free" was the six months she'd spent in jail in 1974.

The next day, the defense said that the pair had been married in Las Vegas on July 4, 1967, even though there was no marriage certificate to prove it. Marino cross-examined Owen: hadn't he been a pimp for the last ten years? "No," said the man who had admitted to police in that 1969 interrogation that his occupation was that of a pimp and had served a six-month sentence for just that crime. Marino pointed out to the court that when Owen and Carol had been convicted in 1973, both had listed themselves as single.

Tempers flared repeatedly. Nahra wanted attorney Burke to make his grunts and groans facing front, so they could be understood. And he admonished Marino to slow down his questioning, which was beginning to seem like badgering. "Objection, objection, objection," the three defense attorneys would chorus now and then. Attorney Sperli produced documents showing that some of Owen's property was listed under the joint names of Owen and Carol, and that she had credit cards in the name of Carol Kilbane. As the day was ending, Sperli commented, "If I haven't shown this was a common-law marriage, then I'm a lady barber."

We'd see about that. In the next courtroom session, still out of the hearing of the jury, I took the stand. All FBI agents are trained in the proper way to testify in court. We know to sit up straight, on the edge of the chair, to address our answers as much to the jury—or, in this case, the judge—as we do to the attorney asking the questions, and to make sure that we do not permit hostile attorneys to prevent us from getting our story out. From time to time Owen had admitted to me that he was a pimp and that Carol was one of his main prostitutes, and I told this to the court, along with the information that I'd been investigating the Kilbanes for years, looking into other murders as well Marlene Steele's.

I testified that I had taken the 1975 statement from Carol and related the circumstances.

I readily admitted that in our most recent conversation Carol said she'd been "insane on drugs" at the time of making the five-page statement. The defense seized on this, of course, but I fought back, getting across the information that I'd talked to Carol for several days before going to Saint Louis, and that while she'd been agitated then, she had been far from insane or high on drugs. Consternation reigned at the defense table when I told them that I had a Bureau-authorized tape recording of one of those conversations and could produce it on request. No way were the defense attorneys going to let that tape into the courtroom, because it gave the lie to their attempt to paint Carol as incompetent mentally when she'd made the statement that incriminated Steele, Robbins, Owen, and Marty. "Objection, objection, objection!" It got so that we always knew when we'd hit a sensitive point with the defense—the chorus of multiple objections was instantaneous.

The very next day, Judge Nahra ruled that Carol Braun was not Kilbane's wife and must testify. Shaughnessy objected, and he was backed up by the three regular defense attorneys, who planned an immediate appeal of the issue. Sperli told the court, "Under no circumstances, regardless of how the Appeals Court rules or what it does, Carol Braun has told me that she will not testify." Nahra said that if Carol refused to testify even after being told to do so, she could be jailed for contempt. "If the court wants to find her in contempt of court, that is the court's decision," said the defense. This attitude seemed to imply that if Nahra sent Carol to jail to punish her for not testifying, that was okay with Carol's supposed common-law husband.

The issue was by no means resolved yet, and there was a fair chance that the appeals court wouldn't see things Judge Nahra's way. While we were waiting for the appeals court, Judge Nahra ordered the prosecution to proceed in presenting its case.

Among the first witnesses for the prosecution was David Lombardo, who had succeeded Steele as the Euclid prosecutor, and the story he told set the tone for the prosecution's case. The two men had been friends; they had met when Lombardo was still in law school and had defended himself on a Euclid traffic charge—Steele was the police prosecutor at that time. Later, Lombardo had gone to work in the Euclid court system, and when Steele was elevated to the judgeship, Steele helped Lombardo become the prosecutor. In either late September or early October of 1968, Lombardo went to see Steele in the latter's chambers, to thank him.

"I told him, anything I can ever do for him in the future, I'd be happy to, because the consensus was that he was going to run for Mayor, and I offered him my assistance." And then Steele surprised him. As Lombardo testified, "He said, 'Do you think that Joe'—meaning my law partner Joe Coviello—'that he could find somebody to kill my wife for me?'"

How had he responded to this, the prosecutor asked.

"I told him he was crazy, in so many words."

They had talked for ten minutes or more, about divorce; Steele let Lombardo know that he wanted one, but that Marlene did not. After a while, Lombardo "made some kind of remark, trying to be funny, because I meant to treat it lightly, and as I was leaving, he said, 'Don't laugh. Some morning you may pick up the paper and see she has had a tragic accident, and you'll know what happened.'" That was the end of Lombardo's conversation with Steele. But on the morning that he learned Marlene had been found dead, Lombardo had been thunderstruck. A few days later, he recounted the "tragic accident" conversation to Euclid safety director Ralph Dunker, who was then in charge of the investigation, and later repeated it to other authorities.

After Lombardo, the testimony turned technical. Patrolman McKibben, who had been first on the scene, told how Marlene's body had been cold to the touch, a fact that did not jibe with Steele's contention that he had called the police immediately on finding his wife dead in their bed.

I was reminded again of the importance of doing an investigation thoroughly, right from the very first few moments of it. This detail, one of many that had been carefully noted by McKibben as he entered the Steele home, figured prominently in the trial eight years later; if he hadn't recorded his observations accurately at that time, his testimony at the trial would have had less impact. In that sense, the ghost of the Sam Sheppard case, which had informed the minds of the investigators since the first moments, had helped in the Steele case, by instilling in them anew the need to be careful and deliberate in accumulating and documenting the evidence.

The most impressive technical witness was Mrs. Mary Cowan, the blood specialist from the coroner's office, a nationally recognized expert on the subject and a veteran of hundreds of trials. Her testimony was a crash course for the jury in forensic trace evidence, laced with the distinctions between running blood, seeping blood, and the various "smudging, staining, jerking, spurting and distorted" blood patterns. Al Lipold took her through the rather grim set of photos of Marlene Steele lying on her deathbed. Again, the investigators had been careful, snapping photos after each layer of bedding and clothing was removed. Together, Lipold and Cowan took apart Steele's version of what had happened that morning in January 1969. For instance, on the matter of pushing or shoving Marlene's shoulder to see whether she was alive, which Steele had said he'd done. If the body had been moved in such a way before the blood dried, Lipold asked, would there have been evidence of it on the pillow?

A: If it were before the blood dried, there would be marked distortion.
Q: And was there any evidence of marked distortion?
A: No, sir.
Q: And what does that indicate to you?
A: No movement of the head.

The most damaging thing Mrs. Cowan had to present was a bit complicated. Steele had claimed he had picked up Marlene's hand, held it in his own, and dropped it downward, all in the moments just after he had rushed into the room and within a minute of hearing the shots. Cowan testified that the dried-blood pattern on that hand matched precisely an area of the face that appeared unbloodied. The rest of the face was a mess, but that spot was clean. Why? Because the hand had been tightly coiled at the face until the blood had dried—a minimum of twenty minutes, Mrs. Cowan estimated—and *then* had been picked up and moved. No other sequence of events could explain the blood evidence. When she had finished, it should have been obvious to any impartial observer that Steele had waited until Marlene's blood had stopped flowing before he had moved her hand, decided she was completely and irrevocably dead, and called the police.

The next morning was Saint Patrick's Day, and the streets were crowded with a parade. Inside, the prosecution was happy to learn that the appeals court had sided with Nahra, and that Carol Braun would soon be called to testify. The defense was cheered by a partial victory, as Nahra ruled that the statement Owen Kilbane had given to police four days after the Steele murder could not be admitted into evidence "at the present time." That statement was considered important, because it would help to establish the prosecution's contention that there had been a conspiracy among the defendants to murder Marlene Steele, but it was not crucial to the case. Later in the day, Nahra decided that the statement could be entered, and the defense muttered to reporters that there were really three prosecutors working in the trial—Marino, Lipold, and Nahra.

The wrangling over Carol's unwillingness to take the stand continued, and was nearing the point at which it would have to be resolved one way or another. In the meantime, Chester Zembala got his inning against Steele, as prelude to the state's star witness, Rickey Robbins.

As had such people as Cowan and McKibben, Zembala, the detective who sat outside Steele's home each year on the anniversary of Marlene's death, had things to report that were devastating to Steele's version of events. Steele had said that he'd heard footsteps downstairs, and the slamming of the door as the unknown assailant ran outside. Zembala recounted how he and his partner had tested out Steele's contentions while Marlene's body was still in the house. "The door would not slam. We must have tried it twenty times," Zembala said. Similarly, "My partner and I, we both tried to run real heavy on our feet and make a clump-clump sound, and we were not able to hear it. Whoever was upstairs was not able to hear it." Outside, they had looked carefully at the footprints. There were, in Zembala's expert opinion, two distinct sets. One showed a "normal short gait," and could only be traced to the end of the house, where the walker looked into the living room, and then returned to the house, Zembala thought those had been made by Steele, because of a pair of shoes that sat inside the house in the midst of a mud puddle. With the second set, "the step in between each footprint was considerably longer than the other set," and led to the ravine; they tracked these prints across a creek, across the abandoned railroad spur, and up onto Green Road, where they had vanished, an indication that the wearer of those boots had then gotten into a car.

Then it was time for Rickey Robbins, whose testimony and cross-examination by all three defense attorneys took two full days. Because of threats made against his life, Robbins had to testify while wearing a bulletproof vest under his sports jacket. Al Lipold led him through the story, pretty much as Rickey had given it in his statements to Walsh and Goodwin, and again to Corrigan. He admitted the shooting of Tedd Browne, what had happened when he'd called Marty Kilbane for help from Camp Pendleton, and what he'd done all through the night and morning of the murder. How the firing pin had fallen out of the gun. How he and the Kilbanes had shot pool while waiting for the moment to go and do the deed. Why he had been willing to do what he had done.

> A: I was afraid that if I didn't do it [the Steele "job"], I'd be told on about the Browne killing. . . . It wasn't a formal threat, but it was brought up a few times . . . every time that I showed I wasn't really interested in it or didn't want to, it was brought up.

Lipold asked him to relate what Owen had said about Marlene Steele.

A: I was told she was a heavy sleeper.
Q: Okay. Anything else?
A: And there was a comment made, and the comment was, "Don't plan on knocking off a quick piece, because she's on the rag."

Rickey had noticed those wet shoes by the door—a detail that had been in none of the newspaper accounts but had figured large in Chester Zembala's notes. He had also knocked the phone off the hook on the way out and left it buzzing, a detail that would also later prove important. With the thousand dollars given him by Owen, Rickey and Marty had bought matching "avocado double-breasted suits" so they could look like gangsters, and he had left some of the money in his mother's mailbox.

On April 4 1969, Rickey testified, he had slit his wrists in a suicide attempt. The complete reason did not come out at the trial but had to do with Sandy, with Robbins's father, and with despondence over his own condition. Rickey had met Sandy on the night of January 9, that is, within hours after the murder; they had quickly become close. But Sandy hadn't wanted to marry an AWOL marine. And the elder Robbins was adamant that Rickey should not continue to be absent without leave; he wanted Rickey to go back and face the music, even if it meant spending time in the brig. Robbins felt the impossibility of resolving the situation, and slit his wrists. After a week in the hospital, though, he did return to the Marine Corps in California, where he was very quickly evaluated by their psychiatric staff and discharged in June of 1969. Released from his duty, he returned to Cleveland, married Sandy, and went to work for the Kilbanes.

When Steele had represented him during the Phillipone shooting in July of 1969, Rickey testified, he believed that Steele did not know that Rickey had killed Marlene. He was "under the impression, until 1973, that no one knew I had done it except Marty, Owen and Larry DiGravio." That impression was countered by Steele's "good job" comment at Owen's sister's wedding in 1973. And the implication that Steele had to know about Rickey's involvement was made more certain by what had happened after Rickey had been arrested in the Browne case. When the newspapers had speculated about the connection between Rickey and Steele in the murder of Marlene, Steele had said to him, "That thing about my wife that's in the paper, don't worry about it, because they are just poking around." It was after that comment that Robbins had dismissed Steele as his attorney.

Lipold's final questions were about the "deal" for Robbins's testimony. Had his sentence been reduced or commuted? It had not, and Rickey testified that he didn't know whether it ever would be.

The cross-examination of Rickey Robbins by three attorneys was quite an exercise, because all the attorneys understood that if they could shake Robbins's story, they'd make a serious dent in the prosecution's case. At the moment, they were winning the trial within a trial that had to do with Carol Braun's testimony, and as they tore into Robbins it was clear that they were hoping for a one-two punch that would result in a hung jury or an acquittal of the defendants. The defense strategy was to imply that, despite his confession, Robbins had *not* been the murderer of Marlene Steele and to insist that he had concocted his story in order to get out of jail. His supposed additional motivation: a wish to get back at Steele for having had to pay the lawyer for representing him in the Phillipone case.

Attorney Burke flourished a letter that Rickey had written from prison to Marty Kilbane, which said. "They are trying to get me to tell them something about the Steele case, and I don't know anything about it." The defense took this as truth and Robbins's recent testimony as deliberate lies. In another letter, Robbins threatened to kill himself rather than spend life in prison. Burke asked rhetorically, "So: now you don't have to kill yourself, do you, Mr. Robbins?" Other attorneys brought up supposedly contradictory details in Rickey's story. He had said that the pool table they'd played on had "sock pockets," so the defense showed a bill of sale for a pool table at Owen's house, a table with sock pockets that had not been delivered to the Kilbane house until well after the night of the murder. Yelsky asked whether Marlene had been lying on her right side or left side when Rickey allegedly shot her. Rickey said one way, then corrected himself and said it was the other way around. (Mary Cowan had made the same mistake on the stand and had corrected herself.) If Robbins couldn't remember which side Marlene had been lying on, Yelsky thundered, then perhaps the entire story had been made up—the details fed to Rickey by Jack Walsh or others privy to the coroner's report and police investigative notes.

To cap their contentions, and much to my annoyance, lawyer Leonard W. Yelsky took a leaf from the book of Robert K. Ressler. He shoved in Robbins's face that awful eight-by-ten-inch color photo of Marlene's bloody head.

"I don't want to look at any pictures," Robbins moaned and averted his eyes.

"That's too bad! You didn't kill this lady, and you don't have to put on any act that you did!"

Robbins continued to stare away from the photo. He was near tears.

"You didn't do this! Just look at it!" Yelsky yelled.

"Do I have to look at the picture?" Robbins asked Judge Nahra.

The judge said he had to, and Robbins did, recovering his composure slightly and pointing to where he had stood in relation to the woman and the bed when he had fired the fatal shots.

Weeks later, after the trial was concluded, Robbins would tell a reporter that for years he had been haunted by a recurring dream: at the moment he had stood by Marlene's bed, instead of shooting her he would tell her that Steele wanted to have her killed, and would run away. But he had not run, he had shot her, and his nightmare would not resolve.

The courtroom tag-team wrestlers then relieved one another, and attorney Sperli asked Rick, "You would do anything to get out of prison, wouldn't you?"

"Anybody would," Robbins agreed. "But I wouldn't lie. I have no reasons to."

But, Sperli pointed out, he *had* lied during the Browne trial, and in their view had plenty of reason to lie now. Then Sperli tried the same tactic as Yelsky had, asking Robbins whether he could look directly at the jury "and tell them that you would not lie to get yourself out of prison."

"As far as this case, I agreed I would not lie," Robbins responded.

"It took you quite a while to turn your face over here," Sperli commented. "You didn't have to muster up your inner self to tell that whopper?"

"No, sir," Robbins answered, but he was badly shaken—and so was the prosecution's case.

The Carol Braun problem finally came to a head in Judge Nahra's courtroom and out of the hearing of the jury. Baby Patrick Ryan was noisy, so Barbara Steele took him into the hall outside the courtroom to allow his mother to give her full attention to the situation inside. The appeals court and Judge Nahra directed that Carol testify in this case, at least to the fact that she had given the statement to McCann and me in 1975. As Carmen Marino forcefully argued, "It is obvious from the acts of the defendants . . . that there is collusion to prevent her from testifying. . . . Each defendant benefits by her not testifying . . . because the statement implicates each and every one of the defendants, including Rick Robbins." As evidence of possible collusion, the prosecution pointed out to Nahra that Shaughnessy, who was representing Carol, was being paid by Owen Kilbane. The implication: that there was a serious question as to whose interests, Carol's or Owen's, were being defended by Shaughnessy. "Do I understand you, Mr. Shaughnessy," the judge asked, "that you have advised this lady that she can disobey an order of this court?" Shaughnessy's face reddened. If as an officer of the court he advised Carol to disobey a court order, that conduct would subject him to penalties. He responded that the decision had been entirely Carol's.

Carol tearfully contended that testifying would do irreparable damage to her marriage, and the judge replied that if she continued to refuse to be sworn as a witness, he would sentence her to six months in jail for contempt of court.

Marino again: "Your Honor, this woman has substantial evidence material to this case, and if she won't testify voluntarily and would rather go to jail, then forcefully bring her to the witness chair if you have to. . . . We don't care if she denies this written statement. Let her deny it to the jury and let the jury decide."

Three times the judge carefully asked Carol whether she would be sworn in, and three times she refused. It was like watching some ancient ceremony, repeated in the same phrases again and again to make sure that there was no misunderstanding as to what was involved. Then Nahra sentenced Carol to six months in jail and ordered her taken away in handcuffs. He told Shaughnessy that his conduct was "completely reprehensible."

Robbins's credibility had been shaken, and now it appeared that we would not be able to introduce Carol Braun's statement into the trial. The prospect of a fiasco loomed.

The situation with Carol Braun remained unresolved. One day, Judge Nahra jailed her; the next,

she was free on bond and she and Owen exchanged
vows in attorney Burke's office. They repeated the
"whither thou goest" verse from the Book of Ruth,
but their vows were common-law and not formal,
probably because they didn't want the prosecution
to say that if this was a formal marriage, that was
evidence they hadn't truly been married earlier.
Within hours of the exchange of vows, the appeals
court sent her back to jail. I went to see her there.

"Why are you doing this to yourself?" I asked.
"We're going to get that statement in, one way or
another, and all you'll get will be time in jail."

"I don't want to talk about it," she cried.

For another few minutes I tried to persuade her
that she could simply attest to having made the
statement to us, even recant it on the stand, if she
needed to. That, I argued, wouldn't hurt her—or
her baby—nearly as much as she was doing by
refusing to testify at all and remaining incarcerated.
She would not be moved.

Ten

"NECESSARY AND RELIABLE"

With the prosecution's two best shots stymied or labeled as less than perfectly credible, it seemed as though the case against Steele and the Kilbanes might unravel. Now a savior came galloping out of the past: Lou Kulis and the nine-and-a-half-hour interview he and Charles Miller had conducted with Steele on February 26, 1969, six weeks after the murder.

As so often happened when what the prosecution wanted to present touched a raw nerve, the defense objected to Kulis as a witness and to the introduction of the taped interview into the trial. Kulis couldn't very well be prevented from taking the stand, since he was a recognized law enforcement detective who had been on the scene in the first hours after Marlene Steele's death, but the defense tried hard to exclude the tape-recorded interrogation. Attorney Burke tried to contend that the tapes were inadmissible because Steele had not known he was being taped. When Kulis said on the stand he thought he'd told

Steele that he was being taped, Burke shouted at him, "You're lying, sir!" An additional problem for the prosecution in regard to the veracity of the taping procedure was provided by the utter disappearance of Charles Miller, a former officer of the Euclid police department, who had sat in on the long interview. In Miller's absence, the defense could argue that it was only Kulis's word against Steele's, and that Steele contended he hadn't known he was being taped, so his answers weren't really under oath.

This whole defense argument against the tapes was balderdash, because a large, bulky black tape recorder had sat in front of Steele, Kulis, and Miller throughout the session, the tape had been changed four times, and Steele had actually been asked about the recording; additionally, Steele had been advised of his rights before he had agreed to the interview.

Judge Nahra ruled that the tapes could be played, but the defense won a partial victory by having certain portions excised before the tapes were heard by the jury. The portions deleted were the accusatory ones, such as the moment when Kulis said Steele must have been "an accomplished liar" to have concealed from Marlene his affair with Barbara Swartz. Had I been on the defense I, too, would have wanted to keep the jury from hearing these portions, because the deleted sections were the most damaging ones to Steele, times when Kulis had flat-out told Steele that his version of events did not jibe with the physical evidence, and Steele in response could not explain the discrepancies. Even with those sections removed, though, the effect of the entire interrogation was to dramatically highlight the contraditions between Steele's recollections and all the other evidence. Also, played at this point in the trial, these old tapes corroborated more recent revelations.

For instance, on the morning of January 9, Kulis had interviewed Kevin Steele in the presence of his grandfather, and Kevin recalled hearing something peculiar at the approximate time of the murder, a humming sound, not a song but some repetitive pattern like music. The jury heard Kulis bring this matter up to Steele, who airily dismissed it. Jurors also were able to compare this story to Rickey Robbins's testimony on the stand. Now that odd sound heard by a small boy eight years earlier, and so carefully noted by Kulis, made sense: it must have been the noise made by the phone that Robbins had knocked off the hook. Kulis had also challenged Steele by means of another bit of information gleaned from Kevin: Steele maintained that he locked the door the very last thing before going to sleep at nights—but Kevin said that it was his mother who always did the locking up. Which was it, sir?

"Third degree," the defense attorneys charged. But their protest was in vain. The total effect of these tapes was to put Steele on the stand just as surely and more effectively than if the former judge had taken the witness chair in front of the jury. Again and again, on the tapes—which took two days of trial time to play for the courtroom—Kulis asked questions that Steele couldn't answer: "Wouldn't any man hearing shots rush down to see if he could stop what was happening? Why didn't you run immediately to the door to see if you could spot the unknown assailant?" "How long was it, precisely, after noting that your wife was dead, that you called the police?" "Did you ever ask a friend about getting in touch with anyone who could get rid of your wife?" "Why, if you shook her body, took her blood-ied hand and face in your hands, was there no blood on you anywhere?"

In the following, typical section of the tape, Kulis utilized his previously conducted interview with Barbara Swartz to try to trap Steele:

Q: Did you ever talk to Barbara about divorcing your wife?
A: Not really. She never pushed it.
Q: Didn't you talk to her about it in November [1968]?
A: Yeh.
Q: So you did talk seriously about getting a divorce?
A: I can't explain this to you, captain.
Q: Try me.
A: We went through periods of ups and downs. In the summer and mid-fall, we were down.
Q: How important was the solidarity of the family to you?
A: Important enough that I didn't push divorce.
Q: I don't think you had any love for your wife in a long time. I don't think your wife's loss bothered you at all. When did Marlene's picture come down from the wall in your office?
A: I think I took it down . . . no . . . it was never on the wall.

At another point, Steele recalled, "When I asked [Marlene] what she wanted for Christmas ... she said 'a divorce.' If I thought she had been serious, I would have said, 'Go ahead.'" Yet at another moment in the long interrogation, Steele said he would not have gone through with a divorce in early 1969, but would have waited to institute divorce proceedings until after the election in the fall of 1969, an election that would have cemented him into his judgeship.

Listening to Kulis's questions and Steele's lame responses—even with the accusatory portions removed—any thinking person almost had to conclude that at the very least Steele had not answered Kulis's queries truthfully. Some of Steele's forthright statements on the tapes managed to make headlines, though: his admission that he had paid prostitutes for sex, that he had discussed divorce with Marlene, that he owed substantial debts to his in-laws, the Gallittos, et cetera. Much more important for the trial was Steele's admission that he had had two lunches on the seventh, thirty-six hours before the murder, one with Barbara and another with Owen Kilbane, and that he had done numerous favors for Kilbane.

After Kulis and the tapes, additional "technical" witnesses corroborated bits and pieces of Robbins's story. One city employee testified that, sure enough, the lights along the stretch of road driven by Marty Kilbane and Rickey Robbins toward the Steele home had been on regular red-green before midnight, and on blinking yellow afterward, a fact that attested to the veracity of Robbins's memory. The log of the television station was offered in evidence to show that the "cowboy movie" to which Steele had referred was a "Zane Grey Theater" episode that went off the air at 1:33 in the morning, so that if he heard shots moments later, there would still have been a half-hour delay before his having summoned the police at 2:11 A.M. That was one more fact that contradicted Steele's version of events. More technical evidence: at the request of prosecutors, Detective Elmer Roubal had bought a gun similar to the one Robbins said he had fired, and experimented with having the firing pin fall out; Roubal was able to reproduce that event, and to report that the gun had afterward fired properly, even with a damaged firing pin.

In an unusual move, the prosecution called Barbara Steele to the stand. Objection, objection, objection! Shouldn't she, the legal wife of a defendant, be precluded from testifying? The law was very specific about such matters, I now learned. She must testify, Judge Nahra ruled, because she was being asked about events prior to the time of her marriage, which were not subject to the usual exclusion granted to testimony on matters that happened during the marriage. Mrs. Steele's answers on the stand helped corroborate much of what the Kulis tapes had informed the jury about her relationship to Steele in the months before the murder of Marlene.

Next, county prosecutor John T. Corrigan took the stand as a witness. Everyone wanted to know about "the deal," the agreement by which Rickey Robbins had testified in this case. Corrigan carefully explained that he had petitioned both the governor and the parole board about a commutation and a reduction in sentence, but that he "gave no guarantee [to Robbins] that this would happen, and as yet it has not happened. Right now, Robbins is still under a life sentence."

However, in cross-examination Sperli got Corrigan to admit that if the charge in the Browne case was reduced to manslaughter, it was possible that Robbins could get out of jail early—very early.

Q: Isn't it true that . . . he could be eligible for parole consideration ten months after his prison time began?
A: I believe that's true.
Q: And hasn't Richard Robbins been in jail almost ten months right now on the Tedd Browne conviction?
A: I don't know. I think so.

Sperli's implied conclusion was apparent: the jury was to understand that it was entirely possible that if the parole board agreed to Corrigan's deal, Robbins could walk away from jail almost as soon as the Steele trial ended. Corrigan's admission of this possibility was another blow to the prosecution.

More of a setback were the continued absences from the stand of former police sergeant Charles Miller and of Larry DiGravio. This meant that all three of the government's "mystery witnesses" were not testifying; the press suggested that, as a result, the prosecution's case was "greatly weakened." Miller had sat in on the Kulis taping of Steele, but his prime importance was that he had interrogated

Owen Kilbane shortly after the murder, and in that interrogation Owen had admitted being single and a pimp, as well as having a business relationship with Steele. Miller could not be found.

Larry DiGravio had been found and then lost again. Earlier, he had been willing to cooperate with the prosecution. I had talked to him, and so had others, and what he'd told us had corroborated Rickey Robbins's recollections. Yes, DiGravio had said in a sworn and witnessed statement to the prosecutor's office, he'd been in Owen's car on the night of the murder and had heard Owen ask Rick and Marty, through the rolled-down windows, whether everything had gone well and whether Rickey still had the gun. DiGravio's continued absence meant that it was likely the Kilbanes had gotten to him and threatened him with harm should he testify for the prosecution. It was also a problem because the prosecutors had mentioned his expected testimony in their opening statement, and it would not sit well with the jury for the prosecution to be unable to deliver on this particular promised evidence.

While Corrigan and others were testifying, along with other FBI agents and the Euclid and Cleveland police authorities, I was out hunting for DiGravio. Judge Nahra had signed an arrest warrant for him as a material witness in the case. Now, if he continued to avoid us, he would be subject to criminal penalties.

After Corrigan, Jack Walsh took the stand to testify to the circumstances of obtaining Rickey Robbins's first oral statement about the murder of Marlene Steele. He talked about how he had obtained Robbins's trust, and how they had become friends, of sorts. Jack testified that he realized there were some minor inconsistencies in Rickey's several statements given this past summer and fall, but that he was convinced that Rickey Robbins was the shooter in the Steele murder. Jack managed to rile Steele's lawyer, Yelsky, when he admitted that he'd received a letter from Robbins but had put it in the garbage because "it had nothing to do with the case."

"So!" Yelsky had shouted. "The only thing he wrote down—a personal letter from your friend Robbins—and you destroyed it!"

Jack just turned a bland face to Yelsky, and that was that.

With Miller, DiGravio, and Braun missing and the state's case about to wind up, Judge Nahra finally had to render a decision on the most complex issue in the case: the statement I'd taken from Carol Braun and my potential testimony. Could I as a witness read that statement for the jury, or must I be prevented from doing so because Carol would not attest to having made it? In the view of the defense, so long as Carol would not attest to the statement, it fell into the category of an "out-of-court declaration" that was, in legal terms, "incompetent hearsay evidence," which must not be permitted into a trial. The "exclusionary rule" for hearsay evidence is one of the foundations of American jurisprudence. Every permitted exception to it has been fought and argued over, and allowing such exceptions is always a difficult decision to make. If Judge Nahra permitted me to read the statement into the record, he risked the possibility that the case might be overturned on appeal. In trying to make up his mind about the admissibility of the Braun statement, one of the things Judge Nahra considered, in addition to the precedents in the lawbooks, was the tape-recorded conversation I'd had with Carol Braun prior to my going to Saint Louis. In it, of course, she had sounded quite lucid and not under the influence of any mind-altering substances—except perhaps anger.

On Friday, April 1, 1977, Judge Nahra announced his ruling. He argued that the circumstances of Carol's refusal to testify were, in effect, an attempt to prevent the truth about the murder from being brought out in court. Nahra ruled that the right of the public, that is, the court, to know the truth outweighed all other considerations. Carol had made the statement to us in 1975 in good faith, had been advised of her rights, had given it in front of two witnesses, and had altered it in her own handwriting and signed it and repeatedly initialed the changes. (Having her cross out, delete and add information throughout the statement, and initial the changes was a technique I had learned back in my army CID days; it virtually guarantees that a statement will hold up in court should there be a question raised as to whether it had been given voluntarily or willingly.) In Nahra's view, the Braun statement had what a later court would call "circumstantial guarantees of trustworthiness that demonstrated its reliability." Moreover, "the evidence was necessary for a just determination of the issues before the court." *Necessary* and *reliable* were the key concepts. Carol's statement was *reliable* not only because we had witnessed it, but also because it was made prior to the date that Rickey Robbins gave his statement; and her statement was *necessary* because it corroborated Robbins's testimony and was essential to the government's case.

And so, despite numerous objections and promises that there would certainly be an appeal of the case because of this ruling, I finally took the stand, statement in hand, on April Fool's Day, 1977.

I've appeared in dozens of trials, and often as a witness whose testimony makes a dramatic difference in the trial's outcome, but never before or since have I been called to testify in circumstances that were so flagrantly theatrical. Just before I was to take the stand, a final attempt was made to have Carol Braun testify. Under protest and struggling against the deputies, she was brought to the courtroom from her cell in the county jail, and Judge Nahra directed the prosecution to call its next witness.

"The state calls Carol Braun," Carmen Marino said in his loud, clear voice.

The courtroom was packed, and the reporters' and spectators' eyes were on Carol, standing there in jail uniform, well within hearing distance of Marino. Many of the jurors looked around, as if wondering who this might be, because they had not been privy to all the wrangling over her appearance. In answer to the summons Carol said not a word, and for several moments, neither did anyone else.

"You may now call your next witness," Nahra

then instructed Marino, who after a short conference, during which Carol Braun was led to a holding cell just outside the courtroom, proceeded to summon me to the stand.

I began to answer Carmen Marino's questions about where, when, why, and how I took the statement from Carol. At every step of the way, the chorus of objections rang out—"hearsay, hearsay, hearsay"—and were for the most part overruled by Judge Nahra. From time to time, a question had to be rephrased to meet some objection, but we managed to get the story out. Each of the phone calls from Carol, each of the movements we'd made in Saint Louis, I detailed for the jury. To show that Carol really had made the statement, for instance, I let them know how my old army CID technique had operated in this instance:

A: She said there were several things in the statement she was not entirely sure about, and I told her if she did not feel comfortable with the items, to strike them from the statement, which she did. There were other areas that she felt she had new recollections that she would like to include, and I told her to include them in her handwriting, and she did.

I read the statement into the record, and out of the corner of my eye I could see the reporters in the room, furiously scribbling notes and champing at the bit to go out and phone in the "dynamite" to their newspapers. For here, in Carol's five-page

Q: Mr. Ressler, you wanted to get Carol Braun piping mad at Owen Kilbane, didn't you?
A: No, sir. Not necessarily get her piping mad. I think she was sufficiently mad when she got to St. Louis.

The defense started in on me about my training. Wasn't I versed in psychology, in ways to break people down and make them do what I wanted them to? Didn't I offer to use hypnosis on Carol? Hadn't I shown her materials in Saint Louis to help her falsely make up a story? I denied all of these contentions. Fortunately, none of the defense lawyers understood that our Behavioral Science Unit at Quantico was the repository of a great deal of information about the workings of criminal minds, or that the course I usually taught was in abnormal psychology. Had they known, they would have hit harder on me about my training in that field. Such tactics would have given me heartburn but wouldn't have essentially shaken my story, which was a simple relating of the facts. All three defense lawyers accused me of "threatening, scaring, harassing, intimidating and deluding" Carol into making the statement. I hadn't done that, so I denied their every accusation, calmly insisting, "I told her to write nothing in that statement that was not the truth."

Perhaps they thought they were going to trap me by asking about visiting Carol recently, and what she'd said, but I readily admitted that I had seen Carol in Cleveland, and that she had not wanted to testify and had wanted to recant her statement. I was perfectly happy to do so, because this way the

227

defense couldn't accuse us of trying to suppress the fact that she now disagreed with something she'd sworn to earlier. I recounted that Carol had told me in December of 1976 that she'd given the 1975 statement when she was "drunk, on drugs and insane."

The Cleveland *Press* wrote that under the tripartite crossexamination, "Ressler was unshakeable."

Eleven

"WHO WOULD KNOW SUCH AN INTIMATE FACT?"

One final prosecution witness followed me, a flawed one: Larry DiGravio. He had come in from the cold after a week in hiding. His purported motive for staying away: that he feared perjury charges because his testimony would contradict the statement he had given to the prosecutors prior to the trial. He now testified under oath that that statement had been given under duress. He hadn't been in the car with Owen on that fateful night, and hadn't known anything about Rick Robbins and the Steele murder. Under cross-examination, though, he did admit changing his story of that night several times when asked by several different groups of people—the Euclid police, Owen's lawyer, the prosecutors. When the Euclid police told DiGravio that Kilbane's alibi for the time of the murder was that he was out drinking with him, DiGravio had retorted that Owen's story "was full of shit."

The defense then began to call witnesses, mostly to impugn Rick Robbins's testimony. Robbins's former cellmate at Columbus testified that Rick had studied newspaper accounts of the Steele murder to "cook up" a participation in it, for the purposes of getting his sentence in the Browne case commuted. In cross-examination, Marino brought out the fact that this cellmate had spent six months in a psychiatric institution in Florida and time under psychiatric observation in Ohio for various mental problems.

Other witnesses included Kilbane's sister, who testified that the pool table hadn't been installed in early 1969, a furniture dealer who said the bill of sale for that table was dated 1970, an attorney who had witnessed Larry DiGravio as he made a tape recording in Sperli's office in which he recanted his statement to the prosecution, a probate court referee who pointed out that Marlene had not left very much property, and another attorney who had tried a case in Steele's court on the morning before the murder and had not noticed him to be especially nervous. In all, the defense presented only six witnesses in a day and a half of testimony. None of the three defendants took the stand in their own defense, nor did Carol Braun become a witness and attempt to deny the validity of the statement she had made to me, something the prosecutors had expected might take place.

In the hall outside the courtroom one morning, Barbara Steele came up to me and started screaming that I had had no right to come into her house and take her husband away, and that I was never to come near her or her home again. Steele was so embarrassed that he tried to ease her away from me. At the urging of the prosecutors, I tried to make myself inconspicuous, to stay away from court some days so as not to give the defendants and their lawyers the chance to cry about an FBI vendetta.

The defense lawyers made their closing statements, some well argued. Yelsky accused the prosecution of orchestrating the case against his client, Steele, and of coaching witnesses. The defense contended, for instance, that all the evidence given by Robbins and in the Braun statement that connected Steele to the murder of his wife was hearsay. They painted Carol Braun as mentally unstable, and pointed out that she had checked herself into a psychiatric facility in December of 1975, though they did not tell the jury that Carol had been discharged two weeks later when no one could find anything wrong with her. They attacked Robbins as a stupid man who couldn't remember what side of her body his alleged victim had been lying on, and who was only testifying to get out of jail. They called him such names as liar, lecher, leech, whore, suicidal maniac, and psychotic killer. Yelsky summed up by saying, "I hope that you ladies and gentlemen of the jury, by your verdict, don't have anything to do with putting a man like that back on the streets." Lawyer Sperli saved some of his greatest fire for that Carol Braun statement, for the agent who had gotten it out of her, and for the FBI's delay in disseminating the statement to the local authorities:

> They knew the condition she [Carol Braun] was in.
> They knew she was mad at her husband. They knew
> this was the time to get her and get something, but

when they came down to it, they really knew it didn't amount to a hill of beans. But ... when Robbins comes forth and when you can put it [the statement] in through the [FBI] agent, it sounds like something, but back then it didn't sound like anything, and they didn't think enough of it to have Ressler follow up on it. Now Mr. Ressler is a nice person. He is obviously a vigorous FBI man. I'm sure he does his job well. But, you know, sometimes you can't have it both ways. . . . Here's a man that got on the plane and went to St. Louis and had another man come from Cleveland to talk to this woman, and would have you believe they didn't follow up on it after that. . . . After investigating it for six years, they put it in a drawer and maybe somebody will pull it out later. Maybe somebody won't. . . . After what this country has been through with Watergate, we know that FBI agents are no different than anybody else. . . .

Then Sperli hit his stride, going back to his cross-examination of me and his theme that I'd been out to get his client.

I don't believe for one minute that he [Ressler] wouldn't do everything he could to get Owen Kilbane in trouble, because . . . they did have an argument. Owen Kilbane got smart with him. He was lippy. He shouldn't have done it, but he did, and that agent never forgot it, and he never will forget it, and if he gets the chance he's going to nail Owen Kilbane. . . .

A moment later, Sperli jumped off this tack and started asking rhetorically what the jury really knew about the "human being" Bob Steele, and whether Steele's uncontrollable sobbing on the morning after the murder wasn't really a reflection of the true and innocent state of his client's mind.

On the prosecution side, Carmen Marino and Al Lipold were very strong. Marino made points when he asked the jury to understand that Robbins had confessed to the Steele murder, whereas he could have just as easily have pinned it all on Marty Kilbane and still merit consideration from the parole board. And Marino brought up the strong evidence of the Kulis tapes. Wasn't it "odd and rare" that Steele says in those tapes

> that at the precise moment he went upstairs to see about his children moving, someone came in the house and murdered his wife? You talk about rolling dice and odds and possibilities — you can't get much further from the truth than that.

In their enthusiasm, though, both prosecutors said things that elicited strong objections from the defense. Marino asked the jury to "think about Carol Braun, how they kept you from hearing her." Objection, objection, objection. Lipold quoted back at the defense the argument of his counterpart, Yelsky, that the jury must acquit Steele and the Kilbanes if they believed Rick Robbins had not killed Marlene; then Lipold said, "The defendants contend that they are not guilty. Not one of them has said, 'We are innocent.' " The chorus of objections followed, based on the obvious fact that the defendants had pleaded "not guilty." Judge Nahra agreed with these objections and instructed the jury to disregard Lipold's statement and to remember that the defendants had indeed pleaded their innocence.

On the other hand, Al Lipold made one of the case's strongest points as he recalled Robbins's relating that Owen Kilbane had told him not to "try knocking off a piece, because she's on the rag." Al characterized this notion as "disgusting" but insisted that the jury put it into proper perspective:

> Robbins had no idea that buried in Dr. Adelson's report was his observation that Marlene Steele had a menstrual pad in place and was in her menstrual cycle. No. Take that one piece of information. Who would know such an intimate fact except Robert Steele? How could Owen Kilbane possibly know that if it hadn't come from Steele? . . . That's truly a fact that ties in the conspiracy between Robert Steele, the Kilbanes and Robbins.

Late in the afternoon of April 7, when the closing arguments were done, Judge Nahra instructed the jury and they retired for deliberations. Their first session lasted only a few hours, and they went to bed early, sequestered in a downtown hotel. It was Holy Thursday, and Easter weekend was just ahead. Everyone hoped that the jury would be finished with its deliberations by then.

Reporters who had attended the trial took an informal poll among themselves; virtually every single one thought that all three defendants would be acquitted. Perhaps this was their cynicism about the judicial system in Cleveland peeking through, for it certainly seemed to me that the prosecution had presented a strong case and that fair-minded jurors would come to the proper conclusion. But we didn't know.

Later, well after the trial was completed and the verdicts handed down, reporter Jim Cox of the *Plain Dealer* talked to nine out of the twelve jurors, and his account gives an insight into what happened during the time when the jury was at its work.

Most states designate as foreman the first person picked for the jury, but at that time Ohio still encouraged juries to elect their own foreman. In this case, the first battle in the jury room, for the post of jury foreman, turned out to be a very important one. Several men were in contention for that post. Thirty-two-year-old graduate business student Casimir (Casey) Matuszewski won more votes than did sixty-four-year-old Walter Zander, a production planner for a printing company, who told everyone that he had twice before been a jury foreman. According to some jurors, Zander was upset about losing, but it would be several days before the jurors were able to understand the roots of his upheaval. Casey proved to be an admirable foreman, using his managerial acumen to start the group of twelve disparate people on the task of trying to decide what evidence to consider first. At the outset, only three of the jurors were willing to vote for conviction.

They had seen some of the more than two hundred exhibits waved around in the courtroom but hadn't examined them closely. Similarly, though they had sat through two days of the Kulis tapes, they hadn't been able to go back and forth over them and analyze them carefully. Now they played parts of the Kulis tapes fifteen to twenty times, and, as one juror remembered, "Something didn't jive."

They didn't believe Rick Robbins, principally because he had so much to gain by his testimony, and because the defense had made capital out of his not remembering which side Marlene had been lying on. Individually and separately, in the hotel in which they were sequestered, many of the jurors looked at their roommates in bed and discovered that they had to grope to describe properly whether someone was on the left or right, facing them or facing away. In the jury room, one man climbed up on the jury table and used an overcoat to simulate a blanket that he pulled over himself. All the lights except one in the bathroom were turned off. No one could tell what side he was lying on. That caused some people to change their minds.

An important factor was the Braun statement, Cox reported. "Her knowledge of small details of the plot—that the shoes Robbins was given to wear weren't his size, and that there would be prearranged signals from within the Steele home—were considered significant by the jury," he wrote. By the second straw vote, there were nine for conviction, three for acquittal. They tacked up on a board the bloody-faced photo of Marlene Steele and let it preside over their deliberations.

The Larry DiGravio business continued to bother the jurors; some jurors believed he had been pressured into making his admission to the FBI and to

the police. Then Zander made a vehement statement: "I know the police do that. I went through
the same thing when the police accused me of murdering my father."

Other jurors were stunned as Zander poured out
a story of what had happened more than forty years
earlier, when he was eighteen. He and his father
had gone fishing, and the father had fallen into Lake
Erie and died; when the father's wallet was recovered from the lake, the money that had been in it
was missing. Detectives had grilled Zander for a
day and a half, accusing him of murder and not
letting up until the coroner ruled that the elder Zander had accidentally drowned.

Zander's tearful confession was a serious problem, one that could have caused a mistrial, because
Zander had not told Nahra about this long-ago
trauma when the judge had asked a routine question
as to whether any previous experience with police
might prejudice Zander's ability to evaluate police
testimony. The jury apprised Nahra of the problem,
and he told the prosecution and defense attorneys
but personally decided that this was not a trial
breaker. Nahra sent a note back to the jurors: "Keep
deliberating."

They did so, with a fifteen-minute break to attend
a nearby church on Easter Sunday. When they
returned, it was with greater zeal to unravel the
mystery. Soon, Zander became the only holdout
against conviction. The possibility of a hung jury
was discussed among the jurors.

Outside, among the trial participants and reporters, that subject also came up. Steele was convinced

that the lengthy deliberations had to mean that the jury could not come to a decision—and that would mean either a costly new trial or a dismissal of the charges. The only matters that controverted Steele's hunch were the jury's requests to the judge to again instruct them about fine points in the law.

In the jury quarters bathroom, Casey was advised by another male juror not to say much in the discussions, because Zander, the lone holdout, was resentful of not being the foreman. Casey kept quiet, and others took up the task of trying to convince Zander. Soon Zander said he believed that Steele and Owen Kilbane were guilty but thought that Marty Kilbane had been simply duped by the others and did not deserve to be convicted.

Patiently people in the room explained the law, that in a conspiracy all of the parties do not have to be fully involved with the act of murder to be equally guilty. Zander now agreed to vote to convict all three defendants. Before sending word to the judge that a verdict had been reached, Casey Matuszewski made what other jurors later characterized as a masterstroke. He asked everybody in the jury room to be silent for three minutes, and to contemplate their decisions and what they were about to do. Then, one by one, each stood and affirmed his or her individual votes. Many jurors cried while doing so. Some jurors couldn't stop crying for twenty minutes.

It was Monday evening, April 11, 1977. In the twenty-third-floor courtroom, the jury's verdict was read and the jury was polled, and former judge Robert Steele, pimp Owen Kilbane, and wheelman

Marty Kilbane stood convicted of first-degree murder. Judge Nahra sentenced them all to life in prison. The defendants showed no emotion in the court, but Mrs. Steele was visibly stunned. This was the eighth anniversary of her marriage to Steele.

The judge refused to permit the convicted men to be released on bond pending the start of their sentences, and ruled that they were to be kept for thirty days in the county jail so that they could straighten out their personal affairs before entering the state penal system.

The verdict relieved and satisfied me. Euphoria at victory, though a staple of fictional trials is hardly ever present on the prosecution side in actual murder cases. After all, winning doesn't mean that the victim gets to come back to life; it means only that the guilty will suffer for their crime. All the local police authorities and the prosecutors who played such important parts in the case, I believe, shared similar emotions. Eight years it had taken. In several police stations around Cleveland and at the Hofbrauhaus bar, parties were held, because the verdict affirmed to the police that their devotion to the cause of justice, so often derided, was real and true, and that sometimes, in this cockeyed world, things did eventually even out and the good guys prevailed.

Mrs. Gallitto had been in attendance during part of the trial but had returned to Florida during the deliberations because they were taking so long. Telephoned with the news of the verdict, she expressed to reporters the feelings of all of us by saying that she was glad it was over, for now she could begin to put the death of her daughter Marlene behind her and get on with life.

Before I went back to Quantico, a few other matters needed clearing up. Another agent and I drove out to Owen Kilbane's house, where spring flowers were just beginning to bud. Owen was in jail, of course, but Carol Braun had been released and was home, and she was the one I had to see. She wouldn't even let me come into the house, just stood there on the porch, defiant, with the baby on her hip, framed by a screen door.

"All right, Carol," I said. "The Steele thing is over and done with. You won't be bothered by Owen anymore; he'll be away for a good long time. Now— what about the murder of Arnie Prunella?"

"I don't care about Arnie Prunella!"

"You gave us a statement about his murder, too, and—"

"Fuck Arnie Prunella!" she screamed in a voice loud enough to wake the neighborhood and the baby at her side. "And fuck Robert Ressler! Get out of my life!"

Her shouted obscenities and the baby's wails rolled over us as we got back into the car, turned around, and headed back to the FBI office in downtown Cleveland.

Part Three

FINAL JUSTICE

Twelve

BACK TO SQUARE ONE

Had this been fiction, the book would have ended right then and there, in April of 1977, with the bad guys being hauled off to jail. Truth is not only stranger than fiction, it is a lot less tidy. In real life, criminal justice cases very often do not end with the defendants' convictions and incarcerations. There are appeals, and other twists. Steele and the Kilbanes were in prison, and so was Rickey Robbins, but there were also serious moves under way to get them all out.

The appeals had one immediate result—to delay the parole board's and the governor's actions on Rickey Robbins. During the trial, defense attorneys had intimated that Robbins's sentence might be reduced to manslaughter and to time already served, and that he might be freed shortly after the conclusion of the trial. But public reaction against a too-lenient deal was strong, so Gov. James Rhodes and the parole board dragged their feet and Rickey continued to serve his sentence in the Browne case, though always housed in prisons at some distance from Steele and the Kilbanes. By early 1979, the parole board, in a split decision, voted not to wholly recommend John T. Corrigan's request that Robbins's sentence be reduced, and Governor Rhodes still hadn't acted upon Corrigan's recommendation for clemency.

Carmen Marino, who worked directly for Corrigan, expressed the feelings of many people when he told the press in early 1979, on the tenth anniversary of the murder, that "Richard Robbins is a rotten little killer who deserves nothing but a long, long time in prison for what he's done. I don't care if he's straightened his life out now, or what. Far as I'm concerned, he's a maggot and I'll regret 'til my dying day that I ever had to make a deal with the likes of him."

So Rickey was still in limbo.

Robert Steele was doing slightly better. In prison, at first he shoveled coal and worked in the laundry, but then he found his true incarcerated vocation: as a jail-house lawyer who advised other inmates on legal problems. As such, he was popular with the inmates. He was also given privileges beyond those afforded most convicts, and rumor had it that these had been arranged through his father's long-term friendships within upper-echelon Ohio political circles. I chafed when I found out about the special treatment Steele was getting, but there was nothing I could do about it. As I later learned, Steele had told Owen and Marty to sit tight and not to do anything foolish, because he was working on ways to get them all out, efforts he said would be crowned

with success in the near future. As they had for ten
years, the Kilbanes continued to believe in Steele's
power in such matters, even from behind bars.

Ten days after the anniversary article, the Ohio
Supreme Court denied the initial appeals of the Kilbanes and Steele. Hurrah! Further appeals were to
be filed, the defendants' attorneys said, but would
take some time. In the meantime, I tried to help the
Bureau pursue the murder of Arnie Prunella, which
had also been firmly linked to Owen Kilbane.

Though after the Steele trial Carol Braun refused
to talk further with us about this matter, we still
had the statement on the Prunella murder that she
had given to Marty McCann and me in August of
1975. Here's what it said. Carol and Owen Kilbane
and Marsha and Arnie Prunella had been friends
and rivals of sorts; Arnie had accompanied Owen
and Carol on trips to Las Vegas, had borrowed a
lot of Owen's money and lost it, and (to quote her
statement) "one way that ARNIE was going to pay
OWEN back the money was by providing his book
of prostitution customers for OWEN to use in
OWEN's prostitution business." Later, according to
Carol, Marsha Prunella suggested that Owen kill
Arnie because of the gambling debts, and Owen
discussed doing so. One evening, after coming home
to Carol, "OWEN told me of the killing of ARNIE
PRUNELLA." He described to Carol how he, his
brother, Martin, and a third man had taken Arnie
out on Owen's boat

*and had beaten him up and then shot and killed
him. OWEN told me how after killing ARNIE that*

*the three individuals had tied a sewer cover to
ARNIE's legs and threw him into Lake Erie. After-
wards, OWEN stated that the three had taken
ARNIE's clothing which he wore and also taken
clothing which they took from the motel that ARNIE
was staying at to one of OWEN's apartment buildings and burned the clothing. . . . Since this time,
OWEN has frequently mentioned the killing of
ARNIE PRUNELLA and when having trouble with
different people has often stated, "I can put that
guy into Lake Erie along with ARNIE and several
others." I have also heard MARTIN KILBANE discuss this murder of ARNIE PRUNELLA on different occasions.*

We looked for other people who had been on the
boat at the time of the murder, to see if we could
convince any of them to turn against the already-
convicted Kilbanes. We had leads to several people,
but they all denied having been on the boat, though
many of them verified that they had heard about
the murder from either Owen or Marty or both. We
had some leads to a man named Phil Christopher,
a friend of the Kilbanes' sister; some stories placed
him on the boat and indicated that he had been the
triggerman for that particular murder. Christopher
wouldn't talk to us, and Carol Braun hadn't mentioned his name, as she had with the hired murderer
of Marlene Steele, Rick Robbins.

Robbins himself told authorities that he had not
only heard the story of Prunella's killing from the
Kilbanes, but that Owen had pointed out to him
the precise location where Arnie's body had been

dumped. Robbins even offered to show the authorities this location. There followed a long and cold charade, during which Rick Robbins enjoyed more than a few nights away from his downstate prison and more than a few days outside of the walls altogether, on a Coast Guard cutter plying the stormy waters of Lake Erie. On one trip, during the winter, the cutter reached home pier just as a woman was trying to commit suicide by jumping into Lake Erie. Joe Harpold dove into the waters and rescued her; he got no thanks from the woman, who had wished to leave this world, but he did receive a commendation for bravery from the Coast Guard.

Several more times, in the company of Harpold, Jack Walsh, and other lawmen, Robbins went out with the Coast Guard to look for the spot where Arnie Prunella's body had supposedly been dumped. As one can imagine, pinpointing a location in the thousands of square miles of undifferentiated waters was an impossible task, and eventually proved fruitless.

Back to square one on Prunella.

On July 5, 1979, the Eighth District Court of Appeals upheld the conviction of the Kilbanes and Steele for the murder of Marlene Steele, but did so on a split decision, 2–1. Since the strands of the decision and the dissent later assumed even more importance, I want to take a moment to discuss them here. Judge John T. Patton wrote the majority opinion, and essentially argued that the state's case had been very strong, that Nahra's decision in the matter of the Braun statement was correct, and that all of the other errors either had been corrected or were of such small bore that they would not have affected the outcome. In Patton's view, the Braun statement was the linchpin of the trial, because it linked the Kilbanes, Steele, and Robbins in a conspiracy to commit murder. In a concurring opinion, Judge J. Pryatel went to the heart of my testimony about Braun and her statement, and how Steele and Kilbanes had damaged themselves by not permitting her to take the stand. Judge Pryatel pointed out that the defense counsels' cross-examination of me

> extracted more information about Carol and her statement than appellants could have done had she taken the stand. A recantation by Carol Braun would have been self-serving, but her recantation through Ressler was a declaration against his interest. Had she testified and renounced her statement, the prosecutor would have pursued her as a hostile witness to prove that the resolution of her differences with Owen and the resumption of living with him were the real causes of her retraction. By not taking the stand, she was spared such an attack.

Justice Leo J. Jackson disagreed with the majority, and rather vociferously—his dissent ran longer than his colleagues' opinions combined. Jackson was black, and he hit very hard on the credibility of Rick Robbins. He was disturbed that the facts of the Tedd Browne murder had not been allowed more prominence in the trial; in particular, he noted that while Robbins had finally admitted that he had killed Browne, he still continued to maintain that he had *not* carved an *N* on the bullet. Jackson faulted Judge

Nahra on proscribing the cross-examination of Robbins on such points.

Quite apart from his concerns about Robbins, the appellate judge also believed that the defendants' constitutional guarantees had been abridged because, in his view, they were not allowed to confront their accusers. For instance, the Kulis tapes had been played; these, as everyone had noted at the time, in effect put Steele on the stand. Jackson viewed this as prejudicing Owen and Marty's rights of confrontation. Similarly, the appellate judge made the point that because the Braun statement had been admitted into the trial but Braun herself had not appeared, Owen was deprived of his right to confront Carol, who in this instance had to be considered his accuser. In Justice Jackson's dissenting view, the Braun statement was also crucial to the outcome of the trial; he made up a chart that graphically demonstrated his view that everything presented in my testimony was hearsay, whereas if the material had been presented by Braun herself, in many instances it would not have been hearsay. He concluded that Carol Braun "did have various motives to give false information to Agent Ressler," and that this alone would argue for a reversal of the verdict. Jackson also disagreed on several other issues with the majority, enough issues, in his view, to warrant reversal.

But the 2–1 appeals opinion was firmly on the side of keeping the defendants incarcerated, and that was what was done.

However, Justice Jackson's dissenting opinion galvanized a new set of defense appeals, this time

Robert K. Ressler and Tom Shachtman

to the federal court system, on the constitutional grounds that Jackson had outlined.

In February of 1981, the first alarums of reversal began to be raised. U.S. Magistrate David S. Perelman said that he was going to recommend to district court judge George P. White, who had the Steele case under consideration, that the defendants receive a new trial. The state rushed to counter the recommendation, but to no avail. On April 2, 1981, Judge George P. White of the U.S. District Court based in Cleveland issued his ruling. The major issue, he wrote, was whether the admission of the Braun statement "denied petitioners the right to confront witnesses against them, as guaranteed by the Sixth Amendment." Judge White cited Judge Jackson's arguments repeatedly in deciding that the rights of all three defendants had been violated, and that they had not received a fair trial. The statement of Braun should not have been allowed, and by itself the Robbins testimony would not have been enough to convict. Therefore, Judge White ordered that the Kilbanes and Steele were entitled to a new trial—one that could not include the Braun statement—and meanwhile, they were to be freed on a writ of habeas corpus.

All of a sudden, the defendants in the murder of Marlene Steele were to be let out of jail. Back to square one on that case, too.

The scene as Steele walked out of prison, observers agreed, was unusual: inmates rushed up to congratulate him, to wish him good luck, and to thank him for all his help. The convicts seemed to think he was a great man, and that his release from jail was a victory.

Thirteen

"GUILTY BUT SILENT"

A few days after his release, Steele was interviewed by the press in his lawyer's office. Reporters found him dressed in a conservative gray suit and salmon-colored tie, his eyes red-rimmed and his hands shaking. He was suffering, he said, from grief over the recent death of his wife, Barbara. His voice broke when he read a statement to the press about her "lonely battle" against brain cancer while he had been in prison.

The prosecutors had decided to appeal Judge White's order, which said that the Kilbanes and Steele must be retried within sixty days or entirely freed. Accordingly, that sixty-day period was put on hold while everyone waited for a three-judge federal appeals panel to decide on the merits of Judge White's ruling—an undertaking that could take quite a while.

Steele told the reporters that he had worked in the prison library to help win his appeal and a new trial, and still maintained his innocence. Moreover,

"I have new evidence that was not available to me during my first trial," evidence that he planned to use if another trial was decreed. He wouldn't say what the evidence was because "I don't want to tip our hand," but he did say that it had come "from people who have moved through prison." If there were a second trial, he said that he would take the stand, and regretted not doing so in the first trial. He claimed to be deeply religious, believed he had profited in the spiritual sense from his stay in prison, but would now lecture and write about the necessity for prison reform.

The second half of 1981 went by without an appeals panel ruling, and so did the first half of 1982. During that year, Owen was reported as gallivanting around in Las Vegas and in California. Steele was working as a legal intern in the office of his former counsel, Leonard Yelsky, and became again known as a man-about-town, squiring around several new ladies.

On July 28, 1982, the decision of the three-judge federal appeals panel was rendered. The judges, by a vote of 2–1, reversed Judge White's decision. It had been a fair trial, and the defendants' constitutional rights had been protected properly, they said. They ordered White's order vacated and the defendants sent back to prison. The lawyers for the defendants immediately appealed this decision, too, saying that the entire ten-member panel ought to rule in the case, since the three-judge panel had been split. While waiting for that appeal to run its course, the defendants remained free on bond.

A few weeks later, a Cleveland Heights street

character named Jeffry Snyder called me at Quantico. I had met him in the early 1970s, and he had helped me on several cases. Jeff was a man who hung around with as many cops as he did with unsavory people, and always seemed to know what has happening on the streets, while having a keen sense of trying to keep the city in good order. He made no bones about ferreting out people, and some thought he was a snitch, though he was always loyal to his own friends. I think he would have liked to have been a law enforcement officer but settled for doing some adventurous assignments with me, over the years. "I'm getting tight with Bob Steele," Snyder said to me on the telephone, "and I told Steele what a good guy you are, and that you would help him if you could."

"Very interesting. Sure I'll help him. What does he want to help *me* with?"

Snyder believed that what Steele had to trade was information on other cases, and that Steele would provide it in exchange for my assistance in getting his life sentence reduced—in the event that the appeal failed and he had to go back to jail again.

Why me? This was the question to ponder. It was clear that Steele was preparing to turn against his former client Owen Kilbane, and he might base his reliance on me on the old chestnut that I had always been out to get Kilbane, and so would look kindly on assistance in this matter. A deeper reading might suggest that Steele realized that I had never lied to him, and that I had been as good as my word. Having promised him back in 1973 that I would bring his wife's killers to justice, I had helped do that, staying on the case for a long time and seeing it through to the conviction of all the parties concerned. Perhaps it was my dogged determination that Steele wanted. Or my integrity. Whatever, he put me back in the game again, whether or not I wanted to be in it.

I talked to Steele briefly on the phone, and he bandied around the phrase the "high seas" crime. Since the murder of Arnie Prunella was referred to in law enforcement circles by this moniker, I understood the reference. "I could give you the nail in the coffin," Steele said about that matter, in another phrase that became equally hard for me to forget. Obtaining permission from my superiors, I flew to Cleveland. On the phone, I had told Steele to go to a certain bar and wait for my signal. He didn't know what that signal would be. My face was still known around Cleveland, and would be especially noted if it appeared in public in conjunction with his. So I had two female agents from the Cleveland FBI office pick up the man-about-town at the bar and bring him to a hotel for Joe Harpold and me to debrief.

We spent two days in that hotel room and spoke frankly (and not so frankly) about several subjects. Steele and I had been mixing it up, I realized, for almost a decade, since the time I first came in contact with him in the summer of 1973 after we inventoried Owen's prostitution-related materials. My longtime adversary looked a lot older than his fifty-two years. Of course I hadn't aged a day.

"I'm still young, and I have a girlfriend," Steele told me. "I don't want to die in jail."

"You should have thought of that before you had your wife killed," I retorted.

He still maintained that he was innocent. Before going further with other matters, I tried to get him to admit, even in a casual way, that he had ordered the killing of Marlene. He wouldn't bite at my suggestions. He offered instead the theory that he had possibly said something in an offhand way to Owen Kilbane—as he had also done to David Lombardo—but that while Lombardo had shrugged off Steele's request to find a killer as just a drunken thought, Kilbane had taken it as gospel and had decided to kill Marlene as a way of furthering himself with the influential judge.

I didn't buy that version, but to say so would not have gotten me anything I wanted. So I threw Steele a bone. In retrospect, this might have been a mistake, but at the time I wanted to lead him on and obtain from him whatever information it was possible to get, so I told him that while I had always felt completely certain about the involvement of Owen, Marty, and Rick in the murder, the extent of his involvement was a bit in question. He was very grateful to hear that. To induce him to say more, I told him that I believed that he, as with most people who commit one-time crimes of passion, was not inherently violent, and was no longer a danger to society. This seemed to be a straw at which he was very willing to grasp.

In response, Steele then offered the closest thing to an admission of guilt that he would ever utter. "You know, Bob," I recall Steele saying to me in the hotel room, "my biggest problem is that I've gone through life with my brains in the wrong head—in my dick. I've never been discreet. I've always chased after women—prostitutes, friends' wives, you name it. If it laid still, I'd pursue it."

Deciding that I'd get no more out of him than this elliptic reference, I returned to the problem at hand. In our preliminary telephone conversation he had intimated that Owen had bragged about killing Arnie Prunella, and had asked for my help in keeping him out of jail. Now I laid out what the deal would be. "We believe Owen was a hit man on several jobs," I said. "You deliver the Kilbanes on the Prunella murder, and on some of the other hits, and maybe I'll say something to the prosecutors."

For two days, then, I did with Steele what I had done with Carol Braun in Saint Louis, seven years earlier: ask questions, jot down notes, have the material typed up into statement form, and take first Carol, now Steele, over the statement word by word to amend, annotate, and then sign it. In the document, dated October 13, 1982, Steele attested that he was discussing the murder of Prunella with us "voluntarily and without coercion. No threats or promises have been made to me . . . Ressler and Harpold have not discussed with me any aspects whatsoever concerning any considerations to be given me with regard to my 1977 conviction in the case of 'State of Ohio vs. Robert Steele.'"

In the course of his long involvement with Owen Kilbane, Steele said in the statement, Kilbane had discussed the murder of Arnie Prunella twice. Kilbane had "a tendency to brag," Steele charged, and several times had come into Steele's downtown office just to chat—not to discuss legal matters but "to establish a social relationship with me." On one of these trips downtown, Kilbane had told Steele that he, Marty, and a third man had taken Arnie Prunella on Owen's boat, shot him, tied a manhole cover on him and dropped him in the lake. Steele had gotten the impression from his talks with Owen that the pimp himself had done the shooting, and had killed Prunella because Arnie had double-crossed him in some business deal.

Kilbane had told the story a second time, around 1970, this time to Barbara Steele. Owen had invited the Steeles to go with him to a racetrack where he had a horse running, and on the automobile journey to the track Owen tried to impress Barbara with how tough a character he was.

"Owen, you're nothing but a pussycat," Barbara had chided him.

At this point, Steele related, Kilbane went into a rage, during which his face became extremely red. "You think I'm a pussycat?" Kilbane asked. "I've killed a man."

Once again, according to Steele, Kilbane related the story of the murder, substantially as he had told it in Steele's office, but this time "in violent terms. I have the impression that Prunella was not even dead when they threw him in the water." Barbara was properly shocked, but when Steele "did nothing to fortify Kilbane's story," they proceeded on to the race with no further mention of the matter.

I had a momentary pang thinking of Barbara Steele, now dead. I had often wondered whether she had ever believed in her husband's guilt; when she had heard Owen's violent insistence that he had killed a man, had she understood that Owen and Steele had, indeed, had Marlene executed?

I also wondered how much of Steele's statement was true, because with Steele, as earlier with Rickey Robbins, we had to take into account that the tale-teller might be saying things only in the hopes that it would reduce his sentence. At the very least, Steele's statement in 1982 was important because it corroborated what Carol Braun had told me about the Prunella murder in 1975. On the basis of those two statements, both from intimate associates of Kilbane, we might be able to go to trial. The question then became, Could we use that Braun statement or not? That all depended on whether the ten-member federal appeals panel would rule on the appeals already made. So, on the Prunella case as well as on the Steele murder, we'd have to wait for the next appeals ruling.

However, Steele wasn't finished singing. He had leads that he said he could give us in several other unsolved murder cases in the area, and we all decided that he would pursue these in further work with Joe Harpold, since I was no longer stationed in Cleveland. Working with the SAC of the Cleveland office, and throwing a lot of resources into the fray, Joe opened a series of investigations under the title of "Clevmurs," based primarily on the information provided by Bob Steele. The Bureau gives code names to all of its investigations—the attempted assassination of President Reagan was REGAT, for example, a name that it didn't take much work to decipher. We lowly agents fantasized that there must be some higher-up at headquarters who spent his entire days at a big leather desk overlooking Pennsylvania Avenue while he brooded about what to call certain investigations. Unfortunately, when the light bulb went on over his head, it wasn't very bright. So we had Clevmurs. Early on in Clevmurs, the former judge even provided Joe with a handwritten introductory note to a well-known Cleveland mob figure saying that Steele would be indebted if the men would help Harpold by providing any new information on certain *corpus delicti*. I thought everyone concerned had been reading too many Mickey Spillane novels.

A month after we had taken the Steele statement, the ten-member panel of the federal court of appeals refused to intervene, and let stand the three-member panel's decision that Judge White's ruling was in error and the original trial was proper. The matter was going to be appealed to the Supreme Court in Washington, but knowledgeable court veterans felt it was unlikely that the Supreme Court would choose to take the case at all.

Now, with a ruling in hand that in effect certified the Braun statement in the earlier case as proper, and which might therefore justify the insertion of a similar statement by Braun in another case, the prosecution made the determination to try to convict the Kilbanes for the murder of Arnie Prunella. The FBI in Cleveland cooperated with the Lakewood police and with several other local jurisdictions to prepare the case. Along with Owen and Marty, a third man, Phillip Christopher, was also indicted by a grand jury. Christopher was currently in jail, in Terre Haute, Indiana, serving a twenty-year federal sentence for a 1972 burglary of $7 million in cash, jewels, and bearer bonds from a California bank. Though Bob Steele believed Owen to have shot Arnie Prunella himself, other informants had indicated that Christopher had been the shooter.

The Kilbanes were re-arrested and taken back to prison. Meanwhile, Steele remained free on bond.

In early 1983, as the time for the Prunella murder trial neared, the newspapers in Cleveland noted that Steele was on the list of potential witnesses, along with Rick Robbins, and tried to find out about their testimony. Carmen Marino, who was going to prosecute the case, wouldn't comment on what Steele might have to say other than to assure everyone that Steele had had nothing to do with Prunella's death. "I don't know anything," Steele told reporters who asked if he would testify. So the newspapers didn't find out about the statement he had given me a few months earlier.

Another interesting potential witness was Carolyn Christopher, no relation to Phil. She had been Steele's secretary, and agreed to be hypnotized in order to recall what Kilbane might have said to Steele in her presence. A two-hour tape of her hypnosis session was played for the lawyers and the judge, Richard J. McMonagle, but not for the jury.

Seeing Owen and Marty at the Prunella trial provided more evidence of the passage of time. They were in their midthirties in 1983, and it was fifteen years after their young punk days—Arnie Prunella had disappeared around Labor Day in 1968. There was Carol Braun, still with Owen; Patrick Ryan Kilbane was of school age, now. Equally telling of time's passage: while many of the potential jurors told Judge McMonagle that they had heard of former judge Steele, only a few in the pool had heard of the Kilbanes. The ones chosen did not know and were not told of the connection between Steele and the Kilbanes.

As the trial began, the defense immediately began to point out that there was no body, no murder weapon, and no specific murder date. They contended that the state could not even prove that the alleged murder victim was dead. "Arnie Prunella had every reason to leave town," lawyer Ralph Sperli insisted; he was again representing Owen Kilbane. "For all we know, [Prunella] may be somewhere else in this country, laughing at ... the predicament Owen Kilbane is in." Prosecutor Carmen Marino countered by telling the jury that Owen had two reasons for having Prunella killed: first, because Prunella had bilked him out of money; and second, because Prunella had talked to the FBI during our probe of Kilbane's prostitution activities.

The trial had no sooner started in earnest than it went offtrack. Phil Christopher was offered the opportunity to have his own case severed from that of the Kilbanes, to plead guilty to manslaughter and then to testify against the Kilbanes. The kicker was that the sentence for manslaughter would run concurrently to the one he was already serving; in effect, then, Christopher would do no additional time for having had a hand in the death of Arnie Prunella. This bargain turned out to be a mistake because there was a loophole in the law. Christopher first agreed to the severance, and it was granted. Then the surprise came. Under a little-known provision of the law, a defendant was allowed to plead guilty without actually admitting guilt for the crime—a version of the plea better known as *nolo contendere*, or no contest. So Christopher did just that, and then refused to testify against the Kilbanes, and neither the court nor the prosecution could now compel him to do so.

After Christopher's plea, Judge McMonagle dealt another blow to the prosecution by not permitting Marino to call any witnesses—such as Bob Steele or Carol Braun—to testify that Owen Kilbane had confessed to murdering Arnie Prunella. McMonagle's reason: the prosecutors had not fulfilled the legal grounds for showing that a crime had taken place! No body, no weapon, no confession by a co-conspirator; in McMonagle's mind, in legal terms that equaled no crime.

"But we've got admissions by Owen Kilbane, by Martin Kilbane and by the other man," Marino protested.

"And those admissions are not admissible by the court," McMonagle responded. He told the prosecutors that their case was "very weak" and gave them another day to come up with something better.

The next morning, the Cleveland *Plain Dealer* printed a front-page headline: "Christopher Guilty but Silent." Defying a gag order from the judge, defense attorney Mark R. DeVan spoke out in order to put to rest the rumors that had started to emerge when Christopher's trial had been severed from that of the Kilbanes. He told the press that his client, Phil Christopher, had made his guilty plea but was definitely not going to testify against the Kilbanes. DeVan said he was talking in order to protect Christopher from the vengeance that prison inmates visited on snitches. Moreover, "he is pleading guilty only to avoid the possibility of a more severe sentence."

Judge McMonagle was furious. He had imposed the gag order in the first place to prevent the jury from finding out about the severance of Christopher—and then, there it was, splashed on the front page of the city's largest newspaper. "I can't conceive the jury would not somehow be exposed to this," the judge commented, and one juror admitted that he had seen the headline. McMonagle told DeVan that he faced contempt charges, a thousand-dollar fine, and a possible year in prison for deliberately defying the gag order. When Sperli made a motion to have a mistrial declared, McMonagle immediately granted it.

The defense lawyers later claimed that the mistrial had been declared at the wrong point for them, because they had the prosecution on the run. Now the prosecution would have several weeks to prepare for a new trial.

It never happened. Without Christopher, the evidence was all still circumstantial, and the case evaporated.

However, in mid-March, the Supreme Court declined to review the Steele case, which meant that the judgment of the appeals panel was the final one on the matter. On March 18, the day on which Bob

Steele had been scheduled to be married to Carol Hugg, a Willoughby Hills widow whom he had known for about eight months, Steele was arrested and sent back to jail. The Kilbanes, already imprisoned, stayed where they were.

But I had the sneaking suspicion that I still hadn't heard the last of any of them.

Fourteen

"THE GOVERNOR MUST BE
ABSOLUTELY MAD"

In June of 1983, just a few months after he had
been returned to prison, Bob Steele began to write
letters to me. In his first one, Steele seized upon
what I'd said in our hotel room meeting, that I did
not consider him at present to be a danger to society.
He wrote that it was just this contention that had
enabled him to trust me and to spill so much about
the Prunella matter and other cases that made up
the Clevmurs investigation. Also, he embraced the
notion that I had some doubt as to his actual degree
of involvement in the murder of his wife. When I
read that, I groaned. What Steele wanted was for
me to use the FBI's clout to make Cuyahoga County
prosecutor John T. Corrigan move from his inflexible
stance of opposition to parole, commutation, or
other ways of reducing Steele's sentence. Steele tried
to make it seem as though his entire hopes depended
on the degree to which I would intercede for him.

I didn't write back. To disabuse him of the idea
that I thought he wasn't completely involved in his

wife's murder would have been a thankless task, and I had nothing else to say. Joe Harpold and John Dunn of the Cleveland office had been pursuing Steele's so-called leads on the other cases in the Clevmurs docket for some time, and each one had taken them many man-hours of investigation and had led precisely nowhere. I now believed that Steele had had only one fish to throw to us, and that was Kilbane; everything else had been rumors that he had repeated in order to stay out of jail.

In early July, when I still hadn't responded to him, Steele sent a second letter along with a clipping from a Columbus newspaper. He was now part of what was called a "shock tour for young toughs," in which teenagers who had committed crimes were taken through the state prison in the hope that a few hours of "reality therapy" would make them change their ways. Steele was still known to inmates as "the judge," the article said. In this second letter, Steele added a new plaint to the ones he'd previously stated: he should be released because he could and would contribute something to society. Once out, he would do community work and continue to warn delinquents against the peril of their ways. By the time his third letter arrived, a week later, Steele's exploits with the teenagers had reached other newspapers, and he included more clippings. In one article, the assistant public defender who started the prison-talk program described Steele's way of asking the kids "to look inside themselves to see what their attitudes are and why they were acting the way they were." Steele wrote me that he would be appearing with the tough-talk program on television, two different channels in two cities, and was going to use these appearances as the basis of a public relations campaign.

I thought that Steele ought to look inside himself and see what his attitude was and why he was acting the way he was. Although I still hadn't responded to his missives, two weeks later Steele wrote a fourth letter, and now added a threat to his plea for intercession. If I didn't do something soon, he was going to make a spectacular new legal filing, one that would get Kilbane out as well as himself—though, he added, he really wanted Kilbane to remain behind bars, because Owen was truly a criminal.

Two weeks later, a fifth letter arrived. Comparing all five letters, I could see that the handwriting was becoming progressively more and more disjointed; the later letters were being dashed off, rather than, as with the first, carefully composed. In this fifth letter, as though he were a jilted teenaged lover, Steele asked whether I even knew how to write, and suggested that I write back using disappearing ink or paper that would dissolve after its message was read, if I was chary of risking the Bureau's wrath to help him. And why, he wanted to know, was Carmen Marino so angry with him? He had never lied about Marino, Steele avowed.

Later in the summer of 1983, Rickey Robbins was released on parole. He had served the last several years of his sentence, which had indeed been reduced to manslaughter, in a western state that had a reciprocal arrangement with Ohio for prisoners who would be in danger in their own states. Out west, he had done such things as build a chapel for a nearby town and work as a fire fighter, jumping into forest fires with other inmate volunteers. His release was done quietly, and he completed the relocation procedure that had begun with the resettlement of his family in 1976. According to Jack Walsh, with whom Robbins kept in touch throughout his incarceration, Rickey at thirty-three was a vastly different man from the violent youth of seventeen who had killed Tedd Browne. Rickey's turnaround did not sound impossible to me, either. As a criminologist who had researched the lives of many murderers, I knew that there was a vast difference between types of people who commit murder. Some kill out of passion, others for revenge, and the very young sometimes do such deeds out of youthful hostility and aggression. These latter killers, of whom Rickey was one, can sometimes be successfully treated and released back into society.

In October, occasional letters to the editor advising that Bob Steele ought to be let out of jail started appearing in local newspapers. I soon learned that these were part of Steele's public relations campaign. In November, the Committee to Free Bob Steele was formed, and took the Robbins parole as an argument for Steele's release. At a well-attended press conference on November 10, 1983, the committee gave out some materials. Their main claim was, as they put it, that Steele's "continued incarceration" was "a travesty of justice." The committee included several lawyer friends of Steele's, two former Cleveland Barons hockey players, some businessmen, the public defenders with whom Steele had cooperated in the shock tour program, and others. Carol Hugg, to whom Steele had become engaged, was a motivating force for the committee, though her name was not on the list of officers. I bristled at the line in the press release that said "certain law enforcement officers whose names must remain undisclosed at the present, but who had a great deal to do with the investigation, now express serious doubts as to any involvement of Bob." Now, it seemed, rather than expressing some slight misgivings as to his full participation in the murder, which is what I had done, I was supposed to have expressed serious skepticism as to whether he'd had anything at all to do with his wife's murder. The former judge's own statement, appended to the press release, contended that he had "never understood the forces that combined to bring about my arrest," but that he was "satisfied that the major factor" in his conviction was that as a judge he had committed "the unpardonable sin of adultery." However, he said, "I have never accepted the responsibility for Marlene's death because I am not guilty."

I read portions of the statements in various newspaper reports that friends sent me. Steele himself forwarded all the committee's released materials, along with a letter, because I had at last written to tell him that I was coming to Ohio around Thanksgiving and would stop to talk with him in prison. His letter enclosing the release mentioned that he was still about to file a strong petition that would knock legal socks off and result in his freedom—but, more than ever, he wanted me to intercede with Corrigan. Now he was telling us precisely how to proceed: we must get the conviction reduced to manslaughter, as with Robbins, so he could get credit for time already served and be released almost immediately. If I behaved as he instructed, he would reward me by not filing his legal petition for "postconviction relief." He even had things worked out so that an important local cleric would praise Corrigan for his good sense in releasing that upstanding citizen, Bob Steele.

Cleveland columnist John Urbancich reviewed all of the committee's materials in his column of November 17, 1983, and commented. "What they don't say, however, is that in spite of all the breast-beating about hearsay and travesties of justice, a jury generally regarded as one of the most intelligent, thorough and methodical in Cuyahoga County crime annals still found enough evidence to convict Steele."

When I went to visit Steele in his Columbus prison in late 1983, I carried with me some important experience. Starting in the late 1970s, I had begun a program in which I had already interviewed nearly a hundred of the nation's incarcerated murderers, including such men as Charles Manson, Richard Speck, David Berkowitz, and Sirhan Sirhan. So I was inordinately familiar with the psychological profiles of violent criminals. Cardinal to any sense of their rehabilitation, in terms of their willingness to live with themselves behind bars, if not in terms of the possibility of their release from jail, is their own eventual acknowledgment of the crimes they have committed. When Joe Harpold and I visited Steele, one thing stood out in his conversation: his continued refusal to admit that he had had anything to do with the death of his first wife.

Absent such an admission, I certainly wasn't going to go to bat for him with Corrigan or with anyone else, and in my visit he got that message, loud and clear. In early January of 1984, I received a last, and very angry, letter from him. He again reiterated that he had helped law enforcement beyond measure by the tips he had given us in the Clevmurs investigation—even though Joe Harpold had told him to his face that no cases were being brought based on his information—and was dismayed to have discovered that I was not the man of integrity he had assumed me to be.

I reeled back in amazement from that last, absurd charge, which gave me a crystal clear insight into how Bob Steele rationalized his own position: He had initially told me things because he had viewed me as a man of integrity who had brought his wife's murderers to justice, but once I refused to believe in his innocence in regard to that murder, I had suddenly lost my integrity and he must therefore chastise me. Despite my bad behavior, his letter went on, he was issuing this last, desperate plea: I must write to Governor Richard Celeste and tell him that I did not feel Steele was a danger to society—and send a copy of any such letter to the committee. I did no such thing, of course.

In the same mail, a friend sent me a clipping of Cleveland *News-Herald* reporter Tom Breckenridge's telephone interview with Kevin Steele, Bob Steele's eldest son. Kevin, now twenty-three, had decided to grant the interview to counter the efforts of the committee to free his father. "Give me an afternoon with them [the committee members] and I'll tell them about the real Robert Steele," Kevin told Breckenridge. "I'll tell them how he abused his children. He murdered his wife and caused all those close to him a lot of pain." The elder Steele had not tried to contact Kevin or his younger brother, Brett, at any time during the past seven or eight years, not even in the eighteen-month period when the former judge was out of jail. Kevin did not want Steele released, and characterized his father as a bad but "brilliant man, sly like a fox," able to dupe such people as Steele's new fiancée, Mrs. Hugg, and the others on the committee.

A dozen days later, Steele made available to Breckenridge and other reporters a letter that he had written to Kevin and Brett. "I did not pay anyone to kill your mother. I did not ask anyone to kill your mother. I never wished your mother dead," Steele wrote. He informed his sons that they had heard only one side of the story, from the Gallittos, who were angry at him for having committed adultery while married to Marlene. Kevin told Breckenridge that his father's letter was a "total scam," a public relations ploy that had only been sent because Kevin had talked to reporters.

One part of Steele's letter to his sons concerned me personally. Steele told his sons that Agent Bob Ressler "had a lot of doubts as to my involvement in your mother's murder but that they wanted my co-defendant (Owen Kilbane) so bad that I was expendable."

Reading that particular allegation, Breckenridge

called me at Quantico. His call presented me with an opportunity to nail this subject, once and for all. I told him emphatically that I "would never go on record as saying Judge Steele was never involved in the murder," because I hadn't been part of the initial police investigation of the facts, since I had come to the case only in 1972. I believed that Steele was guilty as charged, and moreover, "If he [Steele] requests me to come forward to be a spokesman for him and endorse him, I wouldn't do it."

I heard nothing more about the case until mid-1985, when the Ohio state parole board voted 6–0 to turn down Steele's request for parole. Routine stuff. After all, Steele's sentence was twenty-five to life, and he had not even stayed in jail two-thirds of the minimum time, the usual benchmark for parole consideration.

Two years later, at the end of July 1987, along with everyone else in law enforcement who had been connected with the Steele case, I was stunned to learn from the *Plain Dealer* that Ohio governor Richard Celeste had recently—and quietly—commuted Steele's sentence to *ten* years to life, and that the parole board had voted unanimously to recommend his release. At the board's next scheduled hearing for prisoners, near the end of August, Steele was expected to be set free. There was an immediate uproar, accompanied by a flurry of activity from various prosecutors and judges, and a slew of newspaper articles.

"The governor must be absolutely mad," Carmen Marino told reporters, voicing the thoughts of all of us. "That's the kind of conduct that makes people think we hammer only poor people. It was a foolish move. He should have at least contacted the prosecutor's office to get a feel for the victim and the heinous nature of the crime. . . . It's really a joke."

Now the fur started flying. The parole board pointed out that letters about their consideration of the Steele matter had been sent to Corrigan's office and to Judge Nahra. Corrigan and the judicial central office responded that this was technically true, but misleading, because the notification had come in a bunch of about twenty other routine notifications. Usually, in a high-profile case, no such actions are taken by a parole board without calling attention to the upcoming hearing. Even the general public knew that when such people as Charlie Manson or Sirhan Sirhan came up for parole, everybody in the world seemed to learn about the hearing; in Cleveland, Bob Steele's case had similar prominence, but it seemed that a veil had been drawn over the commutation and parole proceedings.

Corrigan, Marino, Jack Walsh, and many others in the Cleveland area who had been intimately connected to the case began to agitate to at least be permitted to make strong statements before the parole board at the time it was scheduled to meet with Steele in late August. I called Carmen and advised him about a case in which I'd been involved as a consultant, in Oregon. There a man who had brutally murdered a woman and had been imprisoned for it had managed to claim that the murder had been done while he was suffering from Vietnam stress syndrome, and his partisans had talked the

governor into commuting his sentence after he had
served only four years. I had worked with the local
prosecutor and helped convince the governor to
reconsider this ill-advised move and keep the murderer in jail for another ten years. I gave Carmen
the name and phone number of the Oregon prosecutor so he could check the legal procedures necessary
to do the same thing with Steele in Ohio.

Just as important, the *Plain Dealer* began an
important investigation into how the Steele commutation had been accomplished, and ran smack into
a wall put up by Governor Celeste, who refused all
requests for information and claimed that he really
knew very little about the case, because everything
had been done by underlings. In particular, Celeste
claimed that he had only been following the recommendations of the parole board in commuting
Steele's sentence.

The parole board postponed the Steele hearing
for a month, to late September, and in the meantime
the newspaper kept up the pressure on Celeste's
office to release all the documents that had to do
with his handling of the case. The paper even sued
the governor under an Ohio law known as the Open
Records Act. On September 11, 1987, the governor's
office settled the suit out of court by turning over
hundreds of pages of documents to the *Plain Dealer*.
Deciphered by reporters Mary Anne Sharkey and
Gary Webb, these documents told quite a tale, one
that showed how Steele had brought pressure on
the governor for a commutation.

In early 1984, shortly after giving up on me, Steele
had had his mother get in touch with an old friend,

Frank Celeste, father of the governor, and ask him to intercede with his son. Frank Celeste and Otto Steele, Robert's father, had been friends for forty years, a fact that Frank cited in his letter to his son, in which he requested that the governor meet with members of the Committee to Free Bob Steele. The elder Celeste also wrote a cover memo to his son's personal secretary; initials and other markings on the filed letter indicated that it had at the very least landed on the desk next to the governor's.

Pressure came also from two other directions. Robert Metz, a college classmate of Steele's, had become a well-known journalist, the managing editor of the Financial News Network in New York City. After Metz had interviewed the governor about an Ohio bank debacle, he had sent Celeste a letter asking him to consider commutation for Steele, and Celeste had written back an assurance to do so "at the appropriate time." The governor's office commented to the newspaper that Metz's letter was the only one on the subject of Steele to which Celeste had made a response; it also said that the governor had not read or seen his own father's letter about Steele.

The clincher for Celeste, the newspaper concluded, came from an obscure and somewhat shady charity named the Robert F. Kennedy Scholarship Fund, Inc. (The fund had no connection to the family of the late senator from New York, which had denounced it as a rip-off and had complained about its use of the Robert Kennedy name.) Celeste's decision to commute Steele's sentence had been driven by that fund's offer of a job for Steele. The *Plain*

Dealer newsroom must have exploded when that fund's name surfaced in the Celeste papers, because the newspaper had been investigating the charity since 1981, and had written a slew of stories about it. Among the many problems with the job offer was that Ohio's secretary of state had revoked the fund's charter two years earlier, in 1985. Moreover, the Cleveland fund had collected many thousands of dollars in contributions but had awarded less than $550 in scholarships in three years while chewing up more than $46,000 in operational expenses.

A man named Jack Craciun III was the fund's director, and the fund operated from his home, which was also the headquarters of Craciun's import business. The chairman of the fund, a Craciun associate, had written to the parole board chairman in 1986 that the fund needed the guiding hand of Bob Steele, and that it would provide a job for him for five years after he was released. Similar letters had gone from Craciun to Celeste. "The governor has just vaguely heard of Craciun," Celeste's office said, but the papers obtained by the *Plain Dealer* showed otherwise. The Craciun family had been political supporters of Celeste, and one of Craciun's letters referred to "our last meeting," in which "you said two things to me about this case [Steele]."

As the story unraveled, it became clear that the fund was at the very least moribund, and had not done business since 1981. Moreover, the job offer to Steele, Craciun's associate admitted, was one that carried with it no paycheck at all; it was strictly a nonpaid position. The governor had not known that this was the case, of course.

What happened next between the governor's office and the parole board was a classic display of neatly choreographed political back scratching. With the job offer in hand, in February 1986 Celeste's office asked the parole board to reconsider its earlier decision not to have Steele's sentence commuted. In June of 1987, the board did an about-face from its 1985 position and voted 6–0 in favor of reconsideration. That permitted the governor, on July 20, 1987, to maintain that he was merely following the board's recommendation when he commuted Steele's sentence—after which the board was similarly able to use the commutation as reason for consideration of immediate parole.

Within days of the appearance of the series of articles in the *Plain Dealer*—and with Steele's parole hearing less than a week away—Celeste realized that he had been had by Steele and scrambled to find a way to reverse his own commutation and to recover from what the *Akron Beacon Journal* called "major political embarrassment."

Wouldn't you know it, his aides managed to find a legal way to get out of the jam. Shortly the governor publicly regretted his "error," and the parole board not only denied parole to Steele but found no reason to reconsider him before another two-year period had elapsed.

Unfortunately for Bob Steele, the quashing of his attempt to use political pressure to bring about his own release had a consequence that he had not intended and would soon regret. Just before Christmas, 1988, I received a "Seasons Greetings" card with best wishes from a post-office box in Lima, Ohio. My new correspondent was Owen Kilbane.

Fifteen

"TO CLEAR THE AIR"

During the Celeste flap the previous summer, Marty and Owen Kilbane had given interviews in which they had publicly lauded the commutation of Steele. "As far as I'm concerned," Marty was quoted by the newspapers as saying, "all the governor did was commute the sentence of an innocent man who probably should have been freed by the courts more than ten years ago."

That interview had puzzled me. I interpreted it to mean that the Kilbanes were maintaining their innocence, and were betting that if Steele was freed, their sentences would also have to be commuted and they would also soon be out. Then Steele's commutation had been overridden, and the Kilbanes' hopes on that score had collapsed.

Now here was a Christmas card from Owen, which included a note that he had seen me on a nationally broadcast Geraldo Rivera television program, where I'd commented on a long interview that Geraldo had done with Charles Manson. "I would like to visit with you at your earliest convenience," Owen wrote.

I had let Bob Steele's 1983–84 letters initially go unanswered, in part because I had already offered him a chance to help himself in the Clevmurs matters, and he had given us little of substance beyond an attempt to get Kilbane. But a letter from Owen Kilbane was a different story. He could have valuable information on a whole host of matters. So I sent him back my own Christmas card, with a note asking him for details of what he wished to discuss with me.

By return mail in early January 1989 he responded. He had initially wanted Carol Braun to get in touch with me, he wrote, but she'd told him to do it himself. (Later I learned that they had been divorced in December of 1988.) Now he wanted "to clear the air" and to ask for my help.

Be more specific, I wrote back. While I personally might be willing to go and see him just to chat, the Bureau wouldn't approve such a trip unless there was the likelihood that the conversation would lead to the solution of crimes that were still on the books as unsolved. In letters and in phone calls from January to May 1989, Owen let me know that he would now be willing to talk freely about the Prunella and Steele cases.

In my job as a supervisory agent in the Behavioral Science Unit at Quantico, I frequently went around the country to lecture and conduct seminars for law enforcement personnel. I was scheduled to do one in abnormal criminal psychology at Kent State University in early May, and received permission from the Bureau to stay out in Ohio a day or two longer in order to debrief the Kilbanes at the Lima Prison. John Dunn, an agent in the Cleveland office who had worked on the Prunella case and was also teaching at the Kent State seminar, sat in on the interview.

It was now twenty years after the death of Marlene Steele. Owen was forty-one; Marty, thirty-nine. As with many inmates who are in jail for long sentences, after a few years inside they had settled down and decided to take advantage of their time by stretching themselves in directions they had never before attempted. Both Kilbanes were almost finished with their college degrees and had decided on undertaking some graduate work. Prior to speaking with them, I had carefully reviewed their prison files and was genuinely impressed by the progress they had made, in school and as persons. In their embrace of education and of mainstream morality, these were different men from the arrogant young dropouts they had been at the time of the murder.

Dunn and I interviewed each brother separately, but their stories were virtually the same. Owen had gotten in touch with me because he had finally realized that Bob Steele had broken a pact with them, one that had held since 1977. Just before their trial, Steele, Marty, and Owen had entered into a joint conspiracy of silence, replete with a solemn oath that they had all sworn. Each pledged not to take the stand or provide testimony during the trial and, if convicted, to continue to maintain silence while Steele, through his influence and political connections, worked to get them out. For some years after they had entered the prison system, the pact held—

especially when all three were sprung on appeal in 1981, an event that seemed to the Kilbanes to be a verification of Steele's power. After they had been sent back to prison in 1982, though, the pact began to crumble. Through sources that he would not name, Owen had gotten wind of my meeting with Steele in the hotel room in 1982, when Steele had told of the Kilbanes' role in the Prunella murder. To Owen, this was evidence that Steele was no longer working to get all of the conspirators out but was only promoting his own welfare. In fact, the Kilbanes had understood that Steele sought to pin the murder solely on them—this, I saw, they could easily have realized from reading news articles that had quoted from the press release of the Committee to Free Bob Steele. Then had come the commutation, which also did not have the Kilbanes attached to it. They had applauded Celeste's action at the time, because it seemed likely to spring them, too, but when the commutation charade collapsed, the reality of their situation hit home: there could no longer be any doubt in the Kilbanes' minds that Steele was working for himself, not for them. Only then had the Kilbane brothers decided to take care of themselves. To do so, they were now ready, after twenty long years, to give me what I had longed to know: the full story of the planning, completion, and aftermath of the murder of Marlene Steele.

It was October–November of 1968. Owen Kilbane had come to know Bob Steele through Carol Braun. They were both guys on the way up, though on different ladders. Steele, the older of the two by more than ten years, was going the legitimate route, seeking political power through his position in the Euclid court system, while maintaining his private law practice on the side. Owen was the aspiring mobster, determined to amass the largest stable of prostitutes on the fringes of Cleveland and to have many businesses funneling money to him. Owen had given Steele some legal work to do, and had been pleased with the results; Steele was a sharp shyster, all right. Kilbane had been even more pleased in July of 1968, when the Euclid police prosecutor had been elevated to the bench. In those days, Owen thought a judge was ten feet tall—the biggest man in Euclid, next to the mayor, and wonderfully powerful. The pimp was tickled to be able to ring up Steele from downstairs in the courthouse and then walk up and press the buzzer outside Steele's office and be invited in for a conference that even secretary Carolyn Christopher didn't know about. Often Steele would sit down with Owen between cases that he was adjudicating and while he was wearing his judge's black robes.

In one of these private-office sessions, Steele asked Kilbane about getting someone to kill his wife. At first Owen thought he was joking and treated the request casually. But the request was repeated several times in different chats in the office, and Owen told his brother, Marty, about it. Marty scoffed, and Owen wasn't too sure about it himself but strung Steele along. How could it be done? Where? Who would do it? Steele had answers for many of Owen's questions. It ought to be done in the house, Steele had said, and while he was home, so he'd be able to control the situation.

Owen had been incredulous. What about the children, the pimp had asked. Steele replied that it would be better for the boys to have it over with quickly, and when he was there to comfort them. Steele assured the Kilbanes that the police were fools, and that he could control any investigation. Certainly there would be some heat, but he could handle it and it wouldn't reach them. He'd even pay $5,000 to have the murder committed, and he didn't expect them to do it themselves.

Marty and Owen had briefly discussed why the judge wanted his wife out of the way. They knew Steele was seeing someone else—the judge's sexual appetites and profligacy were already well known to the Kilbanes—but they didn't realize how serious the relationship was between Steele and Barbara Swartz. No matter: by doing the deed for the judge, they'd have him in their pocket. It was Marty who had come up with a candidate for the shooter, Rick Robbins, an old friend. Everybody in the tough-punk community, and a lot of people outside it, knew that Robbins had killed Tedd Browne, and so was capable of murder. So Marty approached Rick in December, when the marine was home on leave.

Rick was interested, even enthusiastic. Of course, afterward he wouldn't be able to brag about this one as he had done with the Browne murder, but Robbins agreed to do the job, especially when Owen offered him a thousand dollars for the hit. Thereafter, Robbins and the Kilbanes had several discussions about the deed, and Steele was apprised that a shooter had been found.

Now Steele became very specific. In his judge's chambers, between sessions on the bench, he drew the Kilbanes a plan of his house and suggested the way the shooter ought to come in and do the job. He'd arrange to be home, and for Marlene to be asleep. The conspirators would signal one another by telephone, by leaving the door ajar, by lights turned on and off. With the plan firmly in place, all that remained undone was to find the most opportune time, and to obtain a gun. Owen didn't want to use any of his, which might be traceable, so he bought an untraceable one from a friend. The plan was to have Robbins kill Marlene, then hold onto the gun and return it to the Kilbanes, who would melt it down and destroy it along with all the clothes that the killer had worn.

When Robbins called from California and said he wanted to come home, Steele was alerted and the night of January 8–9 was picked for the crime to be committed.

The murder plans worked and the deed was quickly accomplished. After Marty had picked up Robbins in the car, Rick had reported that he'd done the job. Marty expressed disbelief. The shooter held the gun under Marty's nose so that he could smell that it had been recently fired. Back at the Kilbanes' grandparents' home, Rick told the brothers of two minor problems. First, he had urinated outside the house before the execution, so he wouldn't get soiled at the moment of shooting, and second, he had knocked over the telephone in his haste to get out the door. They removed the clothes he had worn, including the oversized boots, and burned them all. Then Marty and Owen hammered the barrel of the gun closed and had it melted down in the incinerator of an apartment building they owned. The bits of melted metal were scattered throughout the trash.

In the aftermath of the shooting, when Steele was much less able to control the investigation than he had claimed, the real problems began. Steele kept the Euclid police at bay, but there was the bloodhound Kulis, who kept coming after them, trying to have Owen take a lie-detector test, something he didn't want to do because his other illegal activities might be the subject of some of the questions. The crux of the difficulties with the damage control was Steele's affair with Barbara Swartz. Kilbane hadn't known that the affair had included trysts in other cities, where Steele had been so arrogantly foolish as to sign in at motels using his own name and credit card. When that affair was brought to light and Steele was forced to resign from the bench, Steele's usefulness to Kilbane declined precipitously. In fact, the police pressure on Kilbane in the six months following the murder, pressure that was brought because of Owen's known connection to Steele, cut the prostitution business in half. However, once the clamor died down and no one was indicted, things started getting better. Steele never offered money to Kilbane for the job, and Kilbane never sought any. But he did extract a considerable amount of legal work from Steele in the years following the murder, and never received a bill or paid Steele anything for that legal work. The reason for not sending bills, and for not proffering payment, was never discussed between them.

As time went by, Bob and Barbara and Owen and Carol would double-date. The men were involved in business together and socialized often. Owen came to believe that Barbara Steele had to have known about the murder of Marlene, but he was never sure of it, and of course Steele and Owen never discussed the murder.

Similarly, in prison, Owen and Marty had never talked about the murder to any of their fellow cons, and hardly ever discussed it with each other, preferring not to think about it but to turn their thoughts to getting out and to furthering their lives.

While listening to the Kilbanes, at various points I thought, This corroborates what Diane told me in 1973; that upholds what Carol Braun said to me in 1975; another revelation validated what Rick Robbins had testified to in 1977. I had been hearing portions of this story from so many people for so many years that it was as though I already knew most of what Owen and Marty had to say, and just needed to have them say it. Hearing their story at last, I experienced no elation, just a quiet satisfaction at the understanding that my belief in the guilt of Steele, the Kilbanes, and Robbins had finally been verified. Whatever small lingering doubts I may have had about Steele's involvement were now entirely erased.

The Kilbanes' version impugned Bob Steele much more so than had any previous witness's. If one believed the Kilbanes—and I did—Rick Robbins's version had been more self-serving than we had known in 1976, when he first told Jack Walsh and Warren Goodwin about his role in the death of Marlene Steele. Carol Braun's version had been the most correct, it turned out, but she hadn't known all the facts or the extent to which Steele had been the moving force behind the planning of his wife's murder. The judge had not simply expressed a wish that it be done and then turned the job over to professional accomplices; he had meticulously arranged most of the details—and had done so while wearing the badge of his power, his judicial robes, and in his judge's chambers.

In exchange for their confessions, the Kilbanes wanted help from me and from Carmen Marino when their parole dates came up, a time several years in the future. I called Carmen and told him what the brothers had said and what they desired. He spoke with Corrigan and called back to say that—as with Rick Robbins, years ago—we must obtain more formal statements before the prosecutor's office could consider what might or might not be done for them; moreover, as I had already suggested to them, Carmen insisted that the Kilbanes must give such statements without any promises having been made. Accordingly, later in the year, after the brothers had been transferred to a prison closer to Cleveland, Dunn and I visited them again and interviewed them with a tape recorder running.

In late 1989, when Bob Steele again came up for parole, the board carefully solicited advice and opinions from all quarters. Brett Steele, Bob's son, sent a letter and copies of letters that he and his brother and grandfather had originally sent to the board in September of 1987 at the time of the Celeste commutation. "Our family is still passionate about this case," Brett wrote in the 1989 letter, part of which made its way into the newspapers. "We do not feel justice will have been served if you let the murderer go after a mere ten years." Brett cited the "new evidence" turned up in the interviews with the Kilbanes as even more reason to keep their father in prison, where, in their view, he belonged for the rest of his life.

A few days before Christmas, 1989, Carmen Marino, Jack Walsh, Warren Goodwin, and I drove down to Columbus to present our findings to the parole board. We testified that Steele should not receive consideration for parole at this time—and, for emphasis, Carmen later repeated to newspaper reporters what we had told the board and released some details of the Kilbane confession. That the judge had carefully planned his wife's murder made headlines throughout the state of Ohio. Shortly, the parole board turned down Steele's bid for early release from prison.

In 1990, after twenty years' service, I retired from the FBI and became a private consultant, author, lecturer, and expert witness.

The main remaining question about the Steele case has been whether the Kilbanes and Bob Steele would ever get out of prison. Rick Robbins, the shooter, has now been free on parole for almost a decade and has been leading a quiet, law-abiding life. Carmen Marino and I disagree about what ought to happen to Steele and the Kilbanes; Carmen wants all three to remain behind bars forever.

I see things differently. As far back as 1982, I told Steele that I did not consider him a danger to society, and I continued to hold that view even though I testified against his release in 1989. At that time, the new evidence the Kilbanes provided seemed to demand further punishment for the former judge, and I acted accordingly to recommend it.

But the next time Steele comes up for possible release, since I will no longer be part of a law enforcement agency, as a private citizen I will probably not oppose his parole. On the other hand, after 1989 I came to the conclusion that I must do more than simply decline to oppose the Kilbanes' parole. Although I could never agree to forget the crime for which they had been convicted, I did feel that they would have now met the state's requirements for serving enough time for that crime—fifteen years. In my work at the FBI, I had come to grips with a society in which serial murders, mass murders, spree killings, drive-by shootings, and violent car-jackings had come to be ever more frequent occurrences. The Kilbanes were taking up prison space that should be used for more violent and dangerous offenders. That is why, for the past several years, I have been supporting the idea that the parole board should release Owen and Marty. I take this position not in simple gratitude for their having provided new information in the Steele case. Rather, I have become convinced that the Kilbanes have both been rehabilitated and can lead productive lives outside prison walls, and that it serves no further social purpose to keep them incarcerated.

At Grafton, the prison near Cleveland, Owen has put together a plan for an ambitious project designed to attack two major social problems: providing employment for ex-convicts and helping with the renewal of decrepit inner-city neighborhoods. One of the largest difficulties facing paroled men is the lack of opportunities for legitimate employment; this lack is the most serious contributing factor to ex-cons being led to commit new crimes rather than to go straight. "Project Renew" would put paroled convicts to work renovating abandoned and foreclosed inner-city properties, and then sell these at market prices and channel the money back to provide income for the released men and seed money for further real estate acquisitions. I find the plan carefully thought out, and believe it has merit and can certainly do no worse than some of the present federal inner-city programs, which have made scant progress in rebuilding our cities and the lives of our ex-cons. For these reasons, in the late summer of 1993, I traveled to Ohio and testified for the Kilbanes at a parole hearing. Despite my positive recommendation, however, the brothers were once again denied parole and will have to wait several years before reapplying.

From time to time I hear from many who were involved in the Steele murder case. Carol Braun has experienced a religious revelation, is busy raising her sons, and is currently writing a book about her journey from prostitution to a more socially acceptable life-style. I'm happy to see it, because I always responded to the decent person that I believed was alive under the tough veneer she used to affect. The other former prostitute, Diane, still calls and writes now and then; she, too, has found religion and is getting her life together. I try to keep in touch with those Cleveland area law enforcement people for whom the Steele case remains an important touchstone. My old boss Marty McCann is director of security at LTV Steel; Earl Gordon worked with him there for some years and has now retired. Andy Vanyo resigned from the Cleveland police force to take a position as director of security for a large resort hotel in Las Vegas. Jack Walsh is now chief of police in Ritchfield, Ohio, while Warren Goodwin heads the security force at a suburban mall. Lou Kulis has recently retired after a lifetime of work. But Chester Zembala is still on the job with the Cuyahoga County sheriff's office, and Al Lipold and Carmen Marino are still the mainstays of the Cuyahoga County prosecutor's office. Joe Harpold is now an instructor at the FBI academy, and other Cleveland office colleagues like John Dunn come to visit when they pass through Quantico.

Rick Robbins is out and, from all reports, doing well. Former judge Bob Steele, who stayed out of prison a bit longer than the Kilbanes did in 1981–82, will again be eligible for parole consideration in 1994. Maybe someday all three will get out of jail and become productive citizens, and that will be the end of the Steele case.

Somehow, though, after more than twenty years of it, I can never rest assured that it's over.

About the Author

Robert K. Ressler, M.S., is a criminologist in private practice and the director of Forensic Behavioral Services, a Virginia-based organization dedicated to training, lecturing, consultation, and expert witness testimony. Mr. Ressler is an expert in the field of violent criminal offenders, particularly in the area of serial and sexual homicide and is often called upon as an expert witness on these subjects. He is a specialist in criminology, criminal personality profiling, crime scene analysis, homicide, sexual assault, threat assessment, and hostage negotiation. He is a twenty-year veteran of the Federal Bureau of Investigation, serving sixteen years in the FBI's Behavioral Science Unit as a supervisory special agent and criminologist, retiring in 1990. He innovated many of the programs which led to the formulation of the FBI's National Center for the Analysis of Violent Crime. He became the first Program Manager of the FBI's Violent Criminal Apprehension Program (VICAP) in 1985.

Ressler's academic affiliations include Instructor of Criminology while at the FBI Academy, adjunct faculty at the University of Virginia and the University of Pennsylvania, and Adjunct Assistant Professor at Michigan State University's School of Criminal Justice. He is a clinical assistant professor in psychiatry in Georgetown University's program on psychiatry and law, and a visiting instructor with the department of forensic pathology at Dundee University, Dundee, Scotland.

Ressler was awarded the *Amicus Award* by the American Academy of Psychiatry and the Law in 1991, and the *Jefferson Award* by the University of Virginia in 1986 and

1988. He is a member of the International Association of Forensic Sciences, the International and American Academies of Forensic Sciences, the Academy of Criminal Justice Sciences, the International Association of Chiefs of Police, the International Homicide Investigators Association, the Vidoqu Society, and other professional organizations.

Robert Ressler originated and directed the FBI's first research program of violent criminal offenders. His interviews and data on thirty-six serial and sexual killers resulted in two published text books, *Sexual Homicide: Patterns and Motives* (1988) and *Crime Classification Manual* (1992), both from Lexington Press. He also coauthored his autobiography, *Whoever Fights Monsters* (1992), from St. Martin's Press. He has testified as an expert witness in civil and criminal cases and has lectured and consulted with law enforcement agencies, universities, writers, television networks, and corporations throughout the U.S. and abroad. His appearances on numerous major network television and radio programs and in articles in major newspapers and magazines worldwide have made him a familiar figure in the United States and abroad and in great demand on the lecture circuit.

Ressler served a long career with the U.S. Army, ten years of which were spent in active duty during the Vietnam era. He served in the military police and as a criminal investigation officer (CID), with the U.S. Army CID Command Headquarters in Washington, D.C. His decorations include the Meritorious Service Medal with oak leaf cluster, the Army Commendation Medal with oak leaf cluster, the Vietnam Service Medal, the Vietnam Campaign Medal, the National Defense medal, and others. He recently retired from the army at the rank of full colonel with thirty-five years of active duty and reserve service. He lives with his family in Virginia.